Exploring woodworking

basic fundamentals

by
FRED W. ZIMMERMAN

Professor, Industrial Education, Technology
Western Illinois University, Macomb

South Holland, Illinois
THE GOODHEART-WILLCOX CO., Inc.
Publishers

Library of Congress Cataloging in Publication Data

Zimmerman, Fred W.
  Exploring Woodworking.

  Includes index.
  1. Woodwork   I. Title.
TT180.Z54   1981   684'.08   81—6923
ISBN 0—87006—398—7

INTRODUCTION

EXPLORING WOODWORKING is a first course which teaches the fundamentals of working efficiently and safely with both hand and power tools. It acquaints you with woods and their characteristics.

EXPLORING WOODWORKING is written using easy-to-understand language. Extra color is used to clarify details, and show woods in natural colors. This text provides constructional details on carefully selected projects, also alternate designs and design variations. It is intended to help you plan in an orderly fashion and to expand your creative abilities.

EXPLORING WOODWORKING tells and shows how to organize and operate a small manufacturing business in the school shop; how to mass produce items with proven student appeal.

EXPLORING WOODWORKING emphasizes the important place woods occupy in our everyday lives. It is the desire of the author that this text will contribute much to your Educational Development.

Fred W. Zimmerman

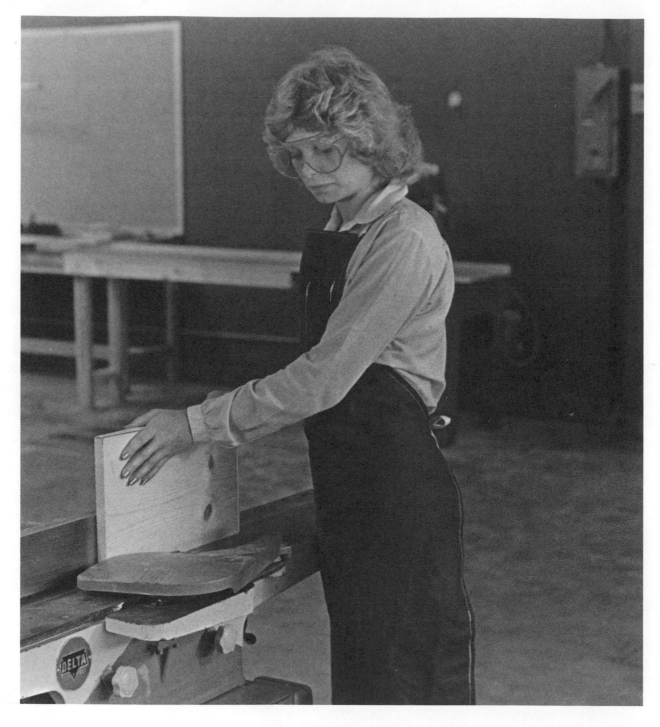

Safety in the school wood laboratory requires safe clothing and good work habits. Note safety glasses, apron, buttoned sleeves and placement of hands on workpiece.

CONTENTS

WOODS. 7

PLANNING. 18

GENERAL SAFETY. 27

LAYING OUT. 29

SAWING. 34

BORING AND DRILLING. 47

FILING, CARVING, AND CHISELING. 56

PLANING. 61

WOOD JOINTS. 74

SHAPING AND ROUTING. 83

WOOD TURNING. 90

USING METAL FASTENERS,
GLUING, AND CLAMPING. 97

SANDING. 110

WOOD FINISHING. 116

HARDWARE. 128

UPHOLSTERY. 132

BUSINESS EXPERIENCE ACTIVITY. 137

CAREERS IN
WOODWORKING INDUSTRIES. 154

PROJECTS. 157

DICTIONARY OF TERMS. 199

INDEX. 205

Student all set to work in school shop. Note apron.

Unit 1
WOODS

Structure and Growth of Wood

Wood is composed of many fiber units or cells, held together with a natural adhesive called lignin. The way the wood fibers are formed and put together determines the grain, strength, weight, and other properties of the wood.

Wood is formed from the center of the tree outward. New wood cells are formed in the cambium layer which is near the bark. The inside of this layer forms new wood cells and the outside forms new bark cells. In the spring, when the year's growth begins, the wood fibers are larger with thin walls, large open centers, and are light colored. This early growth is called springwood. Fibers that grow later in the season are smaller and stronger. They have thicker walls, smaller openings, and are darker colored. This later-grown wood is called summerwood. Each band of springwood and the band of darker-colored summerwood, into which it merges on the outer side, results in a year's growth called an annual ring. The age of a tree can be determined by counting the annual rings, Fig. 1-1. An exception is in the tropics, where growth is almost continuous and annual rings do not appear.

The wood nearest the bark of a tree contains living cells and is called sapwood. As the sapwood becomes inactive it gradually changes into heartwood, this is usually darker in color because of the presence of gums and resins. Medullary rays are rows of cells that run perpendicular to the annual rings toward the pith. They carry sap to the center of the tree. These rays are large in oak, beech and sycamore and small in most other woods. See Fig. 1-1.

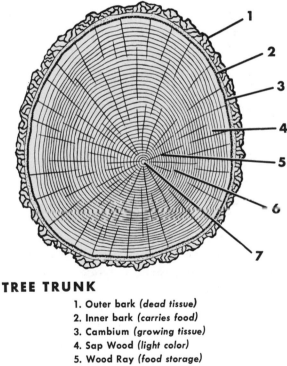

TREE TRUNK

1. Outer bark *(dead tissue)*
2. Inner bark *(carries food)*
3. Cambium *(growing tissue)*
4. Sap Wood *(light color)*
5. Wood Ray *(food storage)*
6. Heartwood *(dark color)*
7. Pith

*Fig. 1-1. Cross section of a tree trunk.
(Frank Paxton Lumber Co.)*

Classification and Identification of Wood

There are several hundred species of trees in the United States, but most of the lumber comes from about 35 species. The other species do not have lumber qualities, adequate size or commercial acceptance.

Trees and the lumber that comes from them may be divided into two main classes, softwood and hardwood. Softwoods are for the most part, products of needle-leaved trees or evergreens such as pine, fir, spruce, cedar, redwood, and cypress. Hardwoods are mostly products of broad-leaved trees such as oak, walnut, birch, maple, hickory, ash and poplar. The terms softwood and hardwood have no direct application to actual hardness or softness of the wood, Fig. 1-2.

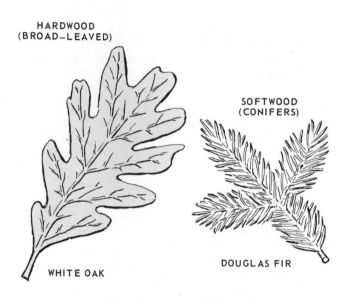

HARDWOOD
(BROAD-LEAVED)

SOFTWOOD
(CONIFERS)

WHITE OAK

DOUGLAS FIR

Fig. 1-2. Wood classification.

Softwoods and hardwoods may in turn be divided into the general classifications of open-grained or porous wood, and close-grained or nonporous woods. Lumber from most broad-leaf trees contains large cells or vessels. When the lumber is cut at the mill, the cells are ruptured, leaving openings or pores. Examples of open-grained woods are oak, walnut, mahogany. Close-grained woods include woods such as pine, birch, gum, maple, basswood, fir. Determining whether the wood is open-grained or close-grained is easy. Open-grained wood is porous and the pores or minute openings are easy to see. In close-grained wood the pores are not readily visible.

Lumbering

The lumber industry is an important contributor to our nation's economy. From forests to wholesaler or retailer the lumber industry provides jobs for over a half million people.

Under the American Tree Farm System thousands of tree farmers are protecting and managing millions of acres of woodlands for continuous crops. On most of our Certified Tree Farms and other well-managed forests, trained foresters supervise the harvest. They decide which trees are to be harvested and make provision for the next crop of timber. Scientific forest management includes proper cutting, tree planting, forest fire prevention, and disease and pest control. Millions of hardy seedlings are grown in tree farm nurseries where they get a good start and are then transplanted by field crews under the direction of company foresters. This means tree growing lands are put back into production as quickly as possible. One crop is harvested while another is started on its way to maturity, Fig. 1-3. With the sound forest management now being practiced we should have a continuous supply of wood for many years to come.

Fig. 1-3. Tree farm nursery.

Lumber Manufacturing Process

When logs arrive at the sawmill they are stored in large piles or in ponds until needed. Water storage of logs is preferred because it prevents end checking, washes off dirt, and makes sorting easy. Logs are usually pulled lengthwise into the mill by a chain or jackladder. Jets of water are used to remove mud and grit, Fig. 1-4.

Fig. 1-4. As logs are pulled into the sawmill, jets of water are used to remove mud and grit.

Logs are rolled one at a time to the carriage where the head sawyer takes over. He is a key man in the production of quality wood products. It is his job to get the maximum quantity of high quality lumber from each log, Fig. 1-5.

Fig. 1-5. The head sawyer cutting a log into huge slabs.

Huge rough slices from the headsaw are transported to trimmer saws where a battery of saws is used to cut up lumber into desired lengths. Each of the spinning circular saws can be raised or lowered independently so that boards can be trimmed to the exact lengths required. Note how two of the saws in Fig. 1-6 are biting their way through a heavy plank. Other saws are used to edge the boards to desired widths.

Fig. 1-6. Trimmer saws.

Most lumber is plain or flat sawed (cut tangent) to the annual rings. This method is cheaper and less wasteful and averages wider boards, Fig. 1-7. Quartersawing (cut paral-

lel to the wood rays) is more expensive and wasteful than plain sawed lumber but results in less warping and checking and exposes more figure in the wood grain particularly in oak, sycamore, beech, and mahogany. See Fig. 1-8.

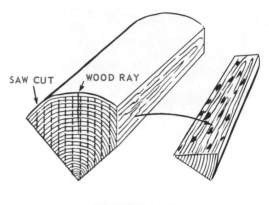

QUARTERSAWED
(Showing figure)

Fig. 1-8. Quartersawed.

Freshly sawed (rough) lumber is carried from the mill with a conveyor belt or chains to a sorting shed where trained workmen sort and grade it. Some of the lumber may be stacked for seasoning, or air-drying, Fig. 1-9. Other lumber may be placed in large ovens for kiln-drying. In large mills, the seasoned rough lumber is usually surfaced

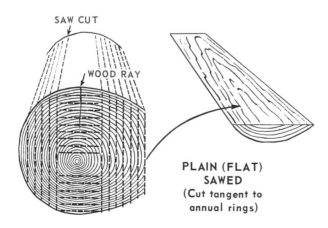

SAW CUT

WOOD RAY

PLAIN (FLAT) SAWED
(Cut tangent to annual rings)

Fig. 1-7. Plain or flat sawed.

Fig. 1-9. Lumber being cured by air-drying.

in a planing mill into finished lumber, Fig. 1-10. Pipes leading from the top of the planer carry away the shavings made by the machine.

Fig. 1-10. Planing lumber.

Moisture Content, Shrinking, Swelling

Wood like most fibrous materials shrinks as it loses moisture and swells as it absorbs moisture. Excess moisture (sap) must be removed from greenwood by drying or seasoning before it is used. Air-drying is done by stacking lumber outdoors where sun and wind will slowly reduce the moisture content to 18 to 20 percent, Fig. 1-9. Kiln-drying is accomplished by drying lumber in a large oven (kiln) at temperatures usually ranging from 120 to 130 deg. F. Humidity, circulation and air temperature are carefully controlled. Kiln-dried lumber will have less moisture content than air-dried, sometimes as low as 4 to 6 percent. During the drying process shrinking begins to occur when the free water is removed.

After drying, all woods have a tendency to reach a balance in moisture content with the surrounding air. This is called equilibrium moisture content. We all know how drawers, doors, and windows tend to stick in damp weather and loosen in dry weather.

Wood actually gets larger as it absorbs moisture and smaller as it loses moisture. Most change takes place across the grain where a board may vary four or more percent in dimension. There is less change in thickness than in width and almost no change in length. Kiln-dried lumber usually varies less in dimension since it is dried to a lower moisture content. This is why kiln-dried lumber is preferred for jobs such as furniture and cabinetmaking.

Defects

Wood that is dried too fast or is carelessly handled and stored often warps or develops other defects. Warping is considered to be the change in a board from a true surface. This includes cup (curved across the grain), bow (surface curved lengthwise), crook (edge curved lengthwise) and twist or or wind (both surfaces and edges curved lengthwise), Fig. 1-11.

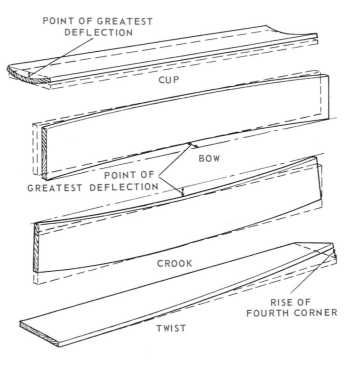

Fig. 1-11. Types of warp.

Small cracks or separations in the end grain of a board which are at right angles to the annular rings are called checks and those which are along or with the annular rings are called shakes. Cracks or splits are separations at the end of a board. See Fig. 1-12. Embedded branches and limbs result in knots which weaken the strength of a board and for many purposes are considered undesirable. An exception is knotty-pine paneling.

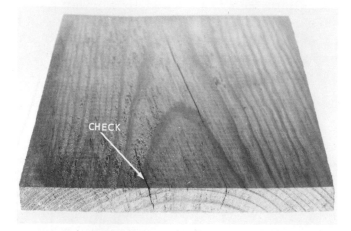

Fig. 1-12. Checks in a flat-grain board.

Grading

Most softwood lumber is divided into three classifications: Yard lumber, which is commonly available in retail lumber yards; structural lumber, used primarily for heavy construction; and factory and shop lumber, which is used for construction of such items as windows, doors and interior trim.

Yard lumber is cut into select (finish) grades and common (utility) grades. Select grades range from A through D, the best grade being B and better. Select grades are used for such things as siding, partitions and finish flooring. Common grades range from numbers 1 to 5 and are generally used as structural lumber. Size, shape and condition of knots are factors in determining these grades.

Softwoods are usually surfaced on four sides to finished dimensions (S4S). Softwoods are available at retail lumber yards in a variety of standard finished dimensions. This is because most softwoods are used for construction purposes. Standard lengths range from 6 to 20 ft. in 2 ft. intervals.

STANDARD THICKNESS AND WIDTH OF SOFTWOOD LUMBER (Dimensions in Inches)

Rough (Nominal)	S4S (Dry)	Rough (Nominal)	S4S (Dry)
1 x 2	3/4 x 1 1/2	2 x 2	1 1/2 x 1 1/2
1 x 4	3/4 x 3 1/2	2 x 4	1 1/2 x 3 1/2
1 x 6	3/4 x 5 1/2	2 x 6	1 1/2 x 5 1/2
1 x 8	3/4 x 7 1/4	2 x 8	1 1/2 x 7 1/4
1 x 10	3/4 x 9 1/4	2 x 10	1 1/2 x 9 1/4
1 x 12	3/4 x 11 1/4	4 x 4	3 1/2 x 3 1/2

Hardwoods are graded according to minimum sizes and the percentage of clear face (surface) cuttings that can be made. First and seconds (FAS) is the best grade in hardwood and must yield about 85 percent clear cuttings. Minimum board size is 6 in. and wider x 8 ft. and longer. The select grade is next best which allows board size of 4 in. and wider x 6 ft. and longer. Number 1 Common is the lowest grade and permits smaller board size with about 65 percent clear cuttings. Standard dimensions for hardwoods are given in thickness only and may be purchased rough or surfaced on both sides (S2S). Hardwoods are sold in random widths and lengths (RW&L). This is because hardwoods are used for furniture and cabinetmaking where maximum yield can be obtained by this method.

STANDARD THICKNESS OF SURFACED HARDWOOD LUMBER (Dimensions in Inches)

Rough	S2S	Rough	S2S
3/8	3/16	1 1/2	1 5/16
1/2	5/16	2	1 3/4
5/8	7/16	2 1/2	2 1/4
3/4	9/16	3	2 3/4
1	25/32	3 1/2	3 1/4
1 1/4	1 1/16	4	3 3/4

Veneer and Plywood

Veneer

Veneer is a thin sheet of wood peeled or sliced. The thickness ranges from 1/100 to 1/4 in. Veneer is made by rotary cutting, plain slicing, and quarter slicing, Fig. 1-13.

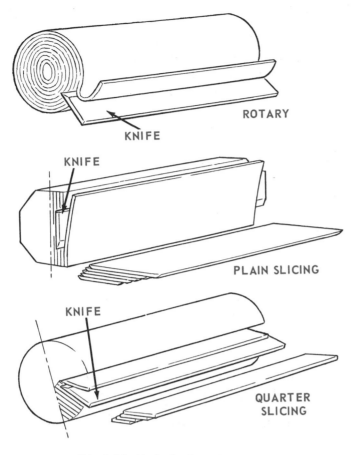

ROTARY

KNIFE

KNIFE

PLAIN SLICING

KNIFE

QUARTER SLICING

Fig. 1-13. Methods of cutting veneer.

Fig. 1-15. Where veneer figures are found.

Fig. 1-14 shows a lathe making a long, continuous sheet of veneer by "unpeeling" log sections specially selected for plywood production. The veneers are then cut to prescribed sizes and are bonded together to produce strong, light plywood. Veneers with grain designs for a variety of uses may be obtained by using the right kind of wood and the correct method of cutting the veneer. Decorative and exotic grain designs are found in some woods by cutting veneer from the tree crotch, burl and stump, Fig. 1-15.

Fig. 1-14. Rotary cutting a continuous sheet of veneer.

Plywood

Plywood is a wood product made of cross-banded layers of veneer and/or lumber bonded together with glue. An odd number (3, 5, 7, etc.) of layers (plies) are used. The grain of the outside veneer layers (face and back) run in the same direction. The inside layer (core) of plywood is built up in several ways. Veneer core is crossbands of veneers, each layer at right angles to the adjacent layer, Fig. 1-16 (Above). Lumber core consists of strips of lumber bonded together, generally as a 5-ply panel of 5/8 in. or more. The core is covered with veneer crossbands over which a face and back of veneer (usually 1/28 in.

thickness) are attached, Fig. 1-16 (Center). Other cores consist of particle board (particles or chips of wood formed with adhesives, heat, and pressure into a homogeneous panel), aluminum or paper honeycomb, foamed plastics, fire retardant treated softwoods and hardboards, Fig. 1-16 (Below).

Plywood for interior or exterior use is available in standard sheets four feet wide and eight feet long. Fig. 1-17 shows pressed panels being unloaded. Press time is generally between two and ten minutes depending upon the thickness of veneers, kind of plywood being glued and number of panels loaded per opening.

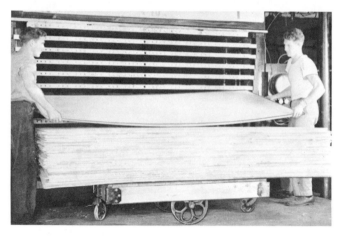

Fig. 1-17. Panels of plywood being unloaded from gluing press.

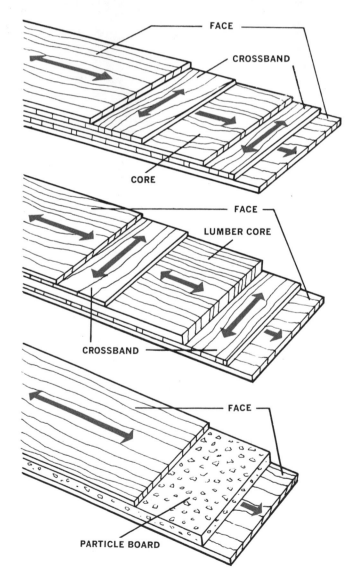

Fig. 1-16. Plywood. Above. Veneer core. Center. Lumber core. Below. Particle board core.

SOFTWOOD PLYWOOD grading is usually specified for both front and back surfaces in letters from A to D such as A/A, A/B, etc. The best grade (N) is a special grade intended for natural finish. Fir plywood is the most prevalent of the softwoods and is available in standard thickness of 1/8, 1/4, 3/8, 1/2, 5/8, and 3/4 in. Softwood plywood is usually sanded on both surfaces (S2S) unless it is intended as sheathing or underlayment (over subfloor).

HARDWOOD PLYWOOD (face and back veneers of 1/28 in. hardwood) is available in standard thicknesses of 1/4 and 3/4 in. Hardwood plywood is graded as premium (best) to good, sound utility, backing and specialty. Specialty grade, the biggest category,

Fig. 1-18. Assortment of hardboard panels.

does not conform in characteristics to any of the other grades. Characteristics are agreed upon by buyer and seller. About 80 percent of all furniture construction is hardwood plywood.

Plywood construction increases strength, reduces warping, eliminates splitting and is comparatively stable in dimension during humidity changes of the atmosphere.

Hardboard, Particle Board and Insulation Board

Through modern research and technology, hardboard, particle board and insulation board are developed from new substances utilizing scrap and waste materials.

Hardboard

Hardboard is made by breaking wood chips down into individual fibers, arranging them into a mat and compressing them with heavy rollers. Lengths of mat (wetlap) are fed into multiple presses where heat, pressure, and lignin (natural adhesive in wood) form them into hard, thin, dry board sheets, Figs. 1-18 and 1-19. The sheets are cut into panels four feet wide and in lengths of 8, 10, 12 and 16 ft. Common thicknesses are 1/8, 3/16 and 1/4 in. Standard hardboard is saturated with oils and resins to make tempered hardboard which is more dense and water repellent. Hardboard is widely used as prefinished wall paneling and siding. Fig. 1-18 is a panorama of newer hardboard panelings including: Wood grains, embossed, striated, vinyls, metallic speckled, smooth melamine covered, perforated and filigree. It is also used in furniture, toys, and for pegboard and sheathing.

Particle Board

Particle board production begins with planer shavings, wood chips and logs. Milling equipment produces wood chips which are screened into desired sizes. Dryers remove excess moisture, then resins and binders are mixed with the wood chips. Forming machines deposit the wood chips on belts forming them into mats.

Fig. 1-19. Industry photo. Forming the mat for hardboard.

Particle mats are cured with heat and pressure, then trimmed and sanded to panel size which is commonly 4 ft x 8 ft. Thicknesses range from 1/4 to over 1 in. Particle board is extensively used as core stock for wood veneers and plastic laminates. It is also used as siding, floor underlayment and for other construction and industrial purposes.

Common edge tools and machines can be used to cut and form hardboard or particle board. For extensive cutting, carbide-tipped tools are often recommended.

Insulation Board

The manufacture of insulation board begins by reducing wood chips to wood fibers by steam or mechanical processes. Bagasse, a fibrous by-product of sugar cane processing is another raw material used. The fibers are combined with water and chemicals using automatic controls. The mixture flows on a broad moving screen where it is formed into large sheets of varying thicknesses by a felting process. The sheets are then dried, cut and trimmed to finished sizes.

Insulation board is manufactured for uses in building construction where a lightweight, rigid panel with good thermal-insulating properties is needed. The insulation value is obtained by millions of tiny air cells developed between the fibers during the felting process. Insulation board is used not only for thermal insulation but also for structural strength and acoustical purposes, particularly when provided with holes or other sound traps. Insulation boards are made for both interior and exterior use. The interior type is usually a uniformly light-colored product with fac-

WOOD IDENTIFICATION

A key element in woodworking is the proper identification of the wood. The insert at the right, which is intended as a guide and an aid to the student in learning to identify various woods, shows typical color and grain characteristics of 40 different species.

BIRD'S-EYE MAPLE

PRIMAVERA

REDWOOD

RED CEDAR

AMERICAN ELM

HOLLY

WALNUT

ROSEWOOD

LIMBA

RED BIRCH

SATINWOOD

WHITE OAK

WHITE ASH

SUGAR PINE

TULIP

RED GUM

HICKORY

AMARANTH

BASSWOOD

CYPRESS

WORMY CHESTNUT

CHERRY

HEMLOCK

VERMILION

LACEWOOD

BALSA

PONDEROSA PINE

EBONY

BEECH

WILLOW

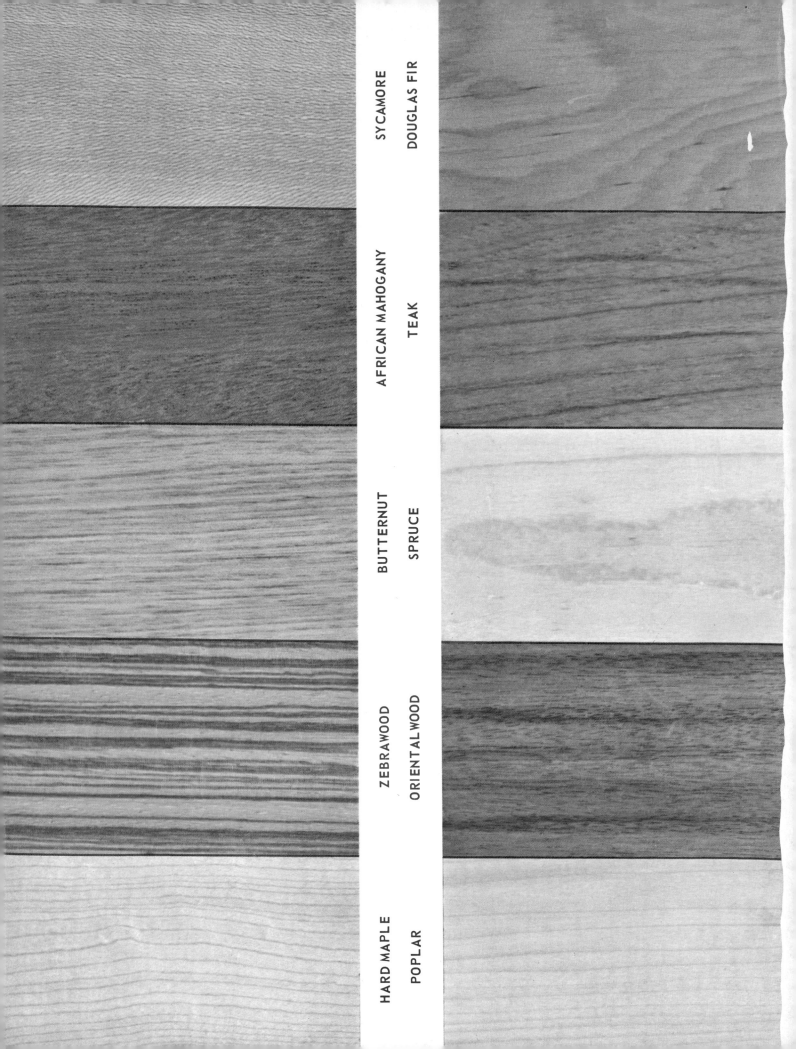

SYCAMORE

DOUGLAS FIR

AFRICAN MAHOGANY

TEAK

BUTTERNUT

SPRUCE

ZEBRAWOOD

ORIENTALWOOD

HARD MAPLE

POPLAR

tory applied paint and is used as wallboard, wall plank and ceiling tile, Fig. 1-20. Exterior type insulation board is either saturated or coated with asphalt to improve its water resistance and strength when wet. Exterior insulation board is used extensively as sheathing and roof insulation. It is also used as insulating form board and sound-deadening board.

Test Your Knowledge - Unit 1

Write your answers on a separate sheet of paper. Do not write in this book.

1. Wood is composed of fiber units held together with a natural adhesive called _____.
2. New wood cells are formed in the _____ layer near the bark.
3. The age of a tree can be determined by counting the _____ rings.
4. Wood nearest the bark of a tree is called _____.
5. Medullary rays which run perpendicular to the annual rings toward the pith carry _____ to the center.
6. Trees and lumber may be divided into two main classes: _____ and _____.
7. Softwoods for the most part are products of _____ leaved trees.
8. Hardwoods are mostly products of _____ leaved trees.
9. Two examples of open-grained wood are _____ and _____.
10. Most lumber is plain or flat sawed (cut tangent) to the annual rings. True or False?
11. Some freshly cut lumber is placed in large ovens for _____ drying.
12. Wood _____ as it loses moisture and _____ as it absorbs moisture.
13. Woods have a tendency to reach a balance in moisture content with surrounding air. This is called _____ moisture content.
14. Warping is a change in a board from a true surface. In cup warping a board is curved _____ the grain. In bow warping the board surface is curved _____.

Fig. 1-20. Installation of thermal-acoustical tile.

15. In making plywood an even number of layers or plies are used. True or False?
16. Hardboard is commonly made in these thicknesses: _____ in., _____ in. and _____ in.
17. In insulation board the insulating value is obtained by _____ cells developed between the fibers.

Research and Development

1. Trace the growth cycle of trees. Why do redwood trees usually live longer than other trees? Use the library.
2. Select four or more small pieces of wood of different kinds. Write the name of each piece on its surface. Then ask your instructor to check for accuracy.
3. Visit a local lumber yard to see how they store and care for lumber.
4. What is being done in your community to support the cause of conservation of our natural resources?
5. Prepare an outline for a short report about the history and development of hardboard, particle board, or insulation board.

Unit 2
PLANNING

Efficient planning helps us to solve problems, avoid mistakes, and use correct techniques and methods.

Designing Products

As we design and construct products in our shop, let us consider some of the objectives sought by industry. To be successful, manufacturers must make a profit from the sale of the products manufactured. Designers must consider sales appeal, sales potential as well as product usefulness.

Manufacturing cost is also important. This cost will include the time and effort necessary to make the product and the cost of needed materials. Another consideration is the suitability of the manufacturer's plant equipment, facilities and personnel.

As we design projects (products) in our shop, we also need to study and apply the principles of good design.

Design Considerations

Function or Usefulness

Is the project needed? Will it perform well for the purpose for which it is intended? Examples: Project intended for use outdoors should be made from a wood that resists weathering. It should be protected with an appropriate finish.

A bookshelf should be designed to hold books of the desired size and quantity.

A hunting bow should have sufficient strength to thrust its arrow powerfully and accurately.

Kind of Wood

This is largely dependent on the use, function and finish of the project. If an opaque finish is planned, we could probably use a wood which is inexpensive, has insignificant grain patterns, but holds paint or enamel well. Basswood, pine, spruce and poplar are excellent woods to use for an opaque finish. If we plan to use a natural or transparent stained finish, we should use a wood offering a desirable color and grain pattern. Birch, oak, walnut, maple and cherry are but a few of the fine woods which are enriched by finishing. Refer to the wood identification section following page 16.

Size

A project should be of the proper size to serve the purpose for which it is intended.

Some sizes of furniture and cabinets are considered as standard. A coffee table is usually 16 - 18 in. high, a desk 29 in. high and a dining table 30 in. high. A chair is usually 18 in. from the floor to its seat. A bathroom vanity is often 31 in. high and a kitchen cabinet base 36 in. high. A search through catalogs and brochures will reveal other standard sizes.

Proportion

Proportion is considered as the ratio of the dimensions of a piece. A coffee table that is 18 in. wide and 42 in. long has a size ratio of 18/42 or 3/7. Generally, an odd number ratio size such as 1/3, 2/5, etc. is more pleasing than an even size ratio such as 1/4, 1/2, etc.

Planning

Durability

We usually should make a project only strong enough to fulfill its purpose. Otherwise, it may appear to be heavy and awkward. We should ask ourselves such questions as: Is the project designed to fit its surroundings? Can it be built with a minimum of time and effort? Is it durable? Are the most appropriate materials being used?

Other Considerations

Economy, harmony and balance are other considerations. Will the project be worth the necessary time and effort? Do the parts blend well together? Does it have eye appeal?

Furniture Styles

Through the years, some of the best designers and craftworkers of their time have developed furniture which is particularly appealing and is known according to the period during which it was created. Furniture created in Europe, particularly during the 18th and 19th centuries is sometimes known as Traditional and French Provincial. Queen Anne and Louis XIV furniture is named for the rulers who ordered the furniture built. Sheraton and Chippendale are named for the craftsmen who originated the furniture. Other popular types of period furniture are Colonial and Early American. Contemporary (modern) furniture reflects the thinking of our present day designers and craftsmen. Contemporary furniture is made with characteristic smooth, trim lines and is of simple construction.

Selecting and Designing Appropriate Projects

Planning in our laboratory involves selecting a project, developing and refining its design, and making other necessary plans to enable us to "think through" its construction in advance.

As a beginner, you will need some specific and detailed information to help guide you in planning a project. After you learn to plan necessary activities, you will need fewer details. To gain experience, it is advisable

Industry photo. Using belt fed, straight line circular saw. (Drexel Enterprises)

Fig. 2-1. Pictorial sketch for a jewelry box.

to utilize some of the existing designs and plans for projects.

Unit 19 will provide you with project ideas and information to aid you in selecting and planning worthwhile projects. Included are projects in varying degrees of difficulty. You should select projects you can make with a minimum of effort and can complete within the allotted time. You are encouraged to select projects which are of particular interest. In designing, use your imagination freely. Developing more than one design for a project will make it possible for you to compare designs and make improvements. You will experience keen satisfaction when you come up with a design that is different and pleasing. Design suggestions may be obtained by visiting shops and stores that specialize in gift items and novelties.

Making a Pictorial Sketch

Sketching your project with a pencil gives you opportunity to make design changes that make it more functional or appealing. Pictorial (three-dimensional) sketches are recommended. Making sketches of your project helps you to plan procedures and helps you to see how its parts fit together. Sketches will also enable your teacher to guide you and give his approval for you to proceed with further plans.

In making a pictorial sketch, draw only the object lines of your proposed project. You can sketch the object lines freehand, then darken them with a pencil and straightedge. First draw the project as it appears from its front. Then draw its top and one side at an angle to the front to provide a pictorial effect. Fig. 2-1 illustrates a pictorial sketch of a jewelry box.

Preparing a Working Drawing

A working drawing provides shapes and dimensions of a project. A final working drawing may be drawn to scale using square, lined paper. This usually consists of two or more views. Detail views (often enlarged) are used to show types of joints and shapes of special or irregular parts.

To start, you should make a pencil sketch and use this as a working drawing of your project. Show the finished sketch to your instructor for suggestions and approval. After your sketch is approved, you should prepare a working drawing, drawn to scale. Fig. 2-2 is a working drawing of the jewelry box shown earlier as a sketch in Fig. 2-1. Two views are given to illustrate the carcass of the jewelry box. Three additional views are given to show the drawer construction. Detail views are used to show the kinds of joints and the shape of the drawer knobs.

Planning

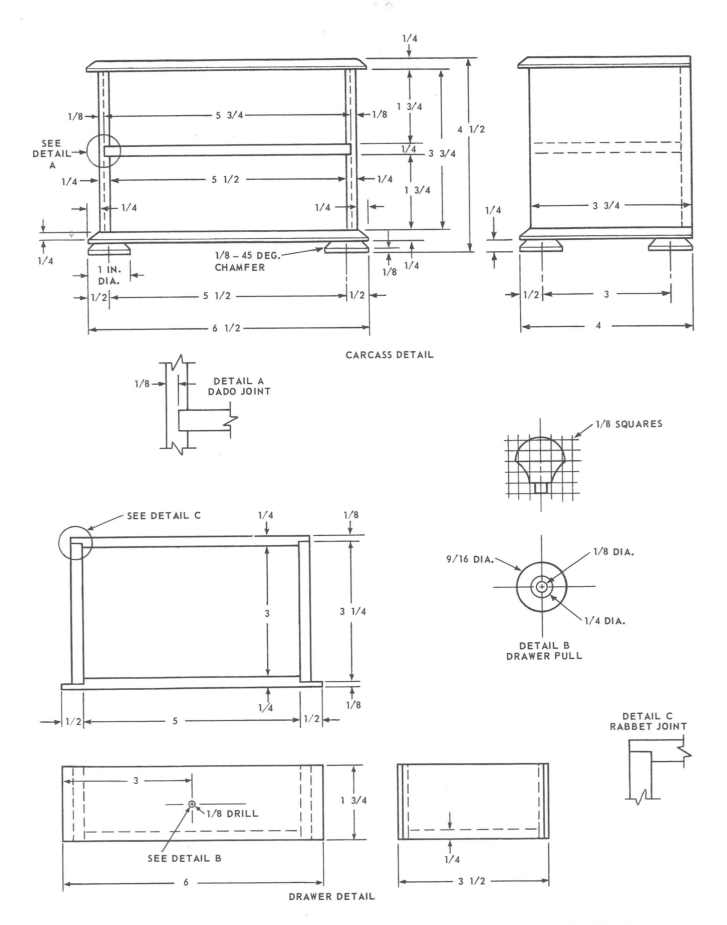

CARCASS DETAIL

DETAIL A
DADO JOINT

1/8 SQUARES

9/16 DIA.
1/8 DIA.
1/4 DIA.

DETAIL B
DRAWER PULL

SEE DETAIL C

DETAIL C
RABBET JOINT

SEE DETAIL B

1/8 DRILL

DRAWER DETAIL

Fig. 2-2. Working drawing for a jewelry box. Above. Carcass detail. Below. Drawer and pull detail.

Fig. 2-3. Completed jewelry box.

Figs. 2-3 and 2-4 illustrate the completed jewelry box and provide alternate jewelry box design suggestions.

Computing Lumber Measurement

We indicate lumber dimensions in the order of thickness (T) by the width (W) by the length (L). The board foot is the unit of measure for lumber. A board foot is a piece of lumber with dimensions (or the equivalent) of 1 in. or less in thickness, by 12 in. wide (distance across the grain) by 12 in. long (distance along the grain). Nominal (rough sawn) sizes are used in computing board measure. Lumber less than 1 in. thick is figured the same as if it were 1 in., but it is usually sold at less cost per board foot. For example, a board 1/4 in. thick, 12 in. wide and 12 in. long is figured as 1 board foot. Lumber which is thicker than 1 in. is figured to the next greater quarter inch. For example, a board 1 1/8 in. thick is figured as 1 1/4 in., and a board 1 3/8 in. thick is figured as a 1 1/2 in. board.

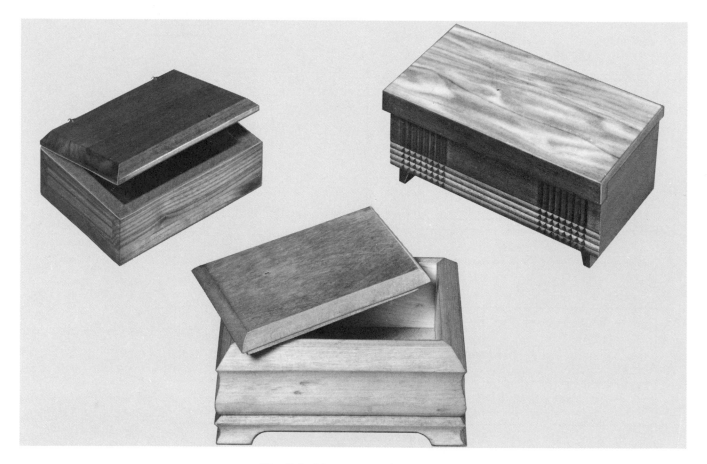

Fig. 2-4. Alternate jewelry boxes.

BILL OF MATERIALS

NAME CHARLES E. HARPER PLANNING DATE MARCH 15 COMPLETION DATE APRIL 22

PROJECT JEWELRY BOX TOOLS NEEDED: TRY SQUARE, MARKING GAUGE HAND SAWS, HAND PLANES, HAND DRILL & BIT, CHISELS, CLAW HAMMER & CLAMPS

STOCK LIST:

No. of Pcs.	Name of Part	Size in Inches (Rough)	Size in Inches (Finish)	Kind of Wood	Bd. Ft.	Bd. Ft. Cost	Cost
2	TOP & BOTTOM (CARCASS)	3/8 x 4 1/4 x 7	1/4 x 4 x 6 1/2	WALNUT	.41	$1.70	$.70
2	ENDS (CARCASS)	3/8 x 4 1/4 x 4 1/4	1/4 x 3 3/4 x 3 3/4	"	.25	1.70	.43
1	SHELF (CARCASS)	3/8 x 3 3/4 x 6 1/4	1/4 x 3 1/2 x 5 3/4	"	.16	1.70	.27
1	BACK (CARCASS)	1/4 x 4 x 6 1/4	1/4 x 3 3/4 x 5 3/4	WAL. PLY G1S	.17 SQ. FT.	1.30 SQ. FT.	.22
4	FEET (CARCASS)	3/4 x 1 1/4 x 1 1/4	1/4 x 1 DIA.	WALNUT	.04	1.70	.07
2	FRONTS (DRAWER)	3/8 x 2 x 6 1/2	1/4 x 1 3/4 x 6	"	.17	1.70	.29
2	BACKS (DRAWER)	3/8 x 2 x 6	1/4 x 1 3/4 x 5 1/2	"	.16	1.70	.27
4	SIDES (DRAWER)	3/8 x 2 x 3 3/4	1/4 x 1 3/4 x 3 1/4	"	.21	1.70	.36
2	BOTTOMS (DRAWER)	1/4 x 3 1/4 x 5 1/2	1/4 x 3 x 5	WAL. PLY G1S	.25 SQ. FT.	1.30 SQ. FT.	.33
2	PULLS (DRAWER)	3/4 x 3/4 x 1 1/4	9/16 DIA. x 5/8	WALNUT	.013	1.70	.02
						TOTAL STOCK COST	$2.96

HARDWARE AND OTHER MATERIALS:

No. of Pcs.	Description	Size	Unit	Unit Cost	Cost
4	FLAT HEAD SCREWS	NO. 4 x 1/2"	EACH	$.01	.04
36	WIRE BRADS	GAUGE NO. 18 x 3/4"	EACH		.07
	LIQUID WHITE GLUE				.07
	SAND PAPER	60, 100, AND 150 GRITS			.15
	FINISH				.25
				TOTAL HARDWARE & MISC.	$.58
				TOTAL PROJECT COST	$3.54

Fig. 2-5. Bill of materials for a jewelry box.

A formula for computing board measure with small pieces of lumber is: Board feet (Bd. ft.) equals the number of pieces times the thickness (T) in inches, times the width (W) in inches, times the length (L) in inches, divided by 12 x 12 (144) or the number of square inches in a square foot, or:

$$\text{Bd. ft.} = \frac{\text{no. of pcs. x T'' x W'' x L''}}{12 \text{ x } 12}$$

EXAMPLE: Compute the board measure of 3 pcs. 1/2'' x 6'' x 9''. Substituting in the formula and cross multiplying we have:

$$\text{Bd. ft.} = \frac{\overset{1}{\cancel{3}}\text{ pcs. x } 1'' \text{ x } \overset{1}{\cancel{6}}'' \text{ x } 9''}{\underset{4}{\cancel{12}} \text{ x } \underset{2}{\cancel{12}}} = \frac{9}{8} \text{ or } 1.125$$

Large pieces are computed as follows: Bd. ft. = no. of pcs. x T (in inches) x W (in inches) x L (in feet) divided by 12, the number of inches in a lineal foot, or:

$$\text{Bd. ft.} = \frac{\text{no. of pcs. x T'' x W'' x L'}}{12}$$

EXAMPLE: Compute the board measure of 2 pcs. 1 1/4 inches thick x 4 inches wide x 4 feet long. Substituting in the formula and cross multiplying we have:

$$\text{Bd. ft.} = \frac{2 \text{ pcs. x } 5''\ (1\ 1/4'') \text{ x } \overset{1}{\cancel{4}}'' \text{ x } \overset{1}{\cancel{4}}'}{\underset{1}{\cancel{4}} \text{ x } \underset{3}{\cancel{12}}}$$

$$= \frac{10}{3} \text{ or } 3.33$$

Plywood is figured by using the square foot unit of measurement.

Preparing Bill of Materials

The working drawing is used to determine the dimensions of the stock in the preparation of a bill of materials. Both rough and finish dimensions are given. Costs are computed according to the rough size dimensions. Rough size dimensions allow for extra stock to be removed in smoothing the parts to finish sizes. Rough size dimensions are obtained by: adding 1/16 - 1/8 inch to the finish size thickness, 1/4 inch to its width (across the grain), and 1/2 inch to its length (along the grain). Hardware and other materials are listed separately. Fig. 2-5 is a bill of materials. Needed tools are listed.

Making a Stock Cutting List

We can make a stock cutting list by grouping together similar rough sizes of stock given in the bill of materials. In this way, we can conserve both time and material as we cut parts to rough dimensions. Fig. 2-6 is a stock cutting list for the jewelry box.

PCS.	NAMES OF PARTS	SIZE	MATERIAL
1	Top, bottom, ends and shelf (carcass)	3/8'' x 4 1/4'' x 30''	Walnut
1	Fronts, backs and sides (drawer)	3/8'' x 4'' x 20''	Walnut
1	Back (carcass) and bottoms (drawer)	1/4'' x 4'' x 18''	Walnut Plywood GIS
1	Feet (carcass)	3/4'' x 1 1/4'' x 5 1/4''	Walnut
1	Pulls (carcass)	3/4'' x 3/4'' x 3''	Walnut

Fig. 2-6. Stock cutting list for a jewelry box.

Tool Selection

Fig. 2-7 illustrates a typical storage cabinet for tools. Tools must be shared and properly cared for so that everyone receives maximum benefit from their use. Always return tools to the storage center after use.

Preparing a Plan of Procedure

We make a plan of procedure to enable us to "think through" in advance the processes we need to use to construct our project. This enables us to organize our work so we can save time, labor and material, and catch minor errors in the drawing, bill of materials, or stock cutting list. Mistakes are much easier to change on paper than with materials. We can sometimes find ways to improve our project design or construction.

You should make your plan of procedure in outline form with enough information to indicate procedures involved.

Jewelry Box Plan of Procedure

1. Check your working drawing, bill of material, and stock cutting list carefully.
2. Select and cut stock given in your stock cutting list. Try to find already-cut stock near the correct sizes.
3. Make carcass parts.
   a. Plane the stock cutting piece to finish thickness.
   b. Saw parts to rough sizes.
   c. Plane and saw parts to finish sizes.
   d. Saw and chisel dados in ends to receive the shelf.
   e. Chamfer edges of the top and bottom.
4. Make carcass feet.
5. Assemble carcass with glue and wire brads or clamps. Attach the feet with screws.
6. Make drawer fronts, backs and sides.
   a. Plane stock cutting piece to finish thickness.
   b. Saw parts to rough sizes.
   c. Plane and saw parts to finish sizes.
   d. Cut rabbet joints at each end of the fronts and backs to receive the sides. Then cut rabbet joints along the bottom edges to receive the bottoms.
   e. Drill 1/8 in. hole in each drawer front to receive the pulls.
7. Make the drawer pulls.
8. Cut plywood to finish sizes to fit the drawer bottoms and carcass back.
9. Assemble drawers with glue and wire brads or clamps. Install the drawer pulls.
10. Smooth surfaces and edges with 60, 100, and 150 grit sandpaper.
11. Apply finish.
    a. Raise grain, let dry, then smooth again with 150 grit sandpaper.
    b. Apply paste wood filler, let dry until it begins to turn dull then remove excess filler by rubbing ACROSS the grain and let dry.
    c. Sand filler coat lightly with 220 grit sandpaper, then apply a coat of sealer and allow to dry.
    d. Sand sealer coat lightly with 220 grit sandpaper, then apply two coats of topcoat finish.
    e. Rub final topcoat with rubbing oil and

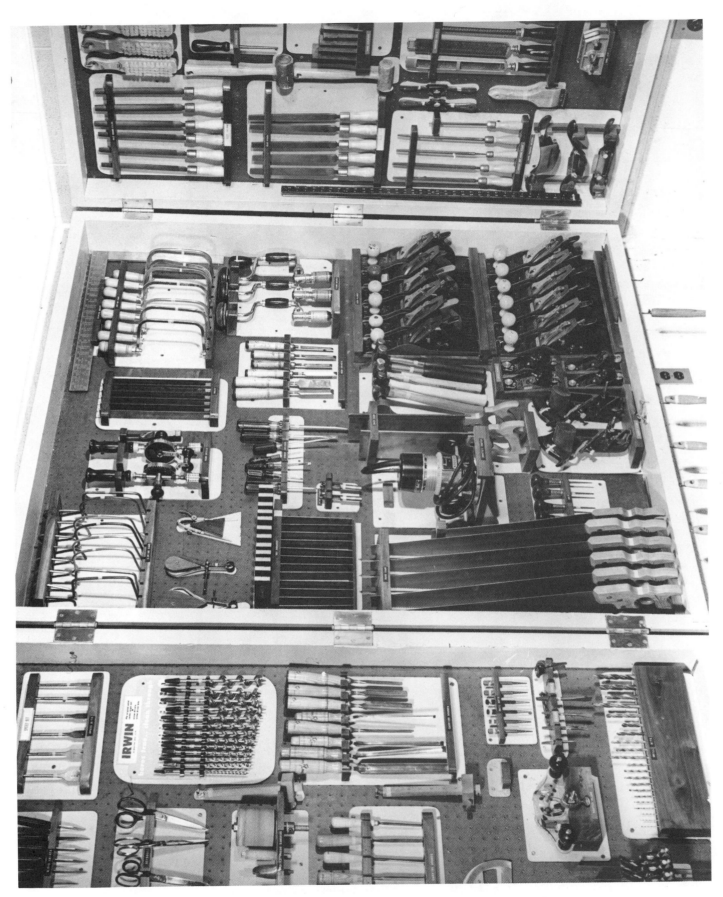

Fig. 2-7. Typical tool storage cabinet.

rottenstone or pumice.
   f. Wax.
12. Attach the carcass back with glue and wire brads or clamps.

Test Your Knowledge – Unit 2

1. To be successful a manufacturer must make a _____ from the sale of the product.
2. In designing projects to be constructed in our shop, three important considerations are: _____ _____.
3. Pieces of Queen Anne and Louis XIV furniture are named for the _____ who first ordered that type furniture built.
4. Contemporary furniture always reflects the thinking of _____ designers. (European, Colonial, or Present Day)
5. Planning in the school laboratory involves selecting a project and developing and refining its _____.
6. A working drawing provides shapes and _____ of a project.
7. The unit of measure for lumber is the _____.
8. Lumber less than 1 in. thick is figured the same as if it were _____ in. thick.
9. _____ size dimensions allow for extra stock to be removed in smoothing parts to finish sizes.
10. To "think through" the processes we need in constructing a project we use a _____ of procedure.
11. In applying finish to a project made of walnut the paste woodfiller should be applied before applying the sealer. True or False?

Research and Development

1. Prepare a short report on a famous furniture designer.
2. How do we decide the difference between good and bad design? Make a chart showing as many characteristics as you can find which suggest good design. Use the library.
3. Choose a project you have a great desire to make. Then make pencil sketches of the project, along with alternate design suggestions.
4. Select several small pieces of wood and compute the number of board feet in each piece. Compute the cost of each board based on current prices and have your instructor check your work.

Fig. 3-1. Drill press safety. Drilling hole in hardwood properly clamped in place. Operator wearing eye shield.

Unit 3
GENERAL SAFETY

Contributions Toward a Safe Laboratory

1. Always think "safety."
2. Wear safety glasses or goggles in danger zones or other designated areas. See Fig. 3-1.
3. Be careful how you handle the property of others. Respect the rights of others.
4. Report even the slightest injury. Small cuts, improperly treated, may cause serious trouble.
5. Notify your instructor of unsafe conditions you observe.
6. Keep the floor clear of excessive litter and scraps of material.
7. Be sure to stack lumber so it will stand firmly.
8. Store clamped stock so it will not fall.
9. See to it that used rags are placed in safety cans.
10. Do your part in keeping finish containers tightly closed.
11. Use the dust collecting system. The air we breathe should be kept clean.
12. Safety should be an important part of every job. Safe work habits acquired now will serve you well for years to come.

Working Safely with Tools and Equipment

1. Ask your instructor to explain any part of your work you do not understand.
2. Assemble tool parts correctly for safe and efficient use.
3. Do not use files without handles.
4. Help keep edge tools sharp.
5. Carry edge tools with edges down and keep them out of your pockets, Fig. 3-2.
6. Clamp all stock securely before using any edge tools.
7. With few exceptions, cut away from you when using edge tools, Fig. 3-3.
8. Report broken tools to your instructor.
9. Store tools in places provided.
10. Protect your eyes from sandpaper dust. Wipe or brush away sandpaper dust instead of using air pressure.
11. Wear rubber gloves to handle dangerous liquids.
12. Close vises so the handles do not protrude in aisles.

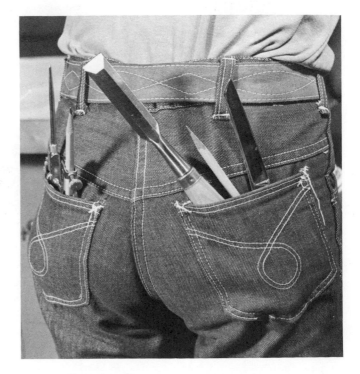

Fig. 3-2. Don't do photo. Sharp-pointed tools in pockets.

Working Safely With and Around Machines

1. Ask your instructor for permission before using a machine.
2. Have your instructor check your setup, before using the machine.
3. Use machine guards. The guards are there for your protection.
4. See that everyone is out of the danger zone before you operate a machine.
5. Stay alert! Keep your mind on the operation of the machine at all times. Do not talk to anyone while operating a machine.
6. Be careful to work within the capacity of the machine.
7. Turn off a machine before making an adjustment, cleaning or lubricating.
8. Pull the plug or turn off the disconnect switch of a machine to change a setup.
9. Remember that you as a machine operator, are in full charge of the machine.
10. Ask for assistance when cutting long or heavy pieces.
11. Wear safe clothing. Remove your coat or sweater. Roll up your sleeves. Tuck in or remove your tie.
12. Use a push stick to cut short or narrow pieces.
13. Care for and use a machine as if it were your own.
14. Make sure the cutting tools are sharp.
15. Turn off a machine after every use.
16. Watch for defects in material such as warp and knots. Check with your instructor before using such material.
17. Use only materials which are free from paint, nails and grit.

Research and Development

1. Make a safety slogan sign that you think will be effective in your laboratory.
2. Obtain for bulletin board use cartoon sketches that depict safety precautions.

Fig. 3-3. Using chisel in wood carving — pushing away.

Unit 4
LAYING OUT

Fig. 4-1. Using a steel rule as a straightedge.

Fig. 4-3. Squaring end of a board with a try square.

In this Unit, we will discuss the use of Rules, Squares, Marking Gauges, Dividers, Bevels and Awls, in measuring and construction procedures.

In laying out projects in wood, it is important that you arrange the design to avoid unnecessary waste of materials. You should give consideration also, to the direction the grain should run, for proper strength and attractiveness of the project.

Rules

A steel rule is used for measuring and as a straightedge. See Fig. 4-1. If you use a wood rule to measure, hold it on its edge for maximum accuracy. Tapes and folding rules are best for measuring long stock, Fig. 4-2.

Squares

Try squares and combination squares are useful for measuring, to check edges for squareness, to square the ends of boards and to lay out hole centers, Figs. 4-3, 4-4, and

Fig. 4-2. Above. Tape rule. Below. Folding rule.

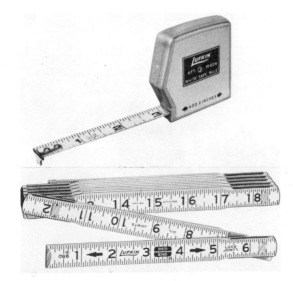

Fig. 4-4. Combination square.

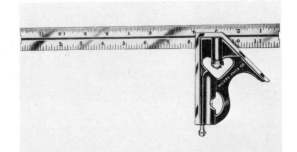

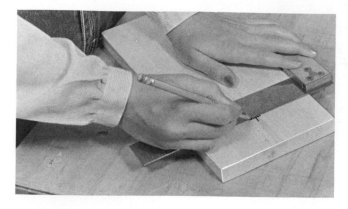

Fig. 4-5. Laying out hole centers with a try square and pencil.

Fig. 4-7. Punching hole centers with an awl.

4-5. A carpenter's square is useful when working with large pieces, Fig. 4-6.

Awls

An awl may be used to punch center locations before drilling holes. It may also be used to punch pilot holes for screws in soft woods, Fig. 4-7.

Marking Gauge

You can lay out lines for joints or chamfers with the marking gauge, Fig. 4-8.

Fig. 4-8. Marking lines parallel to an edge with a marking gauge.

Fig. 4-6. To mark a square line at the end of a board, use a carpenter's square and pencil.

Fig. 4-9. Scribing a circle with pencil dividers.

Dividers

This tool may be used as a compass to scribe arcs and circles, Fig. 4-9, or to step off distances and find centers. Large arcs and circles can be scribed with TRAMMEL POINTS, Fig. 4-10.

Sliding T-Bevel (Bevel Gauge)

You can easily determine and duplicate angles and bevels with this tool, Fig. 4-11.

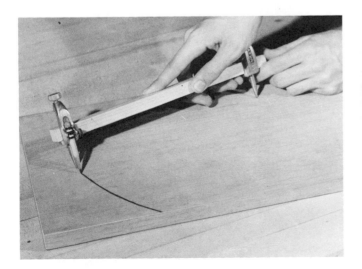

Fig. 4-10. Scribing an arc with trammel points.

Fig. 4-11. Determining an angle for boring with a sliding T-bevel.

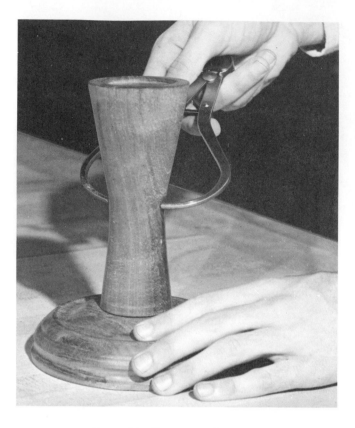

Fig. 4-12. Using outside caliper.

Calipers

Outside and inside calipers are used to measure round stock, Figs. 4-12 and 4-13.

Fig. 4-13. Using inside caliper.

Chalk Line

Straight lines can be quickly made on long boards with a chalk line, Fig. 4-14. You can also use a chalk line to good advantage to lay out true lines, when laying ceiling and floor tile.

Fig. 4-14. Snapping a tightly drawn chalk line.

Changing Design Size

A design which is irregular in shape may be enlarged or reduced in size by following this procedure: Place a tracing paper overlay, laid out in uniform size squares over the design. The design is enlarged by sketching it freehand into larger squares, and reduced by sketching it into smaller squares.

Templates

You can make a full-size pattern of an irregular shape, such as an animal design, on squared paper, attach it to cardboard or hardboard and use it as a permanent template, Fig. 4-15. The same method may be used to make accurate, half or quarter-size patterns.

Test Your Knowledge - Unit 4

1. A steel rule is used for _____ and as a _____.
2. Tapes and folding rules are used to mea-

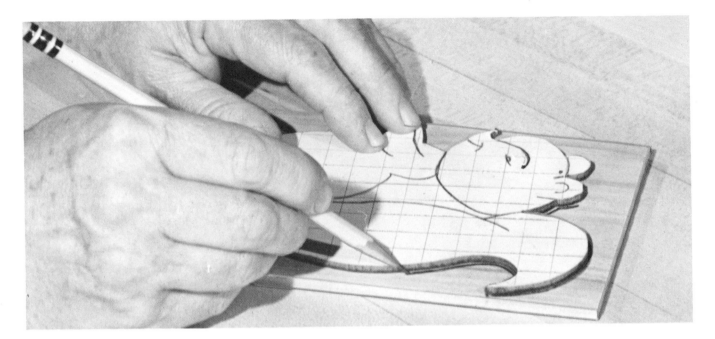

Fig. 4-15. *Tracing around a template onto wood.*

sure_____ pieces.
3. Name three uses for a try square.
4. A marking gauge is useful when laying out _____ or_____.
5. Dividers may be used as a compass to scribe_____ and _____.
6. You can easily duplicate angles and bevels using a_____.
7. Calipers are used to measure _____ stock.
8. The size of a design may be enlarged by sketching it freehand into _____ squares.

Research and Development

1. Obtain from catalogs, illustrations and descriptions of as many kinds of rules as you can find. Use these for a bulletin board display. Discuss the differences.
2. Prepare a short report on using a carpenter's square to lay out a common rafter. Refer to a book on carpentry for this information.
3. Draw a safety poster for your school's woodshop describing the safe use of pointed tools including pencil dividers and awls.

Unit 5
SAWING

In woodworking, it is important that you learn how to use tools properly and safely.

In working with saws be sure to select the proper saw for the job. All saws should be sharp and in good condition. Information on power-operated saws is included so you may see how they are constructed and operated. Whether or not you will be permitted to use power equipment depends on the policies established by your instructor.

Coping Saw

The coping saw is used mostly to cut around curves in stock one inch or less in thickness. While sawing, take quick, easy strokes using only enough forward pressure to keep the saw cutting. Hold the saw straight to help prevent binding.

Two methods are commonly used. If you are using THIN stock (3/8 in. or less in thickness), fasten a V-block as a platform to a bench with a clamp, or in a vise. Using this method, the saw cuts best with a downward stroke so the teeth of the blade point toward the handle, Fig. 5-1. If you are using THICKER stock (1/2 in. or more), fasten it in a vise. Using this method, the saw cuts best with a forward stroke with the saw teeth pointing AWAY from the handle, Fig. 5-2.

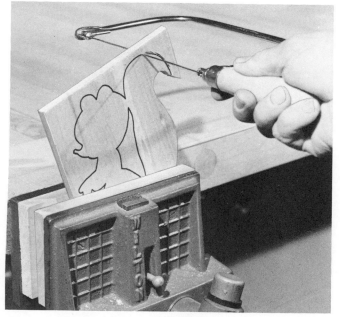

Fig. 5-2. Sawing a curve with a coping saw and vise.

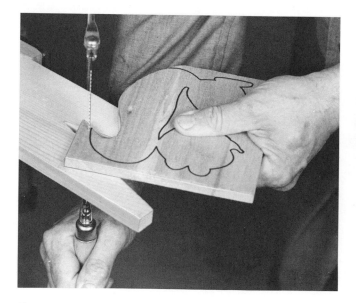

Fig. 5-1. Sawing thin stock with a coping saw and V-block.

Blades may be of the pin-end type or the loop-end type. To change the blade, loosen the handle three or four turns, then press forward on the front end of the frame and insert the blade into the slots provided.

To make an internal cut, drill a 1/4 in. diameter hole in the waste stock, then stick the blade through the hole and attach it to the saw frame.

Hand Crosscut Saw

A HAND CROSSCUT saw is designed to cut ACROSS THE GRAIN on the PUSH STROKE. The front faces of its teeth have an angle of 15 deg. The back angle is 45 deg. See Fig. 5-3, left. BEVELING the edges of the teeth about 24 deg. gives them the appearance and cutting action of a series of knives.

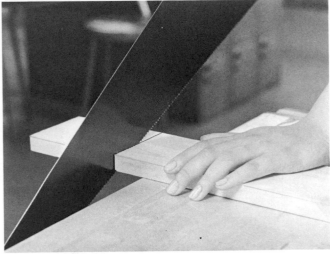

Fig. 5-4. Sawing with a crosscut saw.

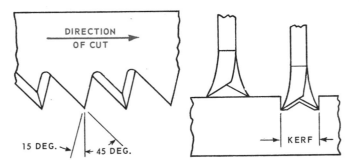

Fig. 5-3. Left. Crosscut saw teeth.
Right. Cross section of teeth.

The teeth are SET (bent to alternate sides) to make the cut or KERF wider than the thickness of the blade, Fig. 5-3, right.

Crosscut teeth score the wood, then the edges of the teeth form a groove and clear the sawdust from the kerf.

Coarseness of a saw is designated by the number of teeth per inch. For example, a saw with 8 teeth per inch is an 8-point saw.

To cross cut, first draw a square line across the end of the board with a try square and pencil. Hold the board firmly against a sawhorse or clamp it in a vise. Start the cut with a series of short strokes, the saw teeth being placed on the outside of the line. Use your thumb placed about two inches above the teeth as a guide. When the saw begins to cut, move your thumb away from the blade and make longer strokes with the saw held at an angle of about 45 deg. Gradually lengthen the strokes using light, uniform pressure. If the saw moves away from the line, twist the han-

dle slightly as you continue sawing to bring it back to the line. As you end the cut, slow and lighten the strokes to prevent splitting, Fig. 5-4.

Hand Ripsaw

This saw is designed to cut WITH THE GRAIN and cuts on the push stroke. The front faces of its teeth have an angle of 8 deg. The back angle is 52 deg. The ripsaw teeth are filed straight across giving them the appearance and cutting action similar to a series of vertical chisels. The saw teeth are set evenly to about 1/3 the thickness of the blade so the kerf made by the saw gives clearance. A 5 point (5 teeth per inch) ripsaw works well for general purpose, Fig. 5-5.

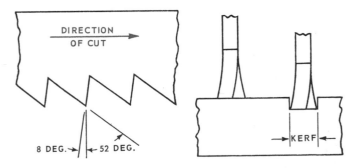

Fig. 5-5. Left. Ripsaw teeth. Right. Cross section of teeth.

To rip, first lay out a straight line along the grain of the board with a square, straight-edge or chalk line. Hold the board firmly against a sawhorse or clamp it in a vise. Hold the ripsaw at an angle of about 60 deg. and saw as with crosscutting, Fig. 5-6.

Fig. 5-6. Sawing with a ripsaw.

Backsaw

A backsaw is used to make fine, accurate cuts as in making wood joints and finish cuts. Its teeth are small; 12 or more points per inch. The blade is thin for narrow kerfs and its back is heavy, hence its name.

To make a finish cut, mark a layout line, Fig. 5-7. As a guide you may clamp a straight board along the line. Use a scrap board beneath to protect your bench top. Keep the blade against the guide as you make slow, light strokes. See Fig. 5-8.

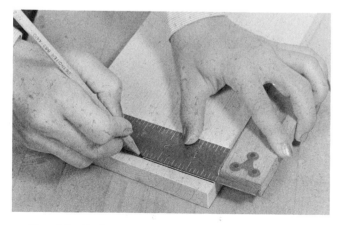

Fig. 5-7. Marking a square line at the end of a board.

Fig. 5-8. Making a finish saw cut with a backsaw and a fixture.

Miter Box Saw

This device is equipped with a special backsaw and cuts angles from 45 to 90 deg. It is especially useful for jobs such as cutting molding, picture frames, etc. See Fig. 5-9.

Fig. 5-9. Cutting a miter with a miter box saw.

Jig Saw

The power driven jig saw (scroll saw) cuts like a coping saw and is primarily designed for curved cuts with thin stock (1 in. or less in thickness). Its size is determined by the distance from the blade to the overarm. A 24 in. jig saw is a popular size and will cut stock this wide. The blade moves up and down, cutting on the DOWNWARD stroke. The motor pulls the blade down and a tension spring in upper sleeve brings the blade up, Fig. 5-10.

Sawing

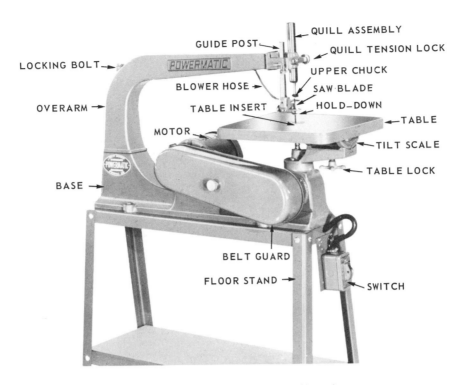

Fig. 5-10. Parts of a jig saw (scroll saw).

Sawing an Internal Cut

Drill a 1/4 in. hole in the waste stock near the line. Loosen the guide post and adjust the hold-down spring to press the stock lightly against the table. Turn the machine by hand to the bottom of the stroke. Place the blade, teeth pointing downward, through the hole into the lower chuck and tighten the thumbscrew. Pull the upper chuck down over the top of the blade and tighten the thumbscrew. Turn the machine by hand to check the adjustments. The blade should be straight vertically, the back of the blade being near the roller support in the guide assembly. HAVE YOUR INSTRUCTOR CHECK YOUR SETUP BEFORE YOU TURN ON THE MACHINE. As you saw, guide the work with both hands pushing forward just fast enough to keep the saw cutting, Fig. 5-11. Bypass sharp bends that you can complete later to help prevent breaking the blade.

Fig. 5-11. Sawing an internal cut with a jig saw.

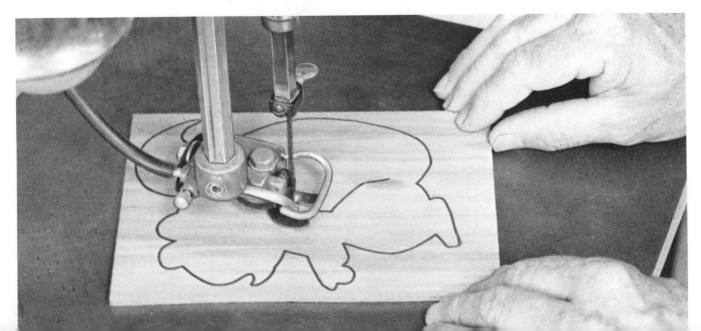

Blades for the jig saw are usually 5 or 6 in. long but vary in size and teeth per inch. They are available to cut wood, metal, plastic and other materials. Manufacturer's catalogs supply information on blade selection. Most work can be done with a blade 0.110 in. wide, 0.020 in. thick and with 15 teeth per inch.

Safety and Care

1. Unplug the saw before making adjustments.
2. Keep your fingers from in front of the saw blade at all times.
3. Turn the saw by hand before turning on the power.
4. Push the stock forward rather than toward the sides.

Portable Jig Saw

This machine, also called a SABER SAW, is designed to be moved around over the work. The blade is heavier than in the table model jig saw and makes a rougher cut. It cuts through 3/4 in. stock with ease. The saber saw is especially useful where curves need to be cut in long stock, Fig. 5-12.

Bandsaw

The bandsaw serves a wide variety of uses. You can make straight and curved cuts, freehand or with a guide. You can cut wood, plastic and metal. The blade of this saw is a continuous band which revolves on two wheels. The size of a bandsaw is determined by the diameter of the band wheels. The upper wheel is adjustable up and down to tighten or loosen the blade. It can be tilted forward and back to adjust tracking of the blade to the middle of the wheel. A 14 in. bandsaw is a popular size, Fig. 5-13.

Blades are available in widths of 1/8 - 1/2 in. and in a variety of tooth sizes and styles. The total length is specified by the manufacturer. A HOOK or SKIP tooth blade is recommended when cutting resinous woods or plastics. A 3/8 in. wide blade may be used to cut a curve with a minimum radius of 1 1/2 in.

Upper and lower guide assemblies need to be checked frequently. ALWAYS CONSULT YOUR INSTRUCTOR BEFORE MAKING AN ADJUSTMENT. For correct adjustment, the blade guides should clear the blade about .003 in. (approx. thickness of note paper) and the roller supports (backing bearings) should clear the back of the blade about 1/32 in.

Cutting with the Bandsaw

Lay out on the stock the cuts you plan to make and consider the sequence of the cuts to be made. SHORT cuts should be made first so that it is unnecessary to back out, Fig. 5-14. Straight cuts should be made before curved cuts for the same reason. Bypass

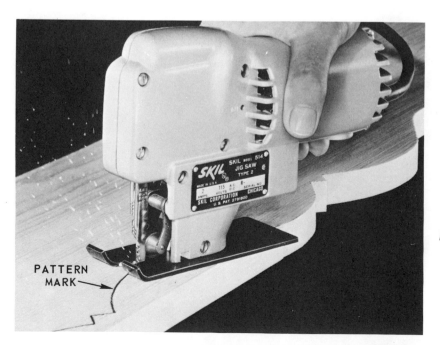

PATTERN MARK →

Fig. 5-12. Sawing curved cuts with a portable jig saw (saber saw). (Skil Corp.)

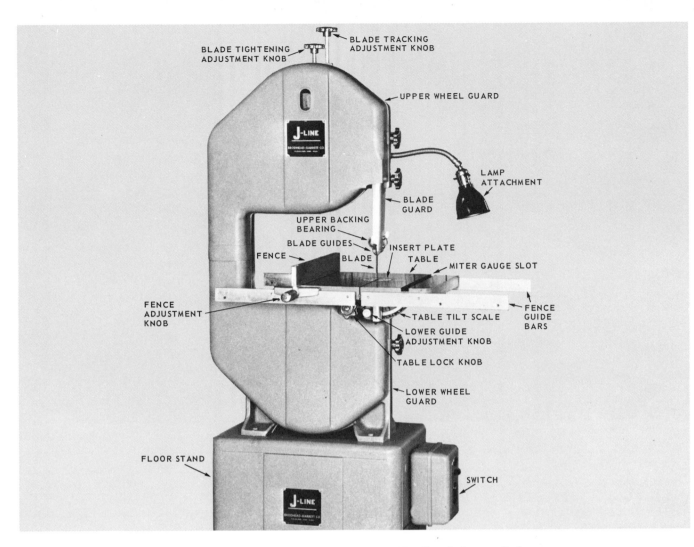

Fig. 5-13. Parts of a 14 in. bandsaw. (Brodhead—Garrett Co.)

sharp curves with longer curves and finish these cuts later. Sharp outside curves can be made by making several saw cuts perpendicular to the curve as RELIEF cuts, Fig. 5-15. Place stock on saw table and adjust guide post so that upper guide assembly is about 1/4 in. above work. HAVE YOUR INSTRUCTOR CHECK THE SETUP BEFORE YOU

TURN ON MACHINE. As you cut, keep your hands to the sides, out of the direct line of the saw blade. Use only enough forward pressure to keep the blade cutting.

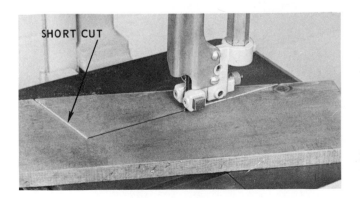

Fig. 5-14. Make the short cut first with a bandsaw.

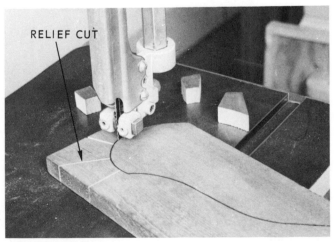

Fig. 5-15. Make relief (clearance) cuts before cutting around sharp curves with a bandsaw.

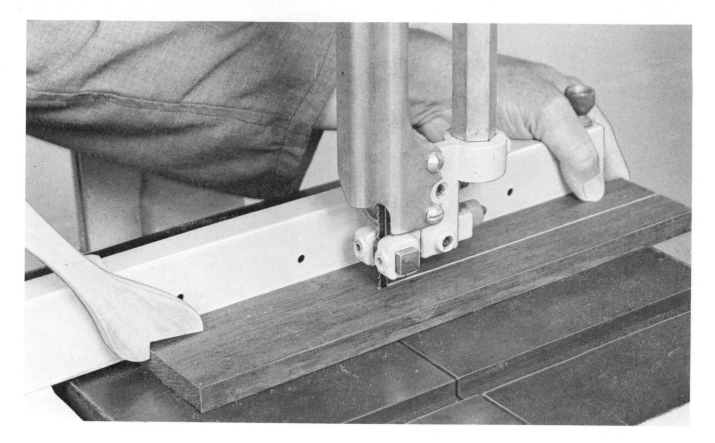

Fig. 5-16. Ripping narrow stock with a bandsaw and a push stick.

To rip narrow, straight stock (less than three inches wide) use a fence and a push stick, Fig. 5-16.

Safety and Care

1. Keep your hands to the side of the blade, away from its path.
2. Should the blade break, step aside and disconnect the machine.
3. Keep your fingers 2 in. or more from the blade at all times. Use a fixture to hold small pieces.
4. Always keep the upper guide assembly 1/4 - 1/2 in. from the stock.
5. To save the blade, push stock forward rather than toward the side.
6. Work within the capacity of the saw. A thick piece must be fed slower than a thin piece.

Circular Saw

The circular saw, often referred to as a TABLE saw, is one of the most productive machines you can use. By practicing a few precautions you can learn to use the circular saw safely and efficiently. The size of a cir-cular saw is determined by the maximum diameter of the circular blade used. The blade revolves at high speed and a guard is kept over the blade for your protection. A movable fence is mounted on the table as a guide for ripping stock to width. A miter gauge is used as a guide for crosscutting and mitering, Fig. 5-17.

Commonly used circular saw blades are the CROSSCUT, RIP and COMBINATION. The crosscut blade has teeth sharpened and set similar to a hand crosscut saw which cuts like a series of KNIVES. The rip blade has teeth sharpened and set similar to a hand ripsaw which cuts like a series of CHISELS.

The plain combination blade has both crosscut and rip teeth and is used for ALL-PURPOSE work. Some combination blades are hollow ground (planer combination) making the blade thicker near the teeth. This provides for clearance of the blade in the saw kerf, eliminating the necessity of setting the teeth. A planer combination blade makes a smooth, accurate cut in crosscutting and mitering, however, blade clearance is usually insufficient for ripping.

Sawing

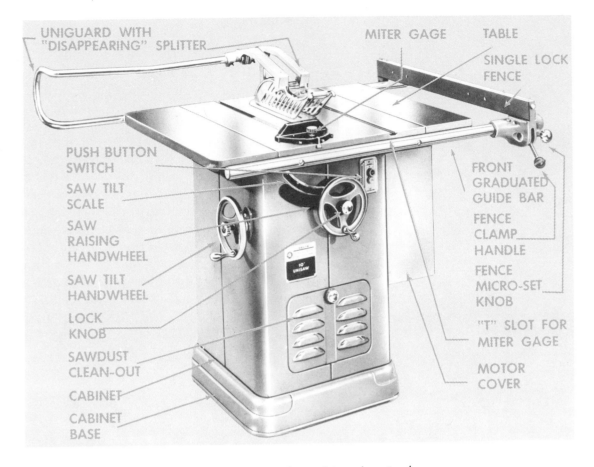

Fig. 5-17. Parts of a 10 in. tilting arbor circular saw.

Safety Note

Warp must be removed from the surfaces and at least one edge of boards to be cut with the circular saw.

Crosscutting

Make a mark on the board where you plan to make a cut. Raise the blade so it projects 1/8 in. above the stock. Lay the board on the table with the true edge against the miter gauge. Align the mark with the saw blade and place the guard over it. Move the fence out of the way (if the board is already square you can clamp a clearance block on the fence and use this block as a gauge for cutting several pieces to the same length). Stand slightly to one side of the blade and turn on the machine. Hold the stock firmly against the miter gauge as you push the gauge slowly along the groove, feeding the stock into the saw. Push the board past the saw blade and turn off the saw. See Fig. 5-18.

Safety Note

Wait until the saw stops before you pick up the piece sawed off.

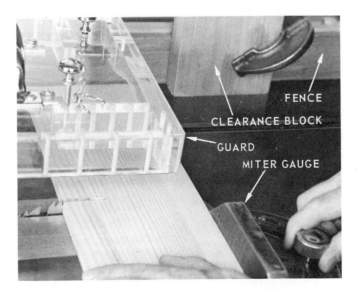

Fig. 5-18. Crosscutting duplicate pieces using a circular saw and clearance block.

Mitering

To saw a miter, set the miter gauge to the angle you desire to cut and proceed as with crosscutting, Fig. 5-19.

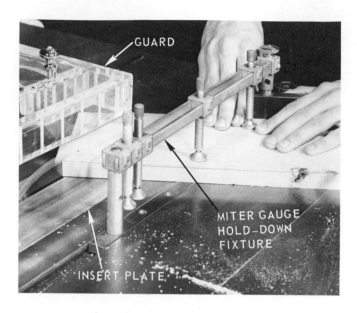

Fig. 5-19. Making a miter cut with a circular saw and a fixture.

Safety Note

For greater safety and accuracy in cutting miters, it is best to use a clamping device with the miter gauge. You can do this by setting the points of two flat head screws through a true-board and then attaching the board to the miter gauge as an auxiliary fence. The screw points act as anchor points to prevent the board from slipping as you make the cut. Another method is to use a miter gauge with a hold-down attachment as a fixture, Fig. 5-19.

Changing the Blade

Disconnect the power to the saw and remove the insert plate (the plate around the saw blade). Place a wrench on the arbor nut with one hand and wedge a board under the saw blade with the other hand. Turn the nut clockwise for removal (most saw arbors have left-hand threads). Remove the nut, collar and saw blade. Replace the desired saw blade by reversing this procedure. Be sure the saw teeth are mounted to cut TOWARD the stock when in operation, Fig. 5-18.

Ripping

Store the miter gauge so that it is protected from damage. Raise the blade 1/8 in. above the stock as in crosscutting. Set the fence by using the scale on the front guide bar. You may want to check this distance by measuring between the fence and the nearest tooth point. Place the guard over the blade. Lay the board flat on the table with the straight-edge next to the fence. Turn on the saw and push the board slowly into the blade. Keep forward pressure only on the piece between the blade and the fence. For pieces narrower than four inches, use a push stick. Continue pushing the board until its entire length is cut and turn off the saw. WAIT UNTIL THE BLADE STOPS BEFORE YOU REMOVE PIECES OF WOOD FROM THE BLADE. See Figs. 5-17 and 5-20.

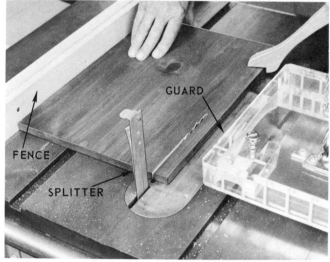

Fig. 5-20. Ripping a board to width with a circular saw. (Guard is removed to view the operation.)

Safety Note

Be sure to use the SPLITTER (sometimes called SLITTER) for ripping operations. The splitter, indicated by an arrow in Fig. 5-20, acts as a metal wedge in the saw kerf, separating the two pieces cut with the rip saw blade to help prevent binding. The splitter is also equipped with metal fingers which hold the board down as it is cut, serving as an antikickback device.

Beveling

A bevel is an angle cut along an edge of a board. To saw a bevel, turn the saw tilt hand wheel to the correct angle and proceed as in crosscutting or ripping. On many circular saws, each turn of the tilt hand wheel moves the arbor 2 1/2 deg. You can set the saw blade to the angle you wish to cut by using the indicator on the saw tilt scale, Fig. 5-17.

Sawing a Rabbet

Lay out the size of the rabbet on the end of the stock and set the blade to this height. Lay the board flat on the table with the marked edge next to the fence. Using a push stick, move the board into the saw as in ripping. Place the surface of the board against the fence and make the second cut, Fig. 5-21.

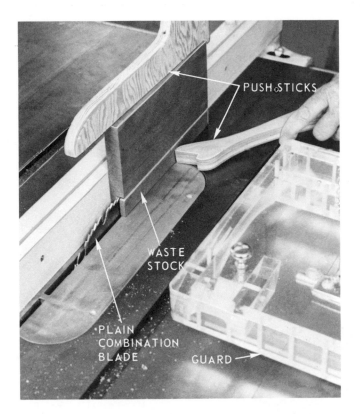

Fig. 5-21. Sawing a rabbet. (Guard is removed to view the operation.)

Safety Note

Be sure the waste stock will fall free at the end of the cut to help prevent kickback.

Resawing

This is a ripping operation to obtain two boards from a thick board.

Mark the end of the board where you plan to make the cut. Raise the blade 1/8 in. above the center line of the board. Place the edge of the board on the table with one of its surfaces next to the fence. Clamp a feather board on the table with pressure applied against the board to be resawed (the feather board acts as a hold-in to prevent the board from being thrown by the saw).

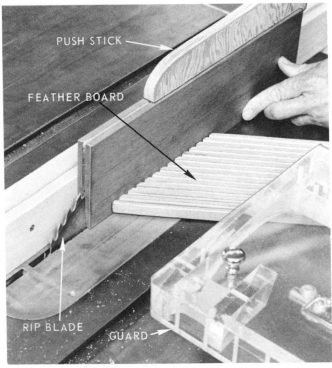

Fig. 5-22. Resawing. (Guard is removed to view the operation.)

To make a feather board, saw an angle of 20-30 deg. on one end of a board and then rip kerfs about 1/4 to 3/8 in. apart and 6 to 8 in. long, Fig. 5-22.

Move the guard against the board as an additional hold-in. Using a push stick, move the board into the saw as in ripping. Complete the cut, turn the board over so the opposite edge is against the table and make the second cut, Fig. 5-22.

Fig. 5-23. Cutting a groove with a dado head. (Guard is removed to view the operation.)

Cutting a Groove or Dado

A GROOVE is a U-shape, square cornered recess cut along the grain of a piece of wood. A DADO is an identical recess cut across the grain.

Grooves and dados are usually made with a dado head. A dado head consists of two saws and a set of chippers with cutting edges varying from 1/16 to 1/4 in. wide. Cuts 1/8 to 13/16 in. wide can be made. The chippers are set up between the saws to the width cut desired. Another type of dado head consists of three parts. In this type the center piece, containing the cutters, is turned to adjust to the width of cut desired.

To cut a groove, adjust the dado head to the width and depth of cut desired. Using a push stick, move the stock slowly into the dado head as in ripping, Fig. 5-23.

Safety Note

When dadoing, keep your hands or push stick in the same position as you would if the dado head were cutting through the stock.

Portable Circular Saw

Carpenters and home craftworkers frequently use this type saw. It is designed to be moved over the work freehand or with a guide. Common sizes are 6 1/4, 7 1/4, and 8 1/4 in. A spring guard covers the blade at the end of each cut, protecting the operator and saw. See Figs. 5-24 and 5-25.

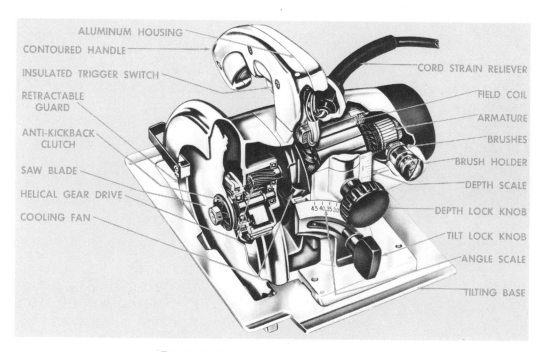

ALUMINUM HOUSING
CONTOURED HANDLE
INSULATED TRIGGER SWITCH
RETRACTABLE GUARD
ANTI-KICKBACK CLUTCH
SAW BLADE
HELICAL GEAR DRIVE
COOLING FAN
CORD STRAIN RELIEVER
FIELD COIL
ARMATURE
BRUSHES
BRUSH HOLDER
DEPTH SCALE
DEPTH LOCK KNOB
TILT LOCK KNOB
ANGLE SCALE
TILTING BASE

Fig. 5-24. Parts of a portable circular saw.

Radial Circular Saw

Although this saw is quite versatile, it is used mostly to cut boards to length. It is sometimes called a CUT-OFF saw. Stock to be cut to length is laid flat with a straight or concave edge against the fence. The saw is then pulled across the stock along the arm track, Fig. 5-26.

Safety and Care

1. Have your instructor check the setup before you turn on the saw.
2. Stand slightly to one side and keep your hands out of the path of the blade at all times.
3. Watch for others. See that no one stands in the path of the saw blade.
4. Cut only stock 1 foot or more in length. Use a hand saw for small pieces.
5. Use the correct blade and fence for the cut being made.
6. Always use a sharp saw blade and a saw guard.

Fig. 5-25. *Crosscutting with a portable circular saw.*

Test Your Knowledge - Unit 5

1. A coping saw is used mostly to make _____ cuts.
2. A coping saw cuts best when used to make _____ strokes with the teeth pointed _____ the handle.
3. A hand crosscut saw is designed to cut _____ the grain on the _____ stroke.
4. On a crosscut saw, the teeth are set to make the kerf _____ than the thickness of the blade.
5. A hand ripsaw is designed to cut _____ the grain.
6. Ripsaw teeth are filed _____.
7. Coarseness of a saw is designated by the number of teeth per _____.
8. A backsaw is used to make finer cuts than

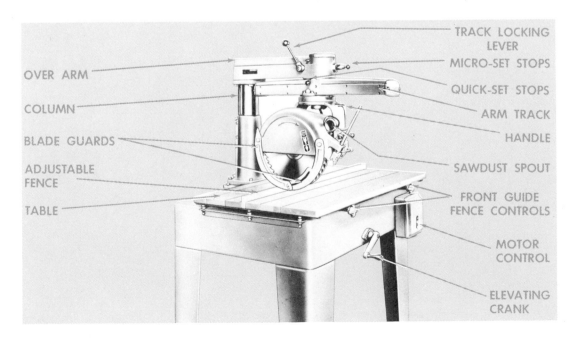

Fig. 5-26. *Parts of a radial circular saw.*

a ripsaw. True or False?

9. A power-driven jig saw cuts on the_____ stroke. The motor pulls the blade _____ and a_____ brings the blade up.

10. A portable jig saw (saber saw) uses a blade that is_____than the table mounted jig saw.

11. The size of a bandsaw is determined by the _____of the _____.

12. A bandsaw may be used to make both _____ and_____cuts.

13. Circular saw size is indicated by the diameter of the_____.

14. A combination blade used on circular saws has both _____ and _____teeth.

15. In using a circular saw, the blade should be set so it projects above the stock about _____.

16. What is a feather board?

17. On a portable circular saw, a _____ _____covers the blade at the end of each cut, to protect the operator and the saw.

18. A radial arm saw is used mostly for:
( ) Cutting boards to length.
( ) Ripping boards to width.

Research and Development

1. Following safety rules is important. Design a safety poster that can be used with a circular saw.

2. Make pencil sketches that show the shape of crosscut, rip and combination circular saw blades.

3. Visit a cabinet shop or other woodworking industry in your community and find out about the power tools used. Report to your class.

Unit 6
BORING AND DRILLING

Hand Tools

In woodworking, holes 1/4 in. and smaller are usually drilled with a hand or power drill. Holes larger than 1/4 in. are bored using an auger bit, expansion or forstner bit.

Brace

A brace is used to hold the bit and to provide leverage needed to turn the bit into the wood. A brace is also used with screwdriver bits to drive screws and with countersinks to provide recesses for screw heads. The brace is made to hold either round or square bit shanks. Its size is designated by the DIAMETER OF SWING (circle made by the brace handle when turned). A 12 in. brace is a common size. The brace is available with a RATCHET (a device for making part of a swing) for close work. See Fig. 6-1, above.

Auger Bits

Auger bits are used to bore holes in wood and other soft materials. They may be purchased in sizes ranging from 3/16 to 2 in. in diameter. The size of a bit is indicated by a number stamped on the tang which shows the diameter in sixteenths of an inch, Fig. 6-1, below.

Boring Straight Holes

Lay out holes to be bored and mark the locations with an awl, Fig. 6-2. In boring, hold

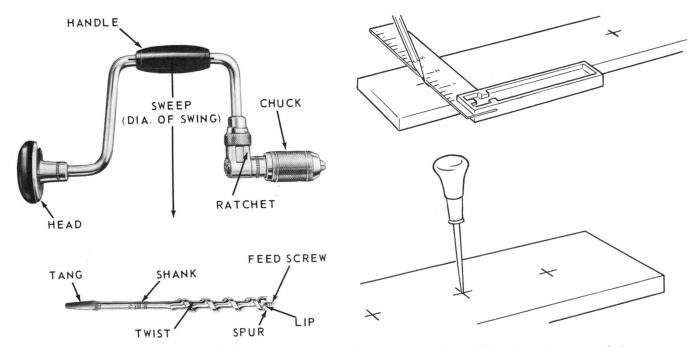

HANDLE

SWEEP
(DIA. OF SWING)

CHUCK

RATCHET

HEAD

TANG

SHANK

FEED SCREW

TWIST

SPUR

LIP

Fig. 6-1. Left. Above. Parts of a brace. Below. Parts of an auger. Fig. 6-2. Right. Above. Laying out holes. Below. Using awl to mark hole locations.

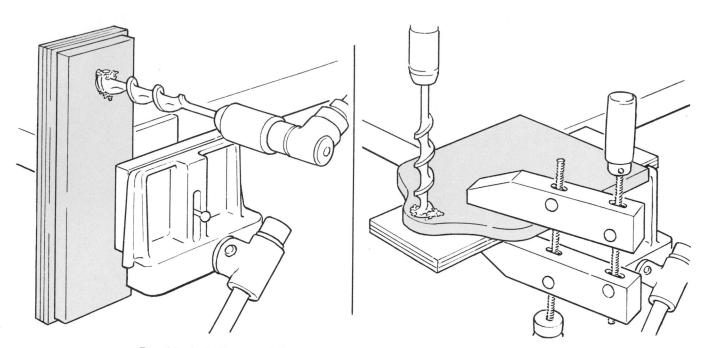

Fig. 6-3. Left. Boring a hole in a horizontal position with a brace and auger bit.
Right. Boring a hole in a vertical position.

the bit straight (perpendicular) to the stock. Use only enough pressure to keep the bit cutting. Use a piece of scrap wood as a back-up board to assure a smooth hole when the bit cuts through the wood. See Fig. 6-3.

Another method is to bore a hole until the feed screw of the bit comes through the board,

then complete the boring of the hole working from the other side.

Boring Holes at an Angle

Lay out holes to be bored and mark the locations with an awl. A bevel gauge set at the proper angle may be used as a guide, Fig. 6-4.

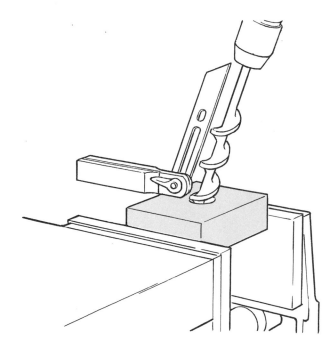

Fig. 6-4. Boring a hole at an angle using a bevel gauge as a guide.

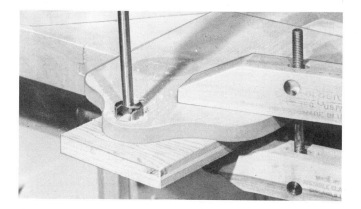

Fig. 6-5. Smoothing the bottom of a hole with forstner bit.

Forstner Bit

A forstner bit which has no spurs, is designed to smooth bottoms of holes bored with other bits. To use this bit, hold the brace as with other auger bits, Fig. 6-5.

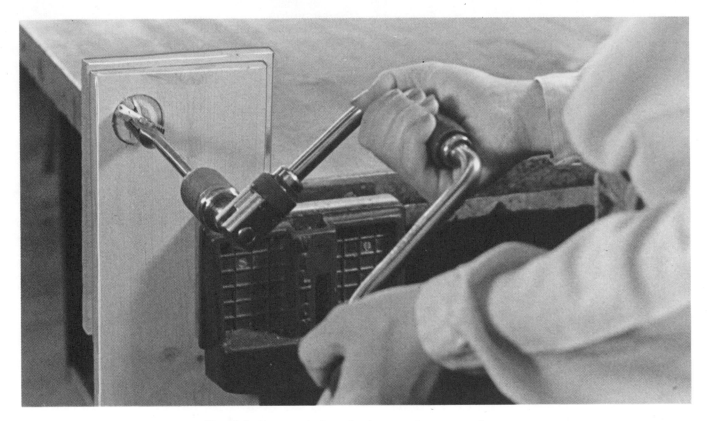

Fig. 6-6. Boring a hole with a brace and expansive bit.

Expansive Bit

Large holes may be bored with expansive bits. This type bit is usually adjustable to bore holes from one to three inches in diameter. Set the expansive bit to the desired size and bore a trial-hole in a piece of scrap stock. Make minor adjustments if necessary, then bore the hole as with an auger bit, Fig. 6-6.

Hand Drill

The hand drill is used with drill bits to drill small holes. It may also be used with a countersink to recess screw heads. The hand drill is made to hold round bit shanks. Bits

are held in a 3-jaw chuck on its front end. The size of a hand drill is designated by the capacity of its chuck (largest bit which will fit in chuck). A 1/4 in. hand drill is a common size. The bit is turned with a handle and geared-wheels, Fig. 6-7.

Automatic (Push) Drill

You operate this tool by pushing the handle. A strong spring returns the handle to its original position. It is fast and efficient to use in making holes less than 3/16 in. in diameter, Fig. 6-8.

Fig. 6-8. Automatic or push drill.

Drill Bits

Round or straight shank twist drill bits are used in hand drills, portable electric drills and drill presses. Twist drill bits made of carbon steel are satisfactory for woods and other soft materials. High speed twist drill

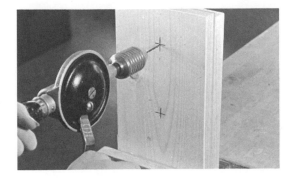

Fig. 6-7. Drilling with a hand drill.

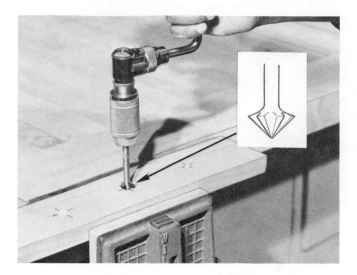

Fig. 6-9. Using a brace and countersink.

ing bit frequently to pull out the chips. If needed, a piece of tape may be used on the drill as a depth gauge. Use a back-up board to assure a smooth hole as the bit cuts through the other side, Fig. 6-7.

Safety Note

If the geared wheels are not covered, be especially careful when handling the hand drill to avoid being pinched by the gears.

Countersinking

A countersink cuts a funnel-shaped recess to receive the head of a flat head wood screw, Fig. 6-9. As you countersink, cut only deep enough so the head of the screw fits flush with the surface of the board.

You may want to cover screws with wood plugs. You can do this by COUNTERBORING the holes with a drill bit slightly larger than the screw heads or by using a special counterboring tool in a portable drill or in a drill press. See Detail 2, Fig. 6-12.

bits (H.S.) which are better for metals and other hard materials, are more expensive than carbon steel bits. Sizes commonly available for school shop use are 1/32 to 1/2 in. in diameter.

Special drill bits (drill points) are made for the push drill. Sizes available are from 1/16 to about 3/16 in. in diameter.

Drilling Holes with a Hand Drill

Lay out and mark locations. In using a hand drill place the point of the drill in a recess made with an awl. Hold the bit straight and use only enough pressure to keep the bit cutting. You control the feed by the pressure you apply. Use less pressure when drilling in hard wood or with small bits. Remove the turn-

Sharpening an Auger Bit

Auger bit should be sharpened only under the supervision of your instructor. You can use a special auger bit file or a flat jeweler's file. File toward the cutting lips with light, even pressure using only enough strokes to make them sharp, Fig. 6-10. FILE ONLY ON THE INSIDE OF THE SPURS.

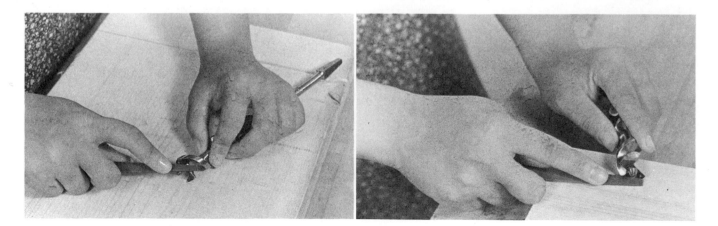

Fig. 6-10. Left. Sharpening the cutting lips of an auger bit. Right. Sharpening the spurs of an auger bit.

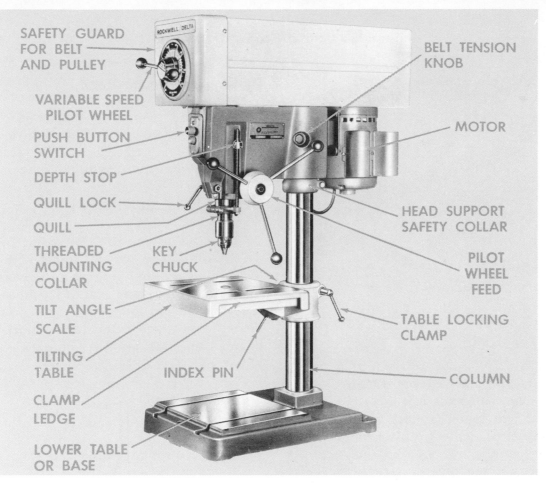

Fig. 6-11. Parts of a drill press.

Drill Press

A drill press is a power tool used to drill holes through wood and other materials. See Fig. 6-11. A drill press can also be used for sanding, routing, shaping and mortising. Drill press size is determined by the distance from the center of the drill bit to the column. For example, a 15 in. drill press will drill a hole in the center of a round piece 15 in. in diameter.

Various drill speeds are obtained by using special drives, or by shifting the drive belt onto different size pulleys. The slowest speed, usually 400 - 600 rpm, should be used to drill holes of one inch in diameter or larger. A speed of 1200 rpm can generally be used to drill holes as large as 1/2 in. in diameter.

Numerous drill bits are available for the drill press and portable electric drill. Among these are twist drills, machine forstner bits, auger and spur bits, speed (spade) bits, circle cutters, plug cutters and Screw-mates, Fig. 6-12. The machine forstner bit cuts like a hand

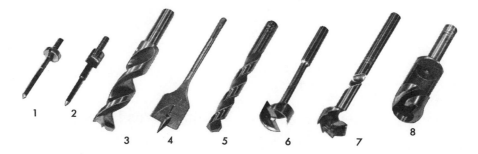

Fig. 6-12. Machine drill bits. 1—Screw-mate. 2—Screw-mate counterbore. 3—Spur machine bit. 4—Speed (spade). 5—Twist drill. 6—Forstner. 7—Multi-spur bit. 8—Plug cutter.

Fig. 6-13. Using a V-block as a fixture while drilling into round stock.

Drilling into Round Stock

Round or irregular shaped stock may be held in a V-block, drill press vise or clamped to the table. See Fig. 6-13. The table may be turned for drilling into large pieces.

Drilling Holes at an Angle

In using a twist drill or auger bit, set the drill table at the correct angle with a sliding T-bevel. Cut the same angle across one end of a scrap piece and clamp the piece over the stock to be drilled. The bevel on the scrap piece is perpendicular to the drill bit which enables the drill point to cut straight into the stock. See Fig. 6-14.

forstner bit. The machine auger bit is similar to a hand auger bit except it does not have a feed screw. The speed (spade) bit has a sharp point and is used without a pilot hole. Circle cutters are usually adjustable to cut large diameter holes. Plug cutters are designed to make short dowels or plugs to cover screw heads. The Screw-mate cuts proper size holes for flat head screws (takes place of two drills . . . drill used to make hole to take shank of screw, and drill used to take threaded portion).

Drilling Through Flat Stock

Lay out and mark holes to be drilled as you would for hand tools. Select the correct size bit, insert it in the chuck, and tighten with chuck key.

Center the table under the bit. Set for proper speed and adjust the depth gauge. Place a scrap board under the work and use some type of mechanical holding device (drill press vise or clamp) to hold the assembly in place.

Turn on the drill. Hold the stock firmly as you bring the bit into the cutting position with the feed lever. Use light pressure. If the hole is deep, remove the bit several times to pull out the chips and to keep the bit from overheating. When the hole is completed, shut off the motor.

If you want to drill several holes only part way through the stock, use the depth stop.

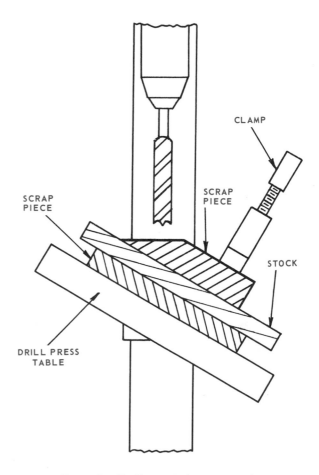

Fig. 6-14. Drilling a hole at an angle.

Drilling Large Holes

Set the circle cutter or hole saw to the correct size. See Fig. 6-15. Adjust the power drill to its slowest speed. The center drill bit should

Fig. 6-15. *Left. Drilling a large hole with a circle cutter. Right. Circle cutter.*

be set about 1/4 in. below the cutter so it will guide and anchor the cutter. Clamp the stock to the drill table, HAVE YOUR INSTRUCTOR CHECK YOUR SETUP. Turn on the power and proceed SLOWLY.

Safety and Care

1. Unplug the drill press before making adjustments.
2. Clamp all stock to drill press table before drilling holes.
3. Have your instructor check your setup.
4. Necktie, if worn, should be tucked in shirt.
5. Use your safety glasses. See that belt guard is in place.
6. See that the chuck key is removed before you turn on the power.
7. Use a sharp drill bit with speed and feed recommended by manufacturer.

Portable Electric Drill

Many craftworkers now use the portable drill because of its efficiency and versatility. See Figs. 6-16 and 6-17. Portable drill size is determined by the capacity of the chuck. Sizes 1/4, 3/8, and 1/2 in. are common. Some portable drills have trigger speed control (TSC) which provides variable speeds. Battery operated and pneumatic portable drills are also available.

Safety Note

Always connect a portable electric drill to a properly grounded outlet.

Fig. 6-16. *Drilling a large hole with a portable drill and dial saw.*

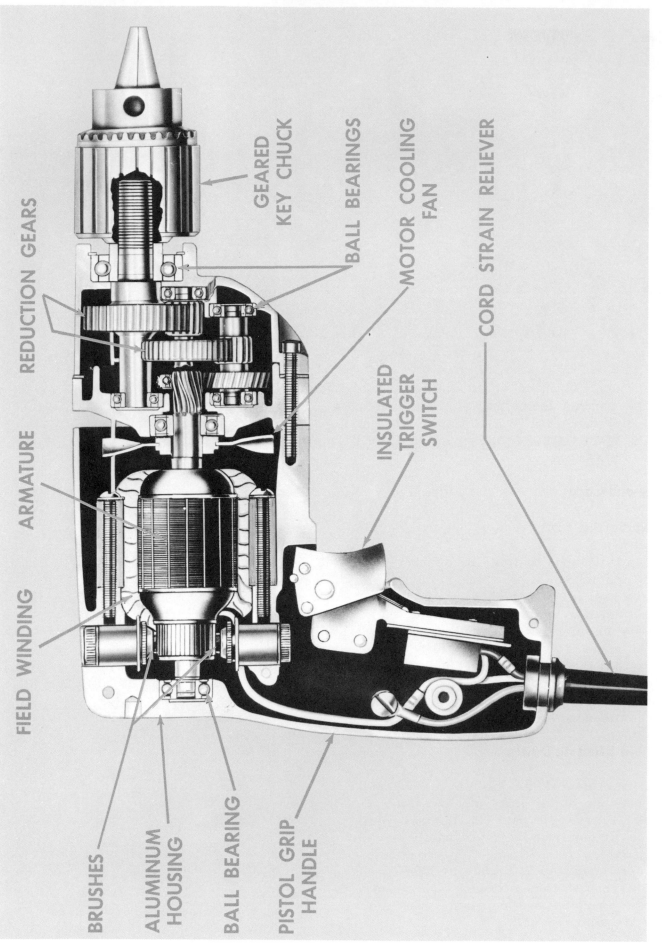

REDUCTION GEARS

GEARED
KEY CHUCK

BALL BEARINGS

MOTOR COOLING
FAN

CORD STRAIN RELIEVER

ARMATURE

FIELD WINDING

INSULATED
TRIGGER
SWITCH

BRUSHES

ALUMINUM
HOUSING

BALL BEARING

PISTOL GRIP
HANDLE

Fig. 6-17. Portable electric drill with parts identified.

Test Your Knowledge - Unit 6

1. A brace is used to hold the _____ and to provide _____.
2. The size of a brace is designated by the _____ .
3. Auger bits usually range in size from ____ to ____ in.
4. Two methods of assuring a smooth hole when an auger bit cuts through wood are _____ and _____ .
5. A _____ may be used as a guide when boring holes at an angle.
6. A forstner bit is designed to _____ .
7. Describe the operation of the automatic push drill.
8. A_____cuts a funnel-shaped recess to receive the head of a flat head wood screw.
9. When sharpening an auger bit, file only on the _____ of the spurs.
10. A drill press can be used for
    a._____ .
    b._____ .
    c._____ .
    d._____ .
    e._____ .
11. Name six types of drill bits available for the drill press and portable electric drill.
12. When drilling round stock, it may be held in a _____ , _____ , or _____ .
13. The portable drill is often used because of its_____ and _____ .

Research and Development

1. How versatile are drilling machines? Find as many attachments as you can that utilize drilling machines. Catalogs issued by power tool manufacturers are good sources.
2. What are some of the advantages in using battery-powered and pneumatic-powered drilling machines?

Unit 7
FILING, CARVING, AND CHISELING

Wood Files

Wood files are used to shape wood and to smooth saw marks from curved and straight edges of wood. Files are identified by the type of teeth and by the cross-sectional shape. Flat, half-round and round files from 8 to 12 in. long are the most common. A set of smaller files is useful for intricate work.

File teeth cut like tiny chisels and may be SINGLE-CUT (rows of teeth running diagonally and parallel across the surface) or DOUBLE-CUT (two rows of teeth crossing each other, running diagonally across the surface).

Using a File

Be sure the file you select for use has a tight-fitting handle. Clamp the stock in a vise close to the edge you are shaping to help prevent vibration and splitting of the wood. File the edge at an angle toward the middle, completing the edge from the other side to prevent tearing the edge. This is especially important when shaping plywood. Use only enough pressure to keep the file cutting. The round side of the file should be used to smooth inside curves, and the flat side for outside curves and straight edges. See Fig. 7-1. Keep the file clean with a wire brush or a file card.

Fig. 7-1. Using a half-round file to shape an edge.

Filing, Carving, Chiseling

Safety Note

Never use a file without a handle.

Shaping an Edge to Rough Size with a Draw Knife

A draw knife has a wide blade and handles at both ends. The blade is sharpened to a keen, beveled edge.

A draw knife is used mostly for shaping edges to rough size. Lay out the contour to be shaped and clamp the stock in a vise. Remove the draw knife from its keeper. Grasp each handle with a firm grip holding the beveled side of the blade down. Pull the draw knife toward you with firm, uniform pressure cutting with or across the grain, Fig. 7-2.

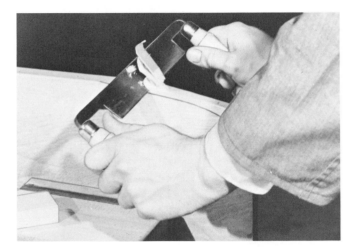

Fig. 7-2. Shaping an edge to rough size with a draw knife.

Safety Note

Always replace the keeper on the cutting edge after use.

Smoothing Curved Edges with a Spokeshave

You can use a spokeshave for jobs such as smoothing freeform shapes, boomerangs, archery bows. Its original purpose was to smooth spokes for wagon wheels and stocks for guns. The spokeshave has two handles and an adjustable blade that cuts similar to a plane iron. It is also sharpened like a plane iron.

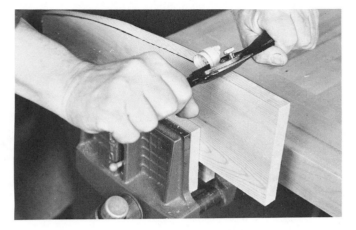

Fig. 7-3. Shaping a curved edge with a spokeshave.

Lay out a curved design on a piece of wood and rough cut the shape with a saw or draw knife. Clamp the piece in a vise close to the edge to be smoothed. The spokeshave may be pulled toward you or turned around and pushed. Adjust the blade for a fine cut. Grasp the tool with both hands and push or pull it along the contour of the edge, cutting with or across the grain. See Fig. 7-3.

Using Gouge to Form Inside of Dish

Gouges are chisels with curved blades. We use gouges (usually outside ground) when shaping the inside of bowls, dishes and trays. Sugar pine, basswood, walnut and mahogany are woods that are well suited for carving.

Lay out a freeform shape on a piece of wood and drill 1/4 in. diameter holes at uni-

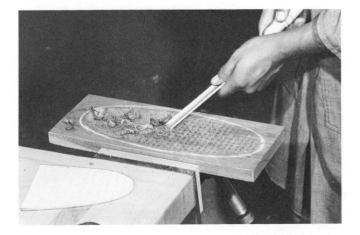

Fig. 7-4. Shaping the inside of a dish with a gouge.

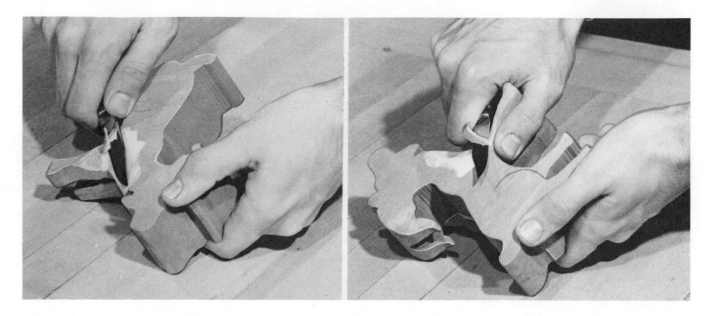

Fig. 7-5. *Left. Using a sloyd knife with a forward stroke to carve an animal figure.*
Right. Using a sloyd knife with a backward stroke to carve an animal figure.

form distances to the approximate desired depth. Clamp the stock in a vise. Start at the outside and work toward the center. Using firm, uniform pressure, guide the gouge with one hand and push with the other, cutting with the grain when possible. Roll the gouge as you cut across the grain. See Fig. 7-4.

Safety Note

When using a gouge, clamp your stock securely and use both hands. Always cut away from yourself.

Carving with Knife

Carving an animal figure (whittling) with a knife is shown in Fig. 7-5. A SLOYD knife, a straight, solid knife is a popular type. A UTILITY knife with changeable blades, Fig. 7-6, can also be used to good advantage. Other uses for a knife include trimming veneer and making accurate layout marks.

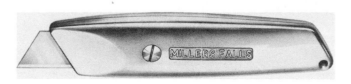

Fig. 7-6. *Utility knife.*

To carve an animal figure, rough cut the shape with a coping saw or jig saw. Hold the figure in one hand and the knife in the other. Then use short, forward and backward strokes working either with or across the grain.

Safety Notes

1. When carving, keep your fingers in such a position they will not be cut if the knife slips.
2. Always keep the knife sharp.

Surface Carving

Carving tools are available in sets with various shapes of cutting edges. These sets include: V-shape and U-shape tools (Veiners), for making outline cuts; gouges, for making background cuts; and straight chisels for other decorative cuts.

You can beautify such projects as jewelry boxes, lamps and book ends with surface carving. Prepare a design and transfer it to the wood surface. Clamp your stock in a vise and cut around the outline of the design with a veiner. Using short, uniform strokes in a forward direction, remove the background with a small gouge, Fig. 7-7.

Fig. 7-7. Carving a background with a gouge.

Safety Note

Always keep your hands behind the carving tool.

Cutting with Wood Chisels

Wood chisels are of two principal kinds, the SOCKET and the TANG, Fig. 7-8. The socket-type chisel is made for heavy work. Its handle is tapered to fit into a cone-shaped recess at the end of the blade. A socket-type chisel is usually driven with a mallet, Fig. 7-8, above. The tang-type chisel is used for lighter work. The back end of the blade which tapers to a point (tang) is driven into the handle, Fig. 7-8, below. Wood chisels 1/8 to 2

in. in widths are readily available. Chisels are ground and honed to a keen edge beveled 25-30 deg. for general work, similar to a plane iron.

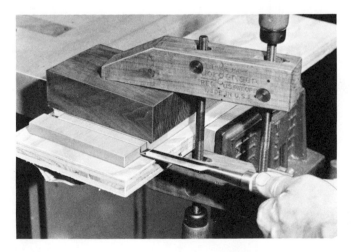

Fig. 7-9. Starting a dado joint with the chisel bevel turned up.

You can use a chisel to trim and shape wood and to make wood joints. Turn the bevel side of the chisel up to make convex cuts, paring cuts and to start dado and rabbet joints, Fig. 7-9. Turn the bevel side down for better

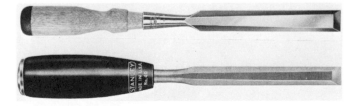

Fig. 7-8. Above. Socket chisel. Below. Tang chisel.

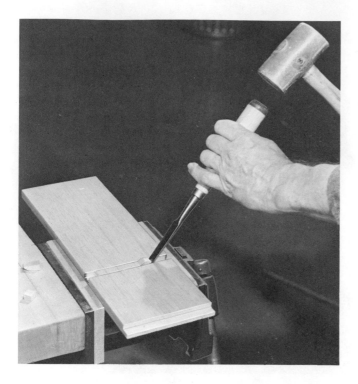

Fig. 7-10. Cutting a dado joint to depth with the chisel bevel turned down.

control when you make concave cuts, or when you cut wood joints to depth, Fig. 7-10.

Safety and Care

1. When using wood chisels always keep both hands behind the cutting edge.
2. See to it the edge is sharp. It is difficult to do satisfactory work with a dull chisel.
3. Lay the chisel on the table with the bevel down to protect its cutting edge.
4. Do not carry a chisel in your pocket.

Test Your Knowledge – Unit 7

1. Wood files are of two principal types: _____cut and _____cut.
2. When shaping plywood it is important to file at an angle toward the middle, and complete the job from the other side. Why?
3. In using a drawing knife, it is advisable to cut ( ) with the grain, or, ( ) against the grain of the wood.
4. A spokeshave was originally used to____.
5. A spokeshave is sharpened like a_____ iron.
6. Gouges are chisels with _____ blades.
7. Three woods that are well suited for carving (whittling) are: _____, _____, _____.
8. Two types of knives used for wood carving are_____and_____.
9. Wood chisels are of two principal kinds: _____ and_____.
10. When sharpening wood chisels, the bevel should be about_____degrees.

Research and Development

1. What are the characteristics of a good carving wood?
2. Prepare a paper on the sources of the woods listed in research question 1 above.
3. Prepare a drawing of a wood chisel and identify the principal parts.

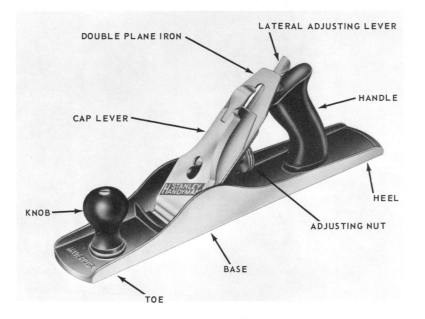

Fig. 8-1. Parts of a hand plane.

Unit 8
PLANING

We use planes to smooth wood surfaces and edges of boards and to make wood joints. Various sizes and types of planes are available. All types operate the same way. Cutting is done by a sharp plane iron. The plane iron cap breaks the wood shavings into wood curls and deflects them out of the plane. See Figs. 8-1 and 8-2.

SMOOTHING PLANES, 6-10 in. long, and JACK PLANES, 11-15 in. long are used for smoothing the face surfaces of the stock. The jack plane is used for all-around work and is a favorite of many craftsmen.

The MODELER'S PLANE is a tiny plane used for small work and the BLOCK PLANE, 4-6 in. long, is a small plane used for end grain and trimming of small pieces of wood. These planes are designed for use with one hand.

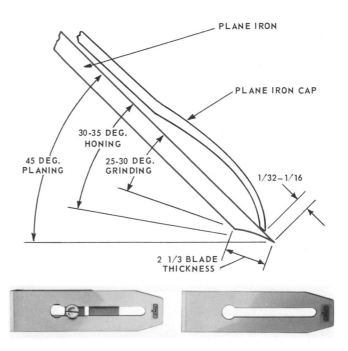

Fig. 8-2. Above. Assembled double plane iron. Below. Double plane iron on the left and a single plane iron on the right.

61

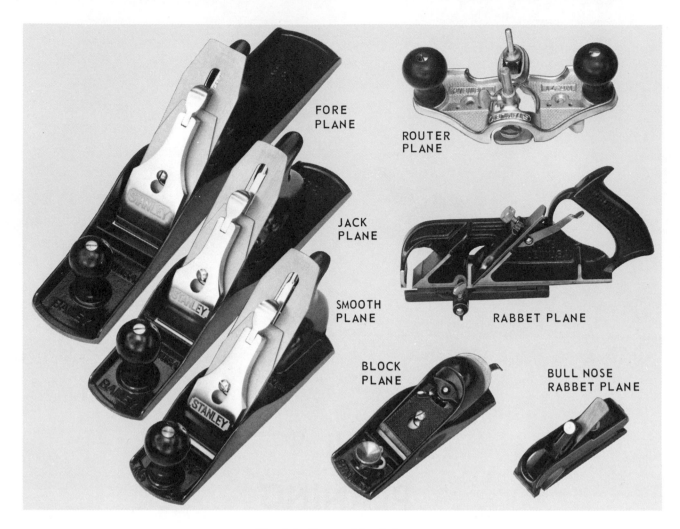

Fig. 8-3. *Types of hand planes.*

FORE PLANES, approximately 18 in. long, and JOINTER PLANES, 22-28 in. long, are used to join the edges of long pieces of stock for gluing.

The ROUTER and RABBET PLANES are used to make wood joints. See Fig. 8-3.

Care and Adjustment of Planes

For satisfactory results, you must keep your plane sharp and properly adjusted. To protect the cutting edge when it is not in use, always lay it on one side or return it to the storage place.

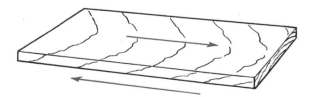

Fig. 8-4. *Note direction of wood grain indicated by arrows.*

Check the plane for sharpness and adjustment before using it. Remove the double plane iron (blade) by lifting the cap lever. A double plane iron consists of the plane iron and plane iron cap, held together with a screw, Fig. 8-2. Replace the blade, sight along the bottom of the base, and adjust the blade parallel to the base with the lateral adjusting lever. Adjust the depth of cut with the adjusting nut (a clockwise direction lowers the blade) so that the cutting edge of the blade is barely visible. Test the plane on a piece of softwood clamped in a vise. A thin shaving indicates a light cut which will produce the smoothest surface.

Planing a Surface

You must plane WITH or along the grain and across it to produce a smooth surface. Torn wood indicates planing AGAINST the grain, a twisted wood grain, or a dull cutting edge. Examine the edges of your board to determine the direction of surface grain. You

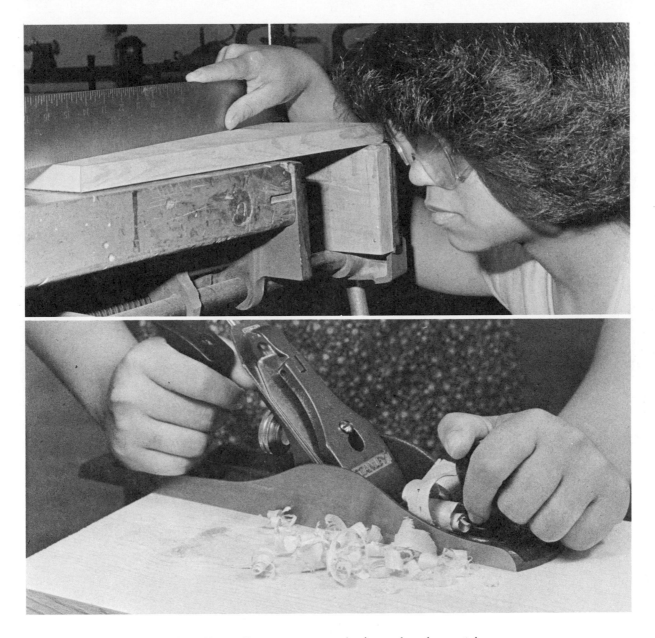

Fig. 8-5. Above. *Using a square to check a surface for straightness.*
Below. Planing a surface with a jack plane.

can also determine the direction of edge grain by examining the surface grain. See Fig. 8-4. Notice that the grain on the top surface runs opposite to the bottom surface. Can you see why?

A plane may be used to remove mill marks (marks made by the cutting knives of a planer or jointer) from the surfaces and edges of a board. A plane may also be used to remove warp and other surface imperfections from the board.

Try your plane on a scrap piece of wood to see if it is sharp and properly adjusted. It should cut easily and smoothly. Clamp your board in a vise. Plane the best surface first. Check for high spots with a straightedge. Remove the high spots by planing diagonally across the surface of the board. Hold your plane level. At the beginning of each stroke, apply pressure on the knob. As you proceed across the length of the board, gradually shift your pressure to the handle. Follow through at the end of each stroke with pressure on the handle. As you continue planing, lap about one third the width of each succeeding stroke over the previous stroke. Check the surface for straightness with a square or rule. The surface you plane straight and true first becomes the WORKING SURFACE OR FACE. See Fig. 8-5.

63

Planing an Edge

Select the best edge and determine the direction of grain. Clamp the board in a vise close to the edge, Fig. 8-6. Plane along the edge, holding your plane level and at a slight angle to the edge to provide a shearing cut. Plane until you obtain a continuous shaving along the length. Check along the length of the edge for accuracy with a straightedge. Test the edge for squareness to the FACE with a try square.

Fig. 8-6. Checking an edge for squareness.

Lay out the width of the board from the finished edge, drawing a line along the length of the board. Plane the second edge to this line and square to the face.

Planing Ends

Planing end grain requires a thin shaving made with a sharp plane. A block plane is often used for planing end grain. The blade of a block plane is made with one piece which is mounted so that its sharpened bevel is UP to deflect the shavings.

Mark a square line across the end of your stock. Clamp your stock in a vise near the layout mark. Set a block plane to make a fine cut. Holding the plane level, use light, uniform pressure and push it toward the middle of the

end. Then, finish the cut from the opposite direction. Be careful not to plane across the end from one direction as this will result in splitting the opposite corner, Fig. 8-7.

Fig. 8-7. Planing end grain with a block plane.

The ends of narrow boards may be planed by using a back-up board against the opposite edge for support and then by planing from one direction.

Measure the length of your stock from the square end and mark a square line. Cut the stock to length with a backsaw. Then, plane the second end square.

Planing Second Surface

Using a marking gauge, mark the desired thickness of your stock from the face surface around the edges and ends. Plane the second surface to this line.

If your stock is free of warp, you can plane the second surface before cutting it to width or length.

Planing Chamfers and Bevels

A CHAMFER is an angle cut made part way across an edge. A BEVEL is an angle cut made across the entire edge.

Using a marking gauge or your forefinger as a guide, lay out lines around the edges of your board. Clamp the board in a vise close to the lines. Holding a plane at the desired angle, plane the chamfer or bevel to the layout lines, Fig. 8-8..

Fig. 8-8. Planing a chamfer.

Using Rabbet Plane

A rabbet plane is used to make rabbet (L shape) joints in the edges of wood. It has adjustable guides for widths and depths of cuts.

Set the guides on the rabbet plane to the desired size of joint. Clamp the stock in a vise near the edge to be planed.

Hold the rabbet plane against the edge of the board. Using firm, uniform pressure, push the plane across the edge of the board. Continue with succeeding strokes until the depth gauge reaches the edge of the board, Fig. 8-9.

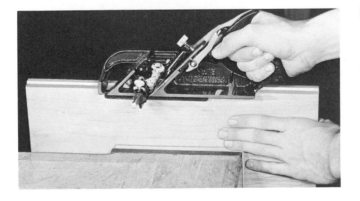

Fig. 8-9. Using a rabbet plane.

Using Router Plane

A router plane is used to smooth the bottom of joints such as dado, rabbet and lap. The blade is mounted in a frame with handles at both ends. The blade, shaped similar to a chisel, is adjustable for depth of cut. An adjustable depth stop controls the thickness of cuts.

Clamp the stock in a vise so the joint to be planed is readily accessible. Place the plane over the joint and set the depth stop and blade

Fig. 8-10. Using a router plane.

for a thin cut. Push or pull the blade across the joint to smooth the bottom of the joint. See Fig. 8-10.

Scraping a Surface

A cabinet scraper is used to smooth flat surfaces after planing. It is helpful in smoothing rough places left around knots and other curly grain or ridges left by the planer. The

65

Fig. 8-11. Using a cabinet scraper.

Sharpening Plane Irons

Sharpening includes grinding and honing. Grinding shapes the cutting edge to a hollow-ground (curved shape made with the grinding wheel) bevel. Honing or whetting on an oilstone further sharpens the cutting surface to a "keen" edge.

Grinding is necessary when the cutting edge loses its hollow-ground bevel or becomes nicked. Plane irons are usually ground to a bevel of 25-30 deg. for general work which forms a bevel in width about two and one third times the blade thickness, Fig. 8-2.

blade, either with or without a holder, is held at an angle of about 75 deg., Fig. 8-11.

You can grind a plane iron by clamping it at 90 deg. to the plane iron cap, then use the plane iron cap as a guide along the tool rest. Another method is to clamp the plane iron in a special sharpening device which is easily moved across the grinding wheel. Grind the plane iron until a small burr appears behind the bevel. During grinding, frequently dip the plane iron in water to keep it cool. Otherwise, excessive heating from the grinding will draw the temper (hardness) from the plane iron, Fig. 8-13.

Sharpening Hand Scraper

To sharpen a hand scraper, clamp it in a vise and draw-file straight across the edge. Hone the edge, then lay the scraper flat on the oilstone and hone both sides. Again clamp the scraper in a vise and stroke the edge several times with a burnisher (hardened steel rod). First, hold the burnisher at 90 deg. to the edge, then gradually raise the burnisher to about 85 deg. This turns the edge over forming a BURR which becomes the cutting edge, Fig. 8-12.

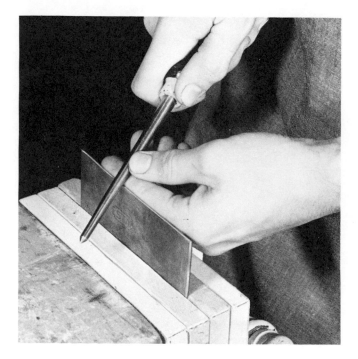

Fig. 8-12. Turning the edge of a hand scraper with a burnisher.

Fig. 8-13. Grinding a plane iron.

To hone a plane iron, apply a few drops of oil on the oilstone. Place the bevel of the plane iron flat on the oilstone, then raise it slightly and push it forward with light, uniform pressure. Stroke the plane iron several times, then turn it over, place it FLAT on the oilstone and stroke the other side to remove the burr. Repeat this process until the cutting edge will slice the edge of a piece of note paper with a clean cut, Fig. 8-14.

After you have sharpened the plane iron, slightly round the corners of the cutting edge on the side of the oilstone to prevent them from digging into the wood during use. Another sharpening method is to grind the cutting edge to a slightly convex curve.

Fig. 8-14. Honing a plane iron.

Jointer

We use a jointer to remove warp and other surface imperfections from the edges and faces of boards, making them straight and true. It is also used to cut chamfers, bevels, rabbets and tapers. The size of the jointer is determined by the length of its cutting knives, usually three, which revolve in a cutterhead at a speed of about 4500 rpm.

A jointer is equipped with two tables, the INFEED (front) and the OUTFEED (rear), and

a FENCE. The OUTFEED TABLE MUST BE SET EVEN WITH THE CUTTING EDGES OF THE KNIVES at the highest point of rotation and locked at this position. The infeed table is adjustable for the depth of cut. The fence is adjustable for different widths and may be tilted for angular cuts. The fence is used to guide stock as it is pushed from the infeed table to and from the outfeed table. See Figs. 8-15 and 8-16.

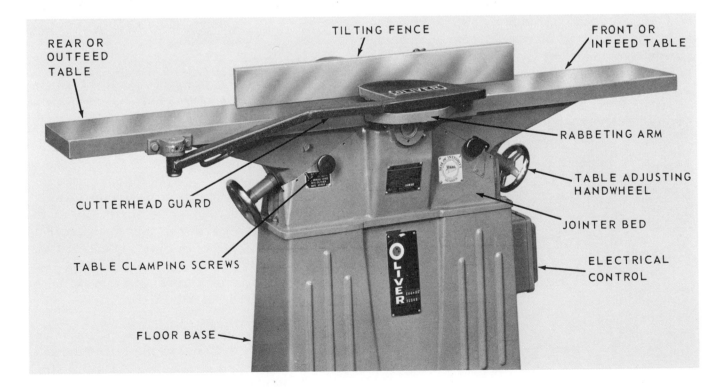

Fig. 8-15. Eight inch jointer with parts identified.

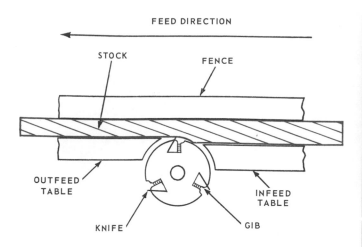

Fig. 8-16. How the jointer works; sectional view of jointer feed tables and cutterhead.

Stock Size and Depth of Cut Limitations

Stock to be smoothed in a jointer should be at least 12 INCHES LONG. Minimum width should be 1 in. and thickness 3/8 in. Your work should be planned so short pieces will be combined with longer pieces and then cut to length after the machining is completed.

Depth of cut recommended depends on the width and hardness of the stock and the rate of feed. Generally, lumber that is hard and wide should be fed slowly. Maximum recommended depth of cut for hardwood is 1/32 to 1/16 in. and for softwood 1/16 to 1/8 in.

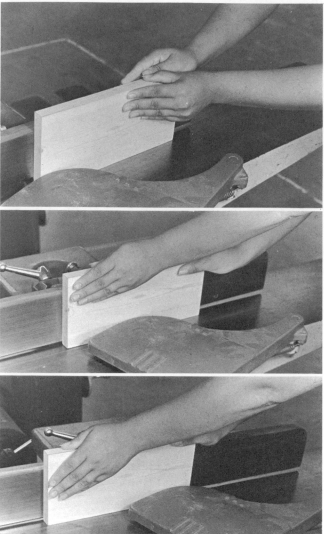

Fig. 8-18. Jointing a board. Above. Applying pressure on the fence and infeed table. Center. Applying pressure on the fence and both tables. Below. Applying pressure on the fence and outfeed table.

Jointing Edges

Adjust the fence so it is square with the infeed table and lock it in place. Check the fence stop for accuracy at this position, Fig. 8-17. Set the depth of cut for 1/16 in. Inspect your stock to determine grain direction. Turn your stock so the knives will cut with the grain. POSITION THE GUARD.

Place the stock on the infeed table and against the fence. Stand to the left of the machine and turn on the motor. With the stock held against the fence and infeed table, push it over the cutterhead, Fig. 8-18 (Above). When

Fig. 8-17. Adjusting jointer fence square with infeed table.

about a foot of the stock has passed the cutterhead, lift your left hand across the cutterhead and apply pressure against the fence and outfeed table with that hand, Fig. 8-18 (Center). At the end of the stroke, use both hands to apply pressure against the fence and outfeed table. BY USING THIS PROCEDURE YOUR HANDS DO NOT PASS DIRECTLY OVER THE CUTTERHEAD, Fig. 8-18 (Below).

When jointing the edge of a long piece, keep both hands on the infeed table, moving one hand to a new position and then the other, until the end of the board is near, then shift the pressure to the outfeed table reaching across the cutterhead.

Narrow pieces, minimum size 12 in. in length and 1 in. wide by 3/8 in. in thickness, can be jointed safely by using a push stick. The left hand should be lifted across the cutterhead to apply pressure to the piece against the fence and outfeed table, Fig. 8-19 (Above).

Chamfering and beveling can be accomplished by setting the fence to the desired angle, locking the fence in place and then jointing the edge to the angle.

Safety Note

Watch where you put your fingers. Keep them away from the cutterhead.

Planing Surfaces

The FIRST surface (working surface or face) is smoothed with a jointer. Set the depth of cut for 1/32 in. Turn your stock so the knives will cut with the grain. Position the guard and turn on the motor. See Fig. 8-16.

If the stock is warped, place it on the infeed table with the cupped surface down. Using a push stick with pressure against the fence and infeed table, push it over the knives toward the outfeed table. Gradually shift the pressure to the outfeed table as you complete the cut, as with jointing. Follow through the piece until the guard snaps back over the cutterhead, Fig. 8-19 (Below).

Rabbeting

Move the fence over toward the rabbeting platform on the left side of the machine, to the width rabbet desired. Lock the fence in place. Set the depth of cut to 1/16 in. and push the stock over the cutterhead. Reset the depth of cut for subsequent cuts until the desired depth of rabbet is obtained.

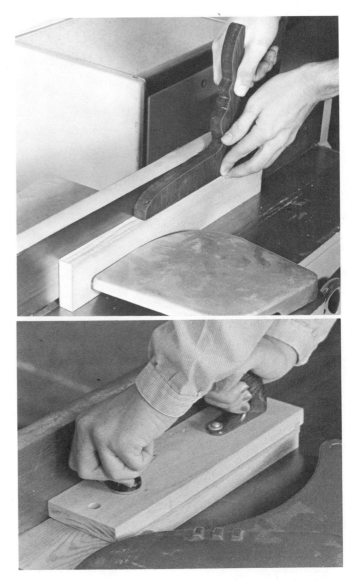

Fig. 8-19. Above. Jointing a narrow board with a push stick. Below. Smoothing a surface with jointer, using a push stick.

Planing Tapers

Attach a block of wood, the thickness of the desired taper to one end of the board. This raises the board so the other end is cut deeper.

Jointer Safety

1. Always secure permission from your instructor before using the jointer.
2. Minimum size stock to plane is 3/8 x 1 x 12 in. Use a jointer only on stock that is free from knots and splits.
3. Keep your hands away from the knives -- always 4 in. or more from the cutterhead.
4. Use a push stick for planing flat surfaces and jointing narrow pieces.
5. See that the area behind the machine is clear before turning on the motor.
6. The jointer knives must be kept sharp. Dull knives cause vibration and poor cuts.
7. Feed your stock so that the knives cut with the grain (feed is OPPOSITE the grain).
8. Surface stock with the cupped (concave) side down so that it has two points of contact with the table.

Using Portable Jointers

The portable jointer is especially useful to the carpenter. It consists of a frame similar to a hand plane into which is attached the motor of a portable router with a special cutterhead fitted in its chuck. The frame is equipped with an adjustable fence for width of cut, and an adjustable front table for depth of cut.

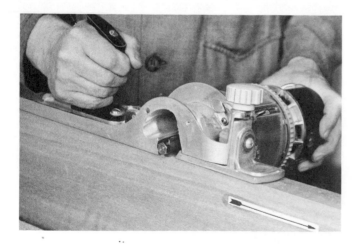

Fig. 8-20. *Jointing an edge with a portable jointer.*

Clamp your stock in a vise with the edge to be jointed accessible. Set the depth of cut for 1/16 in. Place the jointer on your stock and turn on the motor. Push the jointer across

the edge using pressure against the fence. Follow through at the end of the stroke and turn off the motor. Make additional cuts if necessary, Fig. 8-20.

Safety Note

Check adjustments closely before you turn on the motor.

Planer or Surfacer

We use a planer or surfacer to machine stock to exact thickness. A planer is equipped with a cutterhead, usually with three knives, similar to a jointer and cuts the stock on the top surface. The size of a planer is determined by the length of the knives. Common sizes are 12, 18 and 24 in. The machine is equipped with four feed rolls; two upper and two lower. The upper feed roll, usually sec-

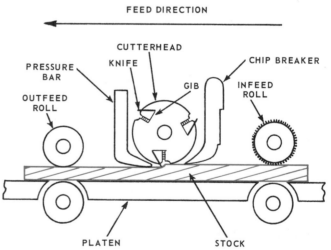

Fig. 8-21. *How the planer works; sectional view of the feed rolls and cutterhead assembly.*

tional, which is milled or corrugated pulls the stock through the cutterhead. The chip breaker, usually sectional, and pressure bar, hold the stock down as it is fed through. Depth of cut is determined by table adjustment. See Figs. 8-21 and 8-22.

To plane a board to exact thickness, plane the first surface on a jointer. Measure the board at its THICKEST point to find its size and set the planer for this size less the depth of cut. Recommended depth of cut is 1/32-1/16

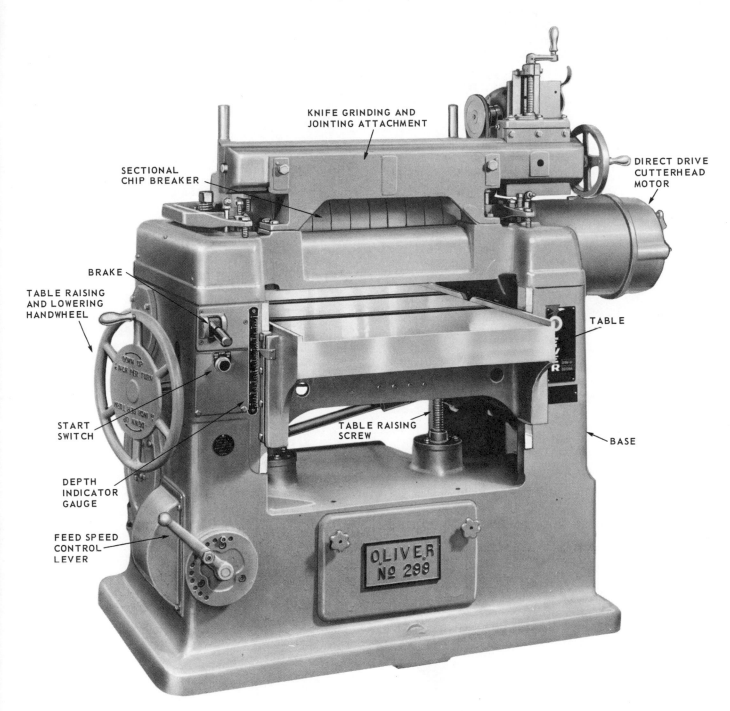

SECTIONAL CHIP BREAKER

KNIFE GRINDING AND JOINTING ATTACHMENT

DIRECT DRIVE CUTTERHEAD MOTOR

BRAKE

TABLE RAISING AND LOWERING HANDWHEEL

TABLE

START SWITCH

TABLE RAISING SCREW

BASE

DEPTH INDICATOR GAUGE

FEED SPEED CONTROL LEVER

OLIVER No 299

Fig. 8-22. 24 in. single surface planer.

in. for hardwoods and 1/16-1/8 in. for softwoods. Turn the board so the knives will cut with the grain and the first (true) surface is down. Grasp the board with both hands, one on either side, hold it horizontally and allow the feed rolls to pull the board across the cutterhead. Walk to the back side of the planer to receive the board or use a HELPER. Reset the depth of cut and make additional cuts until the desired thickness is obtained.

Safety and Care

1. In using planer minimum safe length of rough lumber is 16 in.
2. Hold boards in a horizontal position and with both hands as you feed them into the planer.
3. Feed stock so the planer knives cut with the grain.
4. Wide stock and hard stock should be fed

Fig. 8-23. Industrial photo. Planing a laminated beam.

at slow speeds only.

5. Use only nail, paint and warp-free lumber in the planer.

6. Check with your instructor before making changes in setting for depth of cut.

Test Your Knowledge - Unit 8

1. Planes are used to _____ surfaces and edges of boards and to make wood _____.

2. Six different kinds of planes are:
   a. _____.
   b. _____.
   c. _____.
   d. _____.
   e. _____.
   f. _____.

3. To protect a plane's cutting edge when not in use, _____ or _____.

4. Torn wood indicates planing _____ the grain, a _____ wood grain, or a _____ cutting edge.

5. When planing, check for accuracy with a _____ and test for squareness with a _____.

6. A _____ is often used for planing end grain.

7. Describe the difference between a chamfer and a bevel.

8. L shaped joints in the edges of wood are made using a _____.

9. A router plane is used to smooth the bottom of joints such as _____, _____, and _____.

10. A cabinet scraper is used to smooth:
    a. _____.
    b. _____.
    c. _____.

11. While sharpening plane irons, the plane iron is frequently dipped in water to keep it cool because _____.

12. Describe the procedure to hone a plane iron.

13. A jointer is used to remove _____ and other _____ from boards and to cut _____ , _____ , _____ , and _____.

14. The _____ table must be set even with the cutting edges of the jointer knives.

15. The _____ is used to guide stock as it is pushed from the _____ table to and from the _____ table.

16. The minimum dimensions of stock to be used in a jointer are ___ x ___ x _____.

17. To use a planer or surfacer to machine stock to exact thickness, plane the first surface on a _____.

Research and Development

1. Prepare a paper which traces the history of planing tools and machines.

2. Make a check up to determine the size and type of planers used by industry.

3. Prepare a drawing which shows a typical jointer knife and the bevel to which jointer knives are usually ground when sharpened.

Unit 9
WOOD JOINTS

Many kinds of joints are used to fasten pieces of wood together. Glue is used to strengthen most wood joints. The strongest joints fastened with glue are those involving surfaces and edges of wood, and the weakest joints are those involving the ends of wood. This is why nails, screws, staples and other metal fasteners are used with some joints. Wood dowels, plugs, splines, feathers and wedges are used to strengthen joints to enhance the beauty or to hide the reinforcement.

Butt Joints

A butt joint involves the square end of one piece of wood being attached to the surface of another piece of wood. Butt joints are often used, where the strength is adequate, to save time and effort. Finish or dimension lumber is needed to make accurate butt joints.

To make a butt joint, use a square and mark a line at the end of a smooth board. For a smooth cut saw off the end of the board to the layout line with a backsaw. Attach this end

to the surface of another board with nails or screws. See Figs. 9-1 (Left) and 12-1.

Edge Joints

Edge joints are used to fasten two or more pieces of wood together when constructing table and desk tops, and similar projects.

Boards to be jointed or planed, then edge joined, should be inspected to determine grain direction. You should match the grain patterns so the SURFACE GRAIN OF ALL BOARDS RUN IN THE SAME DIRECTION. This is necessary so the resulting wider board can be smoothly surfaced. END GRAIN OF ADJACENT BOARDS SHOULD BE OPPOSITE to reduce the tendency to warp. Mark reference points on the surfaces of adjacent boards. See Fig. 9-2.

Glued edge joints of boards that are straight and less than 2 ft. long are usually sufficiently strong without reinforcement. See Unit 12 for gluing and clamping processes.

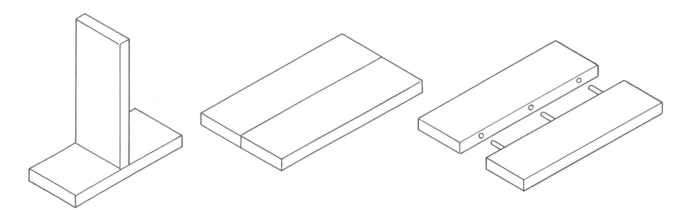

Fig. 9-1. Left. Butt joint. Center. Edge joint. Right. Edge-doweled joint.

Reinforcement of edge joints with dowels is suggested for boards over 2 ft. long. You can easily prepare edges of boards for dowels with a doweling jig. Clamp two adjacent boards together in a vise with the working surfaces facing outward and the edges upward. Mark the locations for dowels across both edges. The diameter of the dowels should be about one-half the thickness of the boards. The dowels

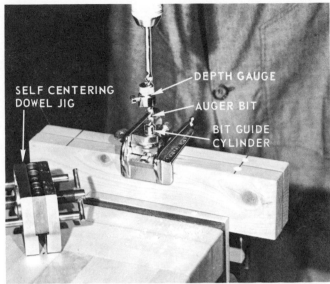

Fig. 9-4. Boring holes for edge-dowel joints into the edges of two adjacent boards.

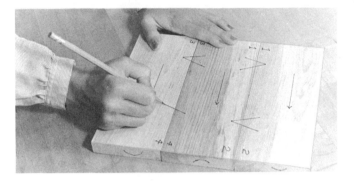

Fig. 9-2. Marking reference points on the surfaces of adjacent boards before attaching them to make a wide board.

should penetrate one inch deep into each board (standard ready-cut dowels 3/8 x 2 in. with spiral grooves are often used with 1 in. stock). See Figs. 9-1 (Right) and 9-3. Adjust the doweling jig and clamp it over one of the layout marks. Attach a depth stop on the bit and bore a hole 1 1/16 in. deep (this provides 1/16 in. clearance). After boring the hole, turn the doweling jig around and clamp it on the opposite side, using the same layout mark, and drill a hole in the other board. Drill all holes before removing the boards from the vise. See Fig. 9-4.

Another method of installing dowels is by using DOWEL POINTS. These are small metal cylinders of standard sizes with sharp center points. To use dowel points, drill holes for dowels in the first piece and insert dowel points into the holes. Press the dowel points into the second piece. This indicates where holes are to be drilled in the second piece.

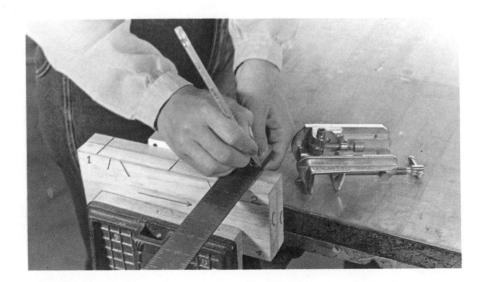

Fig. 9-3. Marking the locations of edge-dowel joints on two adjacent boards.

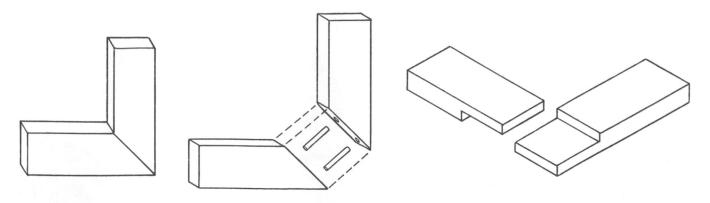

Fig. 9-5. Left. Miter joint. Center. Doweled miter joint. Right. Corner lap joint.

Miter Joints

Miter joints, Fig. 9-5 (Left) are used for jobs such as making corners for frames, and installing molding. Miter joints are often strengthened with wood dowels, feathers or metal fasteners. See Fig. 9-5 (Center).

A miter box is a valuable tool for making miter joints. To make a square corner with a miter joint, cut two pieces of wood to the desired size. Set the miter box saw to 45 deg. and cut the end of one of the pieces to that angle. Turn the saw to 45 deg. on the other side of the miter box, and cut off the end of the matching piece of wood. See Fig. 9-6.

If you are reinforcing the joints with dowels, you can use a doweling jig or dowel points to good advantage when drilling holes.

Lap Joints

Lap joints are made by reducing the thickness or width of each piece to one-half its original size, and then by lapping one piece over the other. Lap joints include half lap, cross lap, edge lap, end lap and corner lap. These joints are very strong when carefully made. See Fig. 9-5 (Right).

To make a lap joint, cut two pieces of wood to the desired size. Lay out one-half the lap joint on each piece. Cut the depth of the joint on each piece with a miter box or backsaw. Using a chisel with the bevel up, cut lightly around the layout lines toward the center until the waste stock breaks free. Smooth the surfaces of the joint with the bevel of the chisel held down. See Fig. 9-7.

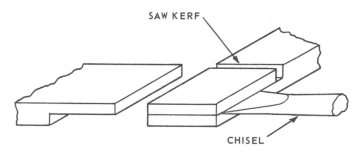

Fig. 9-7. Removing waste stock from a corner lap joint.

Rabbet Joints

A rabbet is an L-shape recess cut at the end or along the edge of a board. The matching end or the square end of a board can be fastened into the recess making a strong joint. This joint is a favorite for making the sides of boxes and chests. It is relatively easy to make and assemble. See Fig. 9-8 (Left and Center).

End rabbets can be made by using a saw with a fixture as a guide. The fixture can be

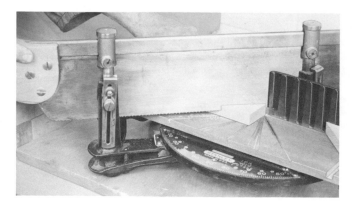

Fig. 9-6. Cutting a miter with a miter box.

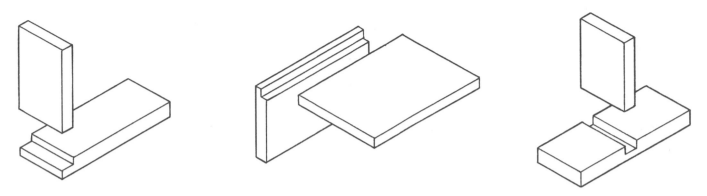

Fig. 9-8. Left. Rabbet and butt joint. Center. Edge rabbet joint. Right. Dado and butt joint.

prepared by attaching a small board of the same thickness as the desired rabbet to one end of a scrap piece of stock. Lay out the width of the joints on the stock with a try square and the depth with the fixture. See Fig. 9-9.

Fig. 9-9. Marking the depth of a rabbet joint with a fixture as a guide.

Fig. 9-10. Using a backsaw to cut a rabbet to depth with a fixture as a guide.

Clamp the stock in the vise together with the fixture. Using the fixture as a guide, saw the joints to depth with a backsaw, then cut each joint to width with a miter box or backsaw. See Fig. 9-10.

A rabbet plane is used to make edge rabbets. Set the rabbet plane guides to the width and depth required. Using uniform pressure, push the plane along the edge of your stock with the grain. Make successive strokes until the required depth is obtained. See Fig. 9-11.

Using a circular saw with a dado head is a good way to make a rabbet joint with machinery.

Fig. 9-11. Cutting an edge rabbet with a rabbet plane.

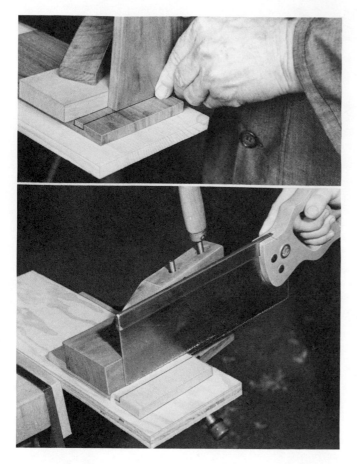

Fig. 9-12. Above. Clamping a straightedge as a guide for sawing a dado. Below. Using a straightedge as a guide for cutting a dado to depth with a backsaw.

Dado Joints

A dado is a square-cornered recess running ACROSS the grain, Fig. 9-8 (Right). It is similar to a rabbet except it is not located at the end of a board. This joint is used extensively to hold shelves in furniture and cabinets. It is also used in drawer sides.

To cut a dado, make the lay out on a suitable board, and clamp a straightedge next to the layout line. Clamp the piece in a vise with a scrap board under. See Fig. 9-12 (Above).

Using a straightedge as a guide, cut the dado to depth with a backsaw. See Fig. 9-12 (Below). Move the straightedge next to the other layout line and make the second cut.

Remove the waste stock with a chisel. Holding the chisel bevel up, start the cut on each side with light raps from a mallet. See

Fig. 9-13 (Above). Turn the chisel over so the bevel is down for better control. Using a mallet, tap the chisel down into the dado, at close intervals, to loosen the waste stock. With firm, uniform pressure, push the chisel toward the center of the dado from each side, Fig. 9-13 (Center).

You can plane the dado to finished depth with a router plane. Adjust the blade and depth stop for the required depth of cut. With uniform pressure, push or pull the router plane

Fig. 9-13. Removal of waste stock from a dado. Above. Starting the cut with the chisel bevel held up. Center. Using the chisel with its bevel held down. Below. Completing the cut with a router plane.

Fig. 9-14. *Left. Laying out a groove with a marking gauge.*
Right. Cutting a groove with a backsaw.

from each side toward the center of the dado, Fig. 9-13 (Below).

Groove Joints

A groove joint is identical to the dado except it is cut along the grain. One of the most frequent uses of the groove is to hold drawer bottoms.

In preparation for making a groove, lay out the size on a soft piece of wood using a marking gauge. See Fig. 9-14 (Left).

Clamp a straightedge on the layout line together with a scrap board beneath as support. Clamp the supporting board in a vise. Using the straightedge as a guide, cut the groove to depth with a backsaw. See Fig. 9-14 (Right). Move the straightedge next to the second layout line and make the second cut.

Remove the waste stock. Turn the chisel so the bevel is up. Using light taps on the chisel with a mallet, start the cut from each side. See Fig. 9-15 (Left). Turn the chisel over, bevel down, for better control. Tap the chisel into the groove to the approximate depth at several locations. With firm, uniform pressure push the chisel WITH THE GRAIN across the groove. Use only enough strokes to cut to the required depth. See Fig. 9-15 (Right). You can also use a router plane to complete the groove.

To cut dados and grooves with power tools, you can use a circular saw and dado head.

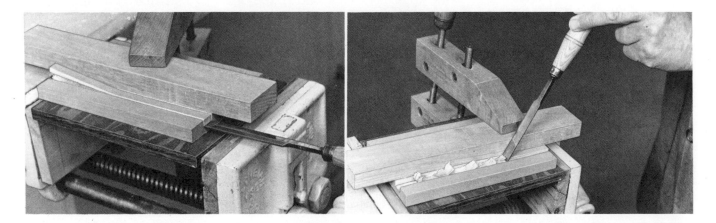

Fig. 9-15. *Removal of waste stock from a groove. Left. Starting the cut with the chisel bevel held up. Right. Using the chisel with its bevel held down.*

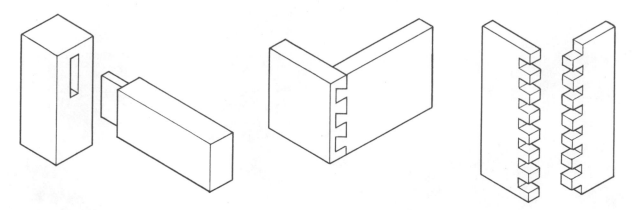

Fig. 9-16. Left. Mortise and tenon joint. Center. Dovetail joint. Right. Box joint.

Mortise and Tenon Joints

We often use mortise and tenon joints, Fig. 9-16 (Left), for the assembly of furniture. A mortise and tenon joint consists of a rectangular recess (mortise) into which fits a rectangular projection (tenon). This type joint is difficult to make with hand tools, but it offers little difficulty when it is made with machinery. It is exceptionally strong when it is accurately made. There are two types, BLIND and THROUGH. The tenon is hidden in the blind type and is partially exposed in the through type.

The mortise should be made first. Lay out the size of the mortise on the stock. Uniformly space marks for holes. Using a doweling jig as a guide, drill the holes to the required depth, allowing 1/16 in. clearance. Smooth the corners and surfaces with a chisel.

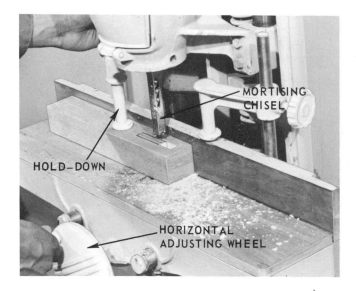

Fig. 9-17. Cutting a mortise with a mortising chisel.

Lay out a tenon to fit the mortise. Cut the tenon to length with a miter box or backsaw, being careful to cut the kerf to the layout line. Cut the tenon to rough width and depth with a backsaw. Pare the tenon to finished size with a chisel, cutting with the grain.

You can make a mortise with a mortising chisel in the mortiser or in a drill press with an attachment, Fig. 9-17. The mortising chisel is a hollow, square chisel fitted with a special drill bit. The two cut simultaneously to make a square hole. The mortising chisel is available in standard sizes of 1/4 to 1/2 in. by sixteenths of an inch. The router can also be used to make a mortise.

A circular saw with a tenoning attachment is often used to make a tenon.

Dovetail Joints

The greatest use of the dovetail joint, Fig. 9-16 (Center), is for drawer construction in the better grades of furniture and cabinets. A dovetail joint consists of wedge-shaped projections, shaped like a dove's tail, which fit into matching recesses. It can be cut by hand with a special saw, but it is best cut with a machine router and a template guide.

To make a dovetail joint, select two pieces of stock, one for a FRONT OR BACK and one for a SIDE. Clamp the piece for the front or back against the guide pin on TOP of the fixture. Then place the piece for a side against the guide pin on the FRONT of the fixture. The inside surface of each piece should face OUTWARD, Fig. 9-18 (Above). Clamp the finger template on top of the fixture. Attach the

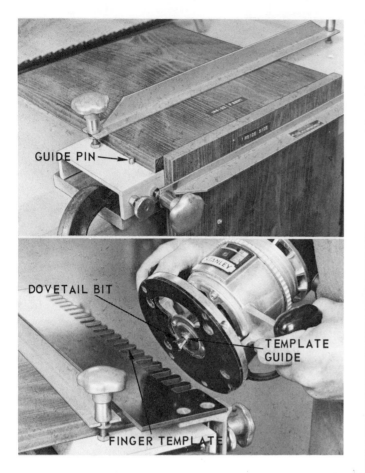

GUIDE PIN →

DOVETAIL BIT

TEMPLATE GUIDE

FINGER TEMPLATE

Fig. 9-18. Above. Clamping drawer parts in a fixture to make a dovetail joint. Below. Preparing the finger template and router for a dovetail joint

template guide to the router and adjust its dovetail bit to the depth recommended by the manufacturer, Fig. 9-18 (Below).

Begin at one side of the clamped stock. Insert the template guide into the finger template from the FRONT ONLY. Turn on the motor, follow the finger template with the template guide to the other side of the stock and turn off the motor. Remove the router by pulling it BACKWARD ONLY. See Fig. 9-19.

Notice that the two pieces of stock are offset when they are cut together so they match when you put them together to make the complete joint. See Figs. 9-16 (Center) and 9-19 (Below).

Box Joints

Box joints are used to make strong or decorative boxes, Fig. 9-16 (Right). The box joint

consists of a series of rectangular-shaped projections and recesses on the edge of one piece which fit into the edge of a second piece. The projections and recesses of the second piece are OFFSET the width of one segment so the two pieces will match when they are put together.

You can make box joints using a fixture on a circular saw.

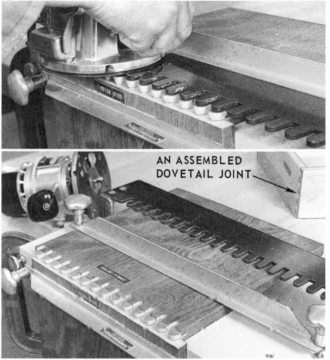

AN ASSEMBLED DOVETAIL JOINT →

Fig. 9-19. Above. Using a router to cut a dovetail joint in a fixture. Below. Completed dovetail joint in a fixture.

Test Your Knowledge - Unit 9

1. _____ is used to strengthen most wood joints.
2. The strongest joints fastened with glue are those involving _____ and _____ of wood, and the weakest joints are those involving _____ of wood.
3. A _____ joint involves the square end of one piece of wood being attached to the surface of another piece of wood.
4. When making edge joints, the surface grain of all boards should _____.
5. In edge joints, end grain of adjacent boards should be opposite to _____.

6. Describe the use of dowel points.
7. A miter box is a tool used for making miter joints, which are used for jobs such as _____ and _____ .
8. Lap joints are made by _____

    _____ .
9. A rabbet is a _____ recess cut at the _____ or _____ of a board.
10. A dado joint is similar to a rabbet joint except it is not located _____ .
11. Describe the difference between a dado joint and a groove joint.
12. A _____ or rectangular projection fits into a _____ or rectangular recess.
13. The greatest use of dovetail joints is for

    _____ .
14. The projections and recesses of the second piece of a box joint are offset the width of one segment so _____ .

Research and Development

1. Which joints are often used to construct house framing? Maybe you can help arrange a visit to a local building site.
2. How does industry use joints? Inspect the cabinets and furniture in your home to see how joints are utilized. You may want to visit a furniture store and cabinet shop.

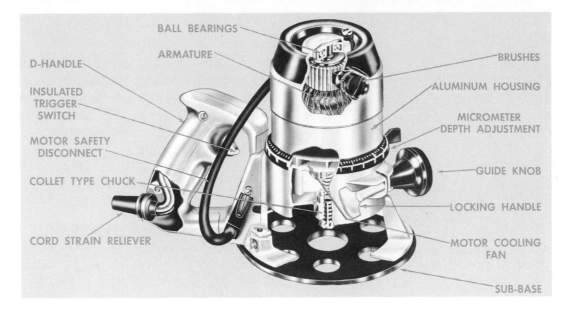

Fig. 10-1. Parts of a portable router.

Unit 10

SHAPING AND ROUTING

Portable Router

The portable router is one of our most versatile machines. See Fig. 10-1. We use it to shape the edges of wood frames and paneling, to rout grooves and mortises, and to trim veneer and laminated plastic. We use the portable router with jigs or fixtures to plane edges and for template cutting.

The size of a portable router is indicated by its horsepower rating and by the capacity of its chuck (bit and shank diameter). The spindle of the router revolves at high speed, usually 20,000-30,000 rpm.

Router Bits

Router bits are usually made from high speed steel. Some bits are tipped with silicon carbide, an extremely hard material, which makes them stay sharp longer than standard bits.

SHAPING BITS are used to form decorative edges. Inside curves are formed with cove bits. Outside curves are formed with rounding over or beading bits. See Fig. 10-2. Other shapes formed on edges are the rabbet, chamfer and combination curve. The tips of shaping bits guide them along the edges of the wood.

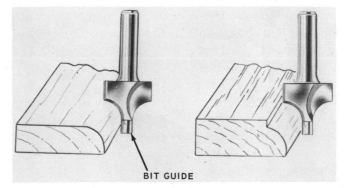

Fig. 10-2. Typical shaping bits. Left. Rounding over bit. Right. Beading bit.

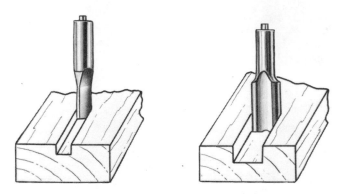

Fig. 10-3. Routing bits. Left. Straight bit, single flute.
Right. Straight bit, double flute.

ROUTING BITS are used to cut dados, grooves, veins, coves and mortises in the surfaces and edges of wood. These bits are guided with a fence attached to the base or with a template and guide. They are sometimes used freehand in a router. Figs. 10-3 and 10-5.

Special bits are available for trimming veneer and plastic laminates. Others are used to make dovetail joints, hinge and lock mortises, and special cuts.

Installing Bits and Adjusting Base

To install a bit in a portable router, disconnect the power cord, loosen the locking handle and remove the router base. Insert the bit into the collet chuck and firmly tighten the chuck. Replace the router base and set the bit to the required depth with the micrometer depth adjustment. Tighten the base locking handle.

If you are using a routing bit you will need a fence. Insert the fence adjustment bars into the router base and tighten the lock screws. Then move the fence to the required width and tighten the lock nuts. See Fig. 10-5.

Safety Note

Tighten lock screws and nuts carefully.

Shaping an Edge

Choose a bit, install it in the router and adjust the depth of cut. Clamp a practice piece

of wood in a vise, grasp the router handles, and turn on the motor. Lightly push the router toward the edge of the stock and allow the bit to make a short cut. Make adjustments if necessary. Hold the router handles with both hands and push or pull it around the edge of the stock. Move with moderate speed using VERY LIGHT PRESSURE against the stock

Fig. 10-4. Shaping an edge with a Roman Ogee-shaped cutter using a portable router.

with the bit guide. Heavy pressure against the bit guide will result in excess friction, and cause the bit to overheat. Complete the edge and turn off the motor. See Fig. 10-4.

Cutting a Groove

A straight bit is used to cut grooves. Select a bit of the correct size, install it in the router and adjust the depth of cut. Attach the fence to the router base and adjust it to the desired width. Clamp a practice piece in a vise and turn on the router motor to make a trial cut. Grasp the router handles with both hands and make a short cut. Make adjustments if necessary. Using pressure against the fence, push or pull the router along the edge of the stock to complete the groove, and then turn off the motor. See Fig. 10-5.

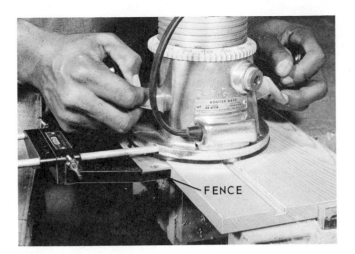

Fig. 10-5. Using a fence as a guide for cutting a groove with a straight bit in a portable router.

Using Templates

Irregular shapes can be cut with a router by using a template and template guide.

You can make a template by cutting the desired shape out of a piece of 1/8 in. hardboard. If you plan to use the template several times, you may want to attach it with hinges to a plywood base.

Clamp your stock to a bench and fasten the template over it. Insert a 1/16-1/4 in. diameter straight bit in the router chuck and tighten it securely. Then attach the template guide to the router base with screws. Fig. 9-18 (Below) illustrates a template guide in-

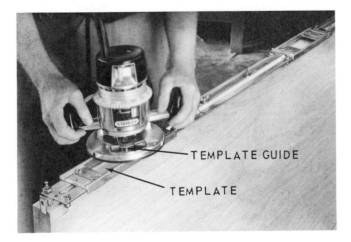

Fig. 10-6. Using a template as a guide to rout recesses in the edge of a door to receive hinges.

stalled. Adjust the bit to the required depth, plug in the power cord, and turn on the motor. Holding the template guide next to the template, push or pull the router around the template. Complete the cut, turn off the motor, and disconnect the power plug. Fig. 10-6 illustrates the use of a template in cutting door hinge recesses.

Trimming Laminated Plastic and Wood Veneer

A special attachment can be fastened to the portable router base for trimming laminated plastic or wood veneer. The attachment has a micrometer adjustment to move its guide to the exact location.

To trim laminated plastic or wood veneer, lay out and cut a rectangle or square-shaped piece of scrap 3/4 in. plywood. Lay out and cut a piece of laminated plastic or wood veneer about 1/2 in. larger than the plywood and stick it onto the surface of the plywood.

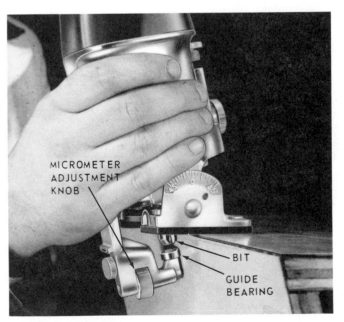

Fig. 10-7. A special router being used to trim laminated plastic.

Insert a trimming bit in the router chuck and tighten it securely. Fasten the trimming attachment securely to the router base and adjust the bit. Use a combination square to check the adjustment.

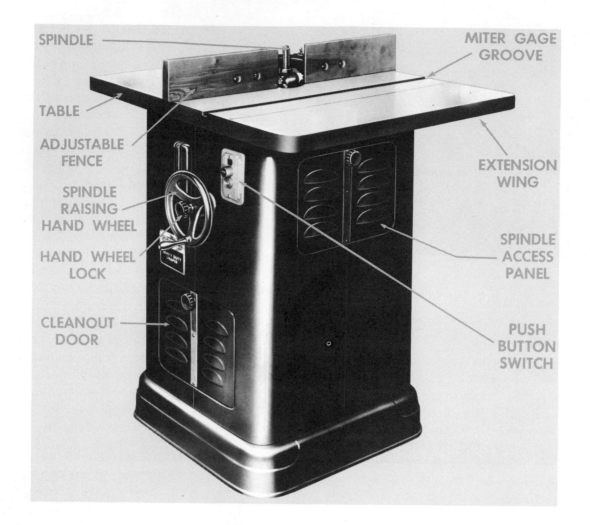

SPINDLE

TABLE

ADJUSTABLE
FENCE

SPINDLE
RAISING
HAND WHEEL

HAND WHEEL
LOCK

CLEANOUT
DOOR

MITER GAGE
GROOVE

EXTENSION
WING

SPINDLE
ACCESS
PANEL

PUSH
BUTTON
SWITCH

Fig. 10-8. Parts of a wood shaper.

Clamp the stock to a bench or in a vise. Grasp the router, connect the power cord and turn on the motor for a trial cut. Lightly push or pull the router toward the stock until the attachment guide bearing touches its edge. CHECK THE CUT AND MAKE ANY ADJUSTMENTS NECESSARY. Continue moving the router around the stock to complete the cut, then turn off the motor and disconnect the power cord. See Fig. 10-7.

Safety and Care

1. Immediately turn off the router motor after making each cut.
2. Disconnect the power cord before making adjustments.
3. Grasp the router firmly, holding the cutter bit away from you, before you turn on the motor.
4. Tighten screws and nuts securely when

making adjustments.
5. Handle the router carefully, and after each cut, lay it on a bench well away from the edges.
6. Use only sharp cutter bits. Protect cutter bits from abuse.

Shaper

The principal uses for a shaper, Fig. 10-8, are to form edges, make moldings and cut grooves. A shaper is used to make both straight and irregular shaped cuts. Templates are used when making duplicate parts.

The size of a shaper is indicated by the DIAMETER OF THE SPINDLE which holds the cutters. Common spindle sizes are 1/2, 5/8 and 3/4 inch. These may be single or double spindle. Most small shapers are single-spindle type. The spindle is adjustable vertically for depth of the cut and may be locked in position. It revolves at speeds of 5,000-10,000 rpm and normally turns in a counterclockwise direction. Most machines are equipped with reversing switches.

Straight stock is usually fed AGAINST THE FENCE. The shaper fence is divided in-to two parts, the FRONT fence and the REAR fence. Both parts of the fence are adjustable.

Curved stock is fed AGAINST A DEPTH GUIDE COLLAR on the spindle.

Shaper Bits

Three-lip solid cutter bits are available in a variety of shapes such as straight, round over, cove, bead, combination, tongue and groove, flute, and door lip, Fig. 10-9. Some bits may be purchased for either left hand or right hand operation. Most bits are made with high speed steel, but some are tipped with silicon carbide to increase durability.

Installing Bits

When possible, bits should be installed to cut from the bottom so stock acts as a partial shield. Space collars may be used over or be-neath the bit to hold the assembly in position

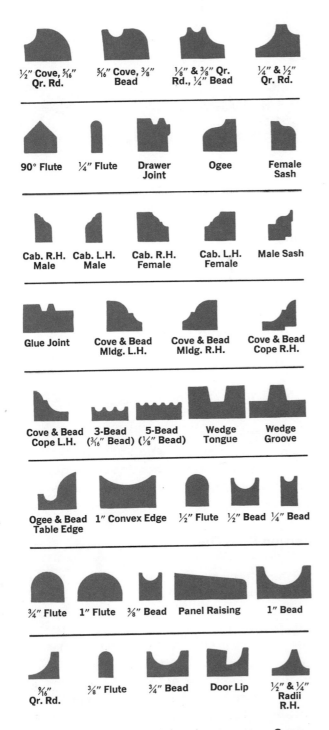

Fig. 10-9. Typical shapes, 3-lip shaper cutters. Cutters are shown half size. (Rockwell Mfg. Co.)

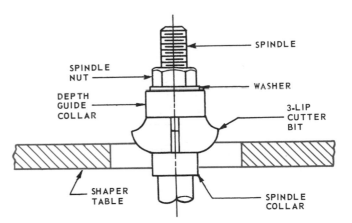

Fig. 10-10. Installing a bit on a shaper spindle.

required to make desired cut. If irregular shapes are cut, a depth guide collar should be placed over or beneath the cutter to regu-late the depth of cut and guide the stock as it is fed across the shaper. See Fig. 10-10.

To install a bit in a shaper, disconnect the power cord and remove the nut from the spindle. If you are forming straight edges of wood against the fence, select the correct cutter and place it onto the spindle. Put one or more space collars over the cutter (as required) and fasten the assembly firmly with the spindle nut. For curved work, you will need one or more depth guide collars assembled next to the cutter.

Forming Straight Edges

For practice select a piece of stock 16 in. or more in length which is free from warp. Install a suitable cutter on the spindle and set the fence in a position so the cutter is correctly aligned with the edge of the stock. Move the fence parallel to the miter gauge slot on the table and securely tighten it. Inspect the grain of the stock to determine its direction. Turn the stock so the CUTTER KNIVES CUT TOWARD THE STOCK and in the direction of the grain.

The process of forming a straight edge with a shaper is similar to that of jointing an edge with a jointer.

Fig. 10-12. Shaping a straight edge of wood against the fence of a wood shaper.

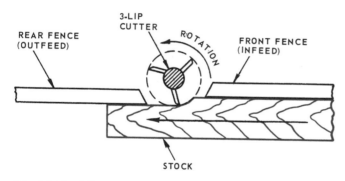

Fig. 10-11. Offset of the shaper fence as an entire edge is shaped (top view).

Place your stock on the shaper table and turn on the motor. With the stock held against the table and the fence, push it over the cutter, Fig. 10-11. When about 2 in. of the stock moves past the cutter, turn off the motor and adjust the second part of the fence to the formed edge. Turn on the motor and continue the stroke. After about 8 in. of the stock passes the cutter, move one of your hands to the other side, then the other hand, and complete the stroke with both hands pressing against the second part of the fence. USING THIS PROCEDURE YOUR HANDS WILL NOT PASS DIRECTLY OVER OR IN FRONT OF THE CUTTER. See Figs. 10-11 and 10-12.

Safety Note

Use only boards free of warp and 16 in. or more in length.

Forming Irregular Edges

Select a practice piece of wood and saw a curve on one edge. Install a suitable cutter and a DEPTH GUIDE COLLAR on the spindle. Fasten a GUIDE PIN in the table in front of the cutter knives. The guide pin acts as a guide and as support when you start the edge of the stock toward the depth guide collar. Turn the stock so the cutter knives cut toward the stock and in the direction of grain.

Position Ring Guard

Place the stock on the shaper table and turn on the motor. With the stock held firmly against the guide pin, push it toward the depth guide collar into the cutter knives. BE SURE THE KNIVES REVOLVE TOWARD YOUR STOCK. Continue to push the stock forward with light pressure AGAINST the depth guide collar. Complete the stroke by keeping light pressure against the depth guide collar as you push the stock past the cutter. Turn off the motor. See Fig. 10-13.

Safety and Care

1. Know where to put your fingers. Keep them away from the cutter.
2. Use only stock that is free of warp and 16 in. or more in length. Use a feather board or other device to help hold stock less than 4 in. wide or 1 in. thick.
3. Be sure the cutter revolves toward the stock and in the direction of grain.
4. Always use a guide pin to help start stock against a depth guide collar. This will help prevent kick-back of the stock.
5. Check adjustments carefully before you turn on the motor.
6. Feed stock at moderate speed. Use only sharp cutters.

Test Your Knowledge - Unit 10

1. The size of a portable router is usually indicated by its _____ rating.
2. Some router bits are tipped with _____ _____ a very hard metal which makes them stay sharp longer than standard bits.
3. Decorative edges are formed with _____ bits, inside curves are formed with _____ bits.
4. The size of a wood shaper is indicated by the diameter of the _____ which holds the cutters.
5. The wood shaper spindle is adjusted _____ for the depth of cut.

Fig. 10-13. Shaping a curved edge of wood against a depth guide collar on the spindle of a wood shaper.

6. Speed of a shaper spindle is usually 5,000 to 10,000 rpm. True or False?
7. _____ lip solid cutter bits are available in a variety of shapes.
8. When installing a shaper bit space _____ may be used over or beneath the bit to hold the assembly in the position required to make desired cut.
9. When operating a shaper, use board free of warp and ____ or more inches in length.

Research and Development

1. Investigate the use of shaping machines during our American Colonial period.
2. See how many different shapes of cutters you can find illustrated in supply catalogs.
3. In what ways are shaping machines used in modern industry? What are the trends toward future use?

Unit 11
WOOD TURNING

We shape cylinders, spindles, bowls, lamp bases, and other items which are round on a wood lathe, using a process called WOOD TURNING. Stock is shaped with special tools held on a TOOL REST as the stock revolves.

Wood Lathe

The size of a wood lathe is determined by the SWING, which is the largest diameter piece that can be turned. Other considerations are the bed length, the maximum distance between centers, and the total length. A popular size lathe is one with a 12 in. swing and bed length of 48 in., see Fig. 11-1.

Woods for Turning

Woods commonly used for turning in school shops are birch, mahogany, hard maple, oak, and walnut.

Fig. 11-1. Parts of a wood lathe.

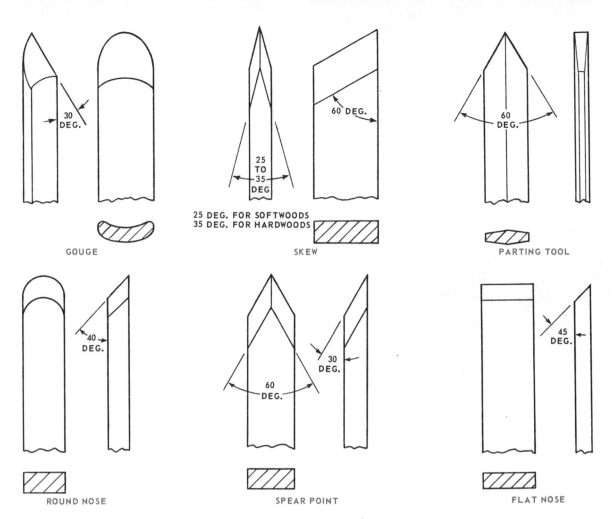

GOUGE

SKEW

25 DEG. FOR SOFTWOODS
35 DEG. FOR HARDWOODS

PARTING TOOL

ROUND NOSE

SPEAR POINT

FLAT NOSE

Fig. 11-2. Turning tools.

Lathe Speeds

All work turned in the lathe should be started with a slow, 400-1000 rpm, speed. This is because stock is often mounted off-center and is not balanced. If turned fast this results in excessive vibration which may throw the stock out of the lathe. After the stock is turned so it is round, a faster speed may be used.

In general, large pieces should be turned more slowly than small pieces. Stock 8 in. or more in diameter should be kept at or below 600 rpm. Small stock, 4 in. or less in diameter, after rough turning to balance the piece, may be shaped at speeds of 1000-1500 rpm.

Turning Tools

Six shapes of turning tools commonly used are shown in Fig. 11-2. The tools are available in various widths and thicknesses.

GOUGE. The principal use for the gouge is to cut rough stock to a round shape. A gouge cuts rapidly, but does not produce a smooth cut or surface. In using a gouge, the convex side should be held down, and the tool should be rolled 30 to 45 deg. in the direction it is being advanced along the tool rest. The cutting edge should be a little in advance of the handle.

SKEW. The skew chisel is used to make finishing or smoothing cuts, cut beads and V-shaped grooves, and to square shoulders.

PARTING TOOL. A parting tool, which is narrow in width, is used primarily to cut straight into the stock to the depth desired, or to make a complete cutoff. The tool is shaped to cut its own clearance so the edge will not be burned.

ROUND NOSE, SPEAR POINT, FLAT NOSE. These chisels are used where the tool shape fits the contour of the work.

Turning tools cut best when the bevels are hollow-ground and honed to a razor-sharp edge with a slipstone. Additional grinding is necessary when a tool is nicked or loses its hollow-ground bevel. Honing should be done at frequent intervals while turning.

Fig. 11-3. Using a mallet to seat a spur center in the end of a piece for spindle turning.

Spindle Turning

In spindle turning, stock is mounted between the lathe centers. Select a piece of stock and cut it about an inch longer than the completed project. If the piece is larger than two inches square, plane or saw off the corners. Fasten the piece in a vise, draw diagonal lines across the corners of both ends, and mark the centers with a punch. Cut saw kerfs about 1/8 in. deep along the diagonal lines of one end. Then drive the SPUR (headstock) center into the kerfs with a mallet, Fig. 11-3.

Insert a CUP (tailstock) center into the tailstock spindle. Some tailstock centers are stationary and are called "dead" centers. These require using grease or wax as a lubricant. Some tailstock centers have bearings which rotate with the stock, requiring little or no lubrication.

Mount the spur center attached to the stock, into the headstock spindle and insert the cup center in the other end of the stock. Turn the stock by hand to seat the cup center in the end of the stock, then lock the tailstock.

Adjust the tool rest parallel to the center of the stock and about 1/8 in. away from it. TURN THE STOCK BY HAND TO SEE THAT IT CLEARS THE TOOL REST. Set your lathe at the slowest speed and turn on the motor.

Place the gouge on the tool rest with one hand on the blade, thumb over the blade and forefinger under the blade, and the other hand on the handle. Turn the blade slightly to make a SHEARING cut. Using your forefinger as a guide, move the gouge carefully along the tool rest. Make additional cuts with the gouge in the same way until the piece becomes a cylinder. When the space between the stock and tool rest reaches 3/8 to 1/2 in., stop the machine and readjust the tool rest. Continue using the gouge until the piece is round. See Fig. 11-4.

To smooth the cylinder, use a skew with a scraping cut by turning its cutting edge at a right angle to the piece. Move the skew along the tool rest as with the gouge to achieve a smooth, uniform cylinder. Scraping cuts are easier to make with the skew than shearing cuts and are recommended until you gain considerable turning experience. Shearing cuts are accomplished by raising the tool rest above center and turning the cutting edge of the skew at an angle to the stock. The cutting edge then cuts as a knife.

Using a parting tool and outside caliper, lay out the necessary diameters along the cylinder, then use other tools to form the desired shape to complete the piece, Fig. 11-5.

Safety Note

Keep the tool rest close to the work and securely tightened.

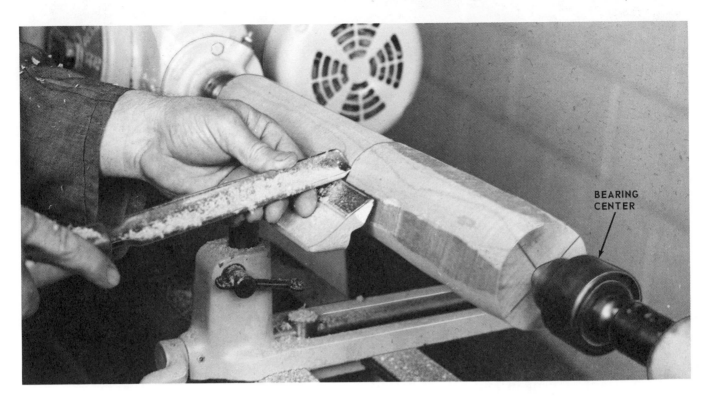

Fig. 11-4. Rough turning spindle stock with a gouge.

Headstock Turning

To make a small bowl, select a piece of stock about 1 in. thick by 5 in. square, and a smaller piece of scrap plywood to use as a separation piece. Cut both pieces round, then attach the plywood to the stock, between

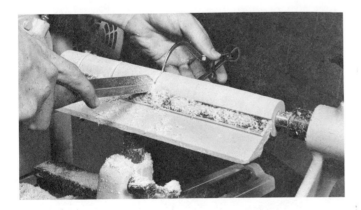

Fig. 11-5. Using a parting tool and outside caliper to check diameters. When checking, the lathe is stopped.

wrapping paper, with glue. The plywood allows you to turn a deeper bowl. The two pieces can be easily separated later, at the glue line, with a wood chisel. Attach a face-

plate to the plywood with No. 12 wood screws, Fig. 11-6.

Remove the spur center from the headstock and mount your stock in the headstock spindle. Set the lathe to its slowest speed

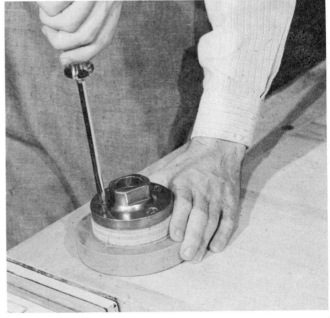

Fig. 11-6. Attaching stock to a faceplate with screws.

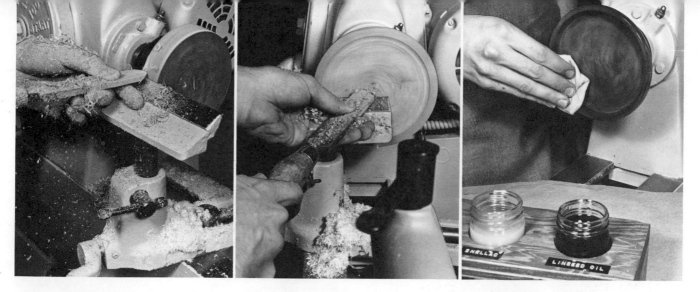

Fig. 11-7. Headstock turning. Left. Shaping the outside of a bowl with a round nose tool. Center. Shaping the inside of a bowl with a round nose tool. Right. Applying a French polish to a bowl.

and turn on the motor. Adjust the tool rest parallel to the center of your stock and about 1/8 in. away from it. TURN THE STOCK OVER BY HAND TO SEE THAT IT CLEARS THE TOOL REST. Rough turn the outside of your bowl with a gouge, then smooth it with a round nose tool, Fig. 11-7 (Left).

Reset the tool rest so it is parallel to the center surface of your bowl. Using a round nose tool held on the tool rest, begin at the center of your bowl and move the tool carefully along the tool rest toward the outside edge. Continue with additional cuts in the same way to obtain a wall thickness of about 1/4 in. and a bottom thickness of about 3/8 in. Fig. 11-7 (Center).

Remove the tool rest, fold a piece of medium or fine sandpaper into a small pad, and use the pad to smooth the bowl. Use a lathe speed of 1500-1800 rpm.

To apply a French polish finish to your bowl use a combination of linseed oil and shellac. Set the lathe to a speed of 600 rpm and turn on the motor. Place a piece of paper under the bowl. Fold a clean cloth into a small pad, apply a small amount of linseed oil to the pad, and rub the oil into the surfaces and edges of the bowl. Apply shellac (3 - 4 pound cut) to the bowl with the pad held lightly against the surfaces. When your bowl is coated, speed up the lathe to about 1200 rpm, and increase the pressure on the pad. Use a few drops of linseed oil on the pad as a lubricant. When the finish becomes shiny,

turn off the lathe, remove the bowl and allow the finish to harden overnight. You will probably want to apply a second coat of French polish, then a coat of wax, Fig. 11-7 (Right).

Chuck for Turning Small Pieces

To make a chuck for turning small pieces of stock, cut a piece of scrap wood 1 in. thick by 6 in. in diameter. Drill a 3/4 - 1 in. diameter hole in the center of the flat surface and fasten it to a faceplate with wood screws.

To use the improvised chuck to turn a small piece of stock, select a piece that is slightly smaller in diameter than the diameter of the hole in the chuck. Drive the piece into the hole in the chuck with a mallet, then turn it to the desired shape, Fig. 11-8.

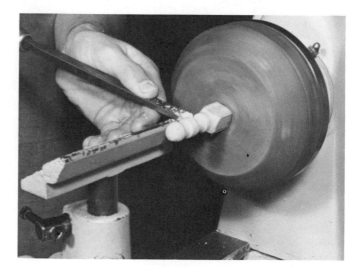

Fig. 11-8. Turning a small piece of wood held in a chuck.

Wood Turning

Safety and Care

1. Roll up your sleeves and tuck in your tie.
2. Clamp work securely and check setup by hand before you turn on the motor.
3. Always begin cutting with a slow speed.
4. Protect your eyes with safety glasses or a shield.
5. Stop the lathe often and check tailstock adjustment.
6. Keep the tool rest close to the work.
7. Hone the cutting tools frequently.

Test Your Knowledge - Unit 11

1. Cylinders, spindles, bowls, and other round items are shaped using a process called _____.
2. The size of a wood lathe is determined by the _____, which is the largest diameter piece that can be turned.
3. Woods commonly used for turning in the school shop include: _____ , _____ , and _____.
4. All work turned in the lathe should be started with a _____ speed.
5. The gouge, used to cut rough stock to a round shape, cuts rapidly and (does) (does not) produce a smooth cut or surface.
6. The skew chisel is used to make _____ cuts.
7. A parting tool is used primarily to cut _____ into the stock or to make a complete cutoff.
8. Turning tools cut best when the bevels are _____ and _____ .
9. Before turning on the lathe, always turn the stock by hand to see that it clears the _____ .
10. To turn a small bowl, the stock and separation piece are attached to the _____ .

Research and Development

1. Sketch six suggested turning projects. Use mail order catalogs and project books for design ideas.
2. When were the earliest wood lathes developed and by whom? Do some research on this and prepare a brief written report.
3. Make a collection of pictures showing products made with the lathe. Newspapers, magazines and catalogs are good sources.

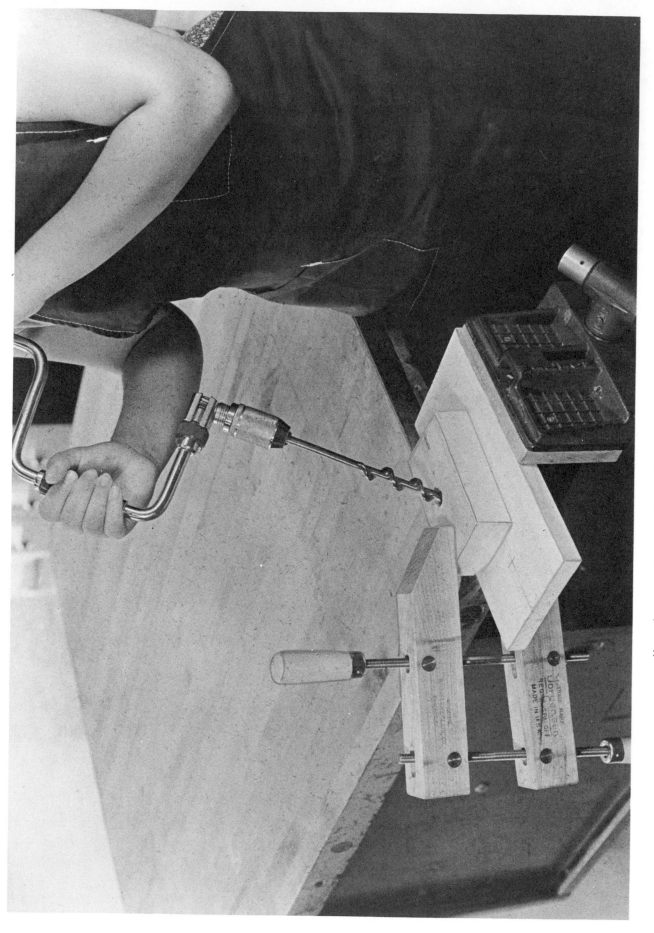

Using fixture made from a piece of 2 x 4 to bore hole at an angle.

Unit 12

USING METAL FASTENERS, GLUING, AND CLAMPING

Nails

Most of the nails we use are made by automatic machines from mild steel; other nails are made from copper, brass and aluminum.

Nail size is indicated by the letter "d", which is the English symbol for penny. Sizes range from 2d nails, which are 1 in. long, to 60d, which are 6 in. long. A wire gauge system is used to determine the diameter of nails. Lengths of smaller nails increase 1/4 in. for each d. For example: 4d - 1 1/2 in., 6d - 2 in., and 8d - 2 1/2 in.

Nails are sold by the pound. The COMMON nail which has a flat head is used in framing and rough construction. The BOX nail also has a flat head, but is smaller in diameter. It is less likely to split the wood. FINISH nails have small round heads which are set below the surface of wood in cabinetmaking and other finish construction. The CASING nail which is heavier than the finish nail has a small, tapered head which like the finish nail, is set below the surface of finish wood. It is often used for door or window casings. Finish nails which are smaller than 2d are called BRADS and common or box nails are referred to as WIRE NAILS. Brads and wire nails are available in several gauge sizes. A No. 16 brad is about 1/16 in. in diameter and almost twice the weight of a No. 20. The ESCUTCHEON nail is used for jobs such as fastening decorative plates around hinges and locks. It has a half-round head which is left exposed. Escutcheon nails are

usually made from copper or brass. RING and SCREW nails have spiral or straight threads. See Fig. 12-1.

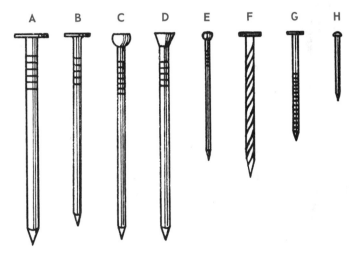

Fig. 12-1. Kinds of nails. A—Common. B—Box. C—Finish. D—Casing. E—Brad. F—Screw. G—Ring. H—Escutcheon.

Nail Hammers

The claw hammer is used to drive nails in cabinetmaking and carpentry. Its size is indicated by the weight of the head. Sizes range from 5 to 20 oz. A 10 oz. hammer works well in driving small nails, but a heavier hammer, 13 to 16 oz., is needed when driving large nails.

Nail Sets

Nail sets are used to set the heads of finish and casing nails below the surface of wood. Nail sets are available in tip sizes of 1/32 to 1/8 in. diameter.

Driving Nails

Nails used in cabinetwork are usually driven straight into the wood. Nails used in rough framing are often driven at an angle (toenailed) to increase the strength of the joint. Toenailing is usually practiced to fasten the end of one piece to the surface of a

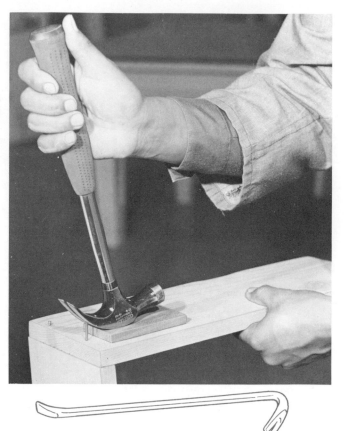

Fig. 12-3. Above. Pulling a nail with a claw hammer. Below. A wrecking bar.

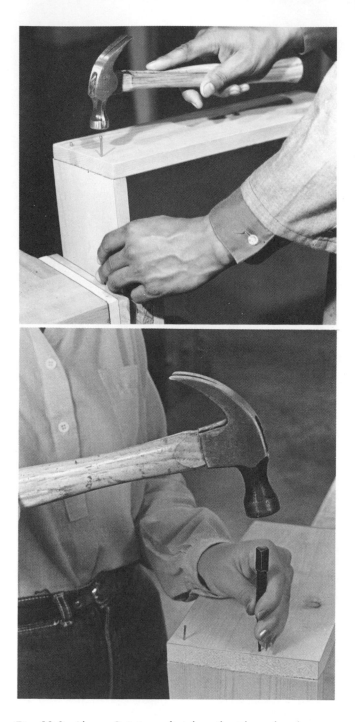

Fig. 12-2. Above. Driving a finish nail with a claw hammer. Below. Driving a finish nail head below the wood surface with a nail set and claw hammer.

second piece. Offsetting the placement of nails (staggering) helps to prevent splitting, and bending over the ends of nails (clinching) greatly increases the strength of the joint. A small hole should be drilled before driving a nail into hardwood. (If the correct size drill bit is not available, you can improvise by cutting the head from a nail, and using the nail as a drill bit.)

To fasten with finish nails, use a 10 - 13 oz. hammer. Select two pieces of wood and clamp one of the pieces in a vise. Using light taps with the hammer, start two nails into the surface at one end of the second piece. Place the second piece over the first piece and hold each end flush with the other. Drive each nail through the second piece into the first piece, keeping your eyes on the nail. To avoid bending the nail, strike it squarely with the face of the hammer. Drive each nail until just the head is exposed, then drive the nail below the wood surface using a nail set. See Fig. 12-2 (Above and Below).

Pulling Nails

Small nails, 8d or less, may be removed with a claw hammer. To remove large nails, often called SPIKES, a special steel bar called a WRECKING BAR should be used. See Fig. 12-3. Pulling nail with a hammer is also shown in Fig. 12-3.

Screws

We use screws to fasten hardware and pieces of wood which may need to be disassembled. As screws are turned (driven) with a screwdriver into holes drilled to receive them, they make threads in the wood, and hold a great deal more than nails.

Many kinds and sizes of screws are made from wire in automatic machines, from mild steel, brass, aluminum and other metals. Finishes include bright, blued, zinc chromate, brass, copper, nickel, and chromium. Sizes are given in diameter by gauge from 0 (smallest) to 24 and in lengths from 1/4 to 6 inches.

FLAT HEAD screws are designed so the heads fit flush with the surface of the wood or slightly below it. The entire screw is measured to determine its length. Heads of ROUND HEAD screws fit on top of the wood surface so the length is determined from

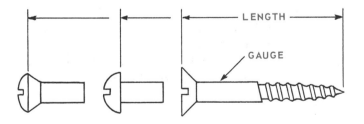

Fig. 12-4. Determining the length of screws. Left. Oval head. Center. Round head. Right. Flat head.

under the head to the tip of the screw point. Heads of OVAL HEAD screws are partially recessed into the wood surface. The length is determined by measuring from the point of recess to the tip of the screw point. See Fig. 12-4.

Fig. 12-5. Using a common screwdriver to drive a flat head screw with a slotted head.

Heads of screws may be slotted to take a regular screwdriver or recessed to take a Phillips screwdriver.

Screwdrivers

Screws with slotted heads are driven with a "regular" screwdriver. A variety of sizes should be available to fit different size screws. The tip of the screwdriver should fit the screw slot. A screwdriver that is too large may damage the screw slot and tear the wood. One that is too small is inefficient and may break. You can often use a screwdriver tip in a brace to good advantage. Screws with Phillips heads are driven with a Phillips screwdriver. With speed control, screwdriver tips can be used effectively in an electric or pneumatic drill, Figs. 12-5 and 12-6.

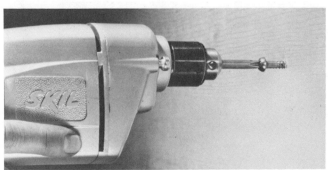

Fig. 12-6. Using a Phillips screwdriver in an electric drill to drive a round head screw with a Phillips head.

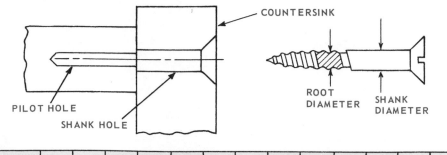

NO. OF SCREW	1	2	3	4	5	6	7	8	9	10	12	14	16	18
SHANK	5/64	3/32	3/32	7/64	1/8	9/64	5/32	11/64	11/64	3/16	7/32	15/64	17/64	19/64
PILOT	—	1/16	1/16	5/64	5/64	3/32	7/64	7/64	1/8	1/8	9/64	5/32	3/16	13/64

Fig. 12-7. Drill sizes for setting common screws.

Installing Screws

To set screws two different sizes of holes are needed. One (clearance hole) should be the size of the SHANK. For flat head screws, the top side of the clearance hole is countersunk to receive the screw head. The pilot (anchor) hole should be a little smaller than the root diameter of the screw thread. See Figs. 12-5, 12-7 and 12-8.

If you are counterboring for the screws, you can use a plug cutter to make wood plugs from the same kind of wood and glue the plugs in place over the screws. When the glue sets, you can trim the plugs flush with the wood surface.

Miscellaneous Fasteners

Fig. 12-9 illustrates a typical assortment of fasteners which are useful in various

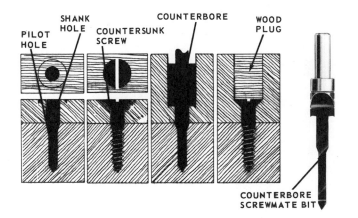

Fig. 12-8. A special counterbore screwmate bit drills the pilot hole, shank hole, and counterbore for a wood plug.

phases of woodworking. These are identified as:

A. Hanger bolt to fasten legs to a table with an attaching plate.

B. Lag screw to hold braces and other supports. This has a square head which is turned with a wrench.

C. Stove bolt with nut to attach parts which need to be easily disassembled.

D. Corrugated fasteners to reinforce miter and end-butt joints of softwood.

E. Upholstery tacks for use in unexposed areas to hold webbing and fabrics in place.

F. Screw cup hooks.

G. Screw eyes.

H. Rubber headed nails.

I. Upholstery nails for use in exposed areas to hold upholstery covering in place.

J. Lazy Suzan bearings.

K. Bar of staples used in a stapling gun or hammer.

L. Chair brace to strengthen chair joints.

M. Tilt-base leg glide for a leg base.

N. Carriage bolt to hold heavy pieces together. A nut is used to hold the bolt in place.

O. Attaching plate to fasten a leg to a table with a hanger bolt.

Concrete Fasteners

Fig. 12-10 illustrates some of the fasteners which are available for attaching wood to masonry:

A. Masonry nail for attaching to solid concrete or a mortar joint. This is a heavy-duty nail. A pilot hole should be drilled with a masonry bit to receive the nail.

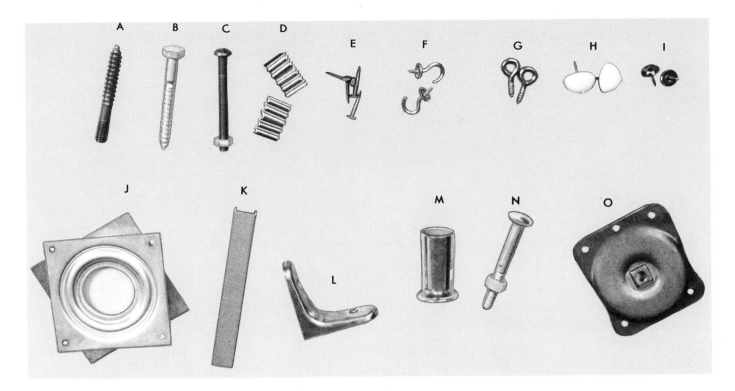

Fig. 12-9. Miscellaneous fasteners. A—Hanger bolt. B—Lag screw. C—Stove bolt. D—Corrugated fasteners. E—Upholstery tacks. F—Cup hooks. G—Screw eyes. H—Rubber headed nails. I—Upholstery Nails. J—Lazy Suzan bearings. K—Strip of staples. L—Chair brace. M—Tilt-base leg glide. N—Carriage bolt. O—Attaching plate.

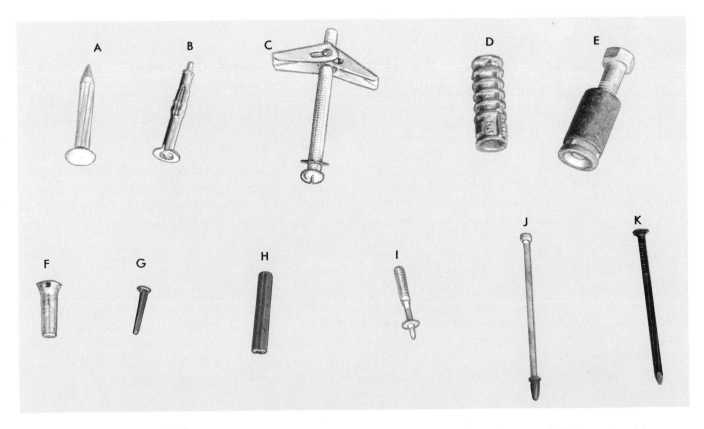

Fig. 12-10. Concrete fasteners. A—Concrete nail. B—Hollow wall screw anchor. C—Wing-toggle bolt. D—Lead lag screw plug. E—Machine screw anchor. F—Lead screw anchor. G—Plastic anchor. H—Plastic plug. I—Ram set bolt. J—Ram set nail. K—Concrete nail.

B. Hollow wall screw anchor for attaching to a hollow wall. A hole large enough to receive the outside jacket of the anchor is drilled into a hollow wall. The screw is removed from the anchor, then the jacket is inserted into the hole. The screw is replaced in the anchor and tightened. This causes the sides of the jacket to flare, holding the anchor firmly.

C. Wing toggle bolt for anchoring to a hollow wall. A hole is drilled in the wall, then the wings are folded and inserted through the hole. The wings spring outward, inside the wall. As the bolt is tightened, the wings are held firmly inside the wall.

STAPLE CROWN (SIDE VIEW)

Fig. 12-11. Side view cutaway of a driven staple with diverging points.

D. Lead screw anchor for lag screws. A hole is drilled with a masonry bit and the anchor is inserted in the hole. A lag screw is placed in the lead anchor and is turned, forcing the anchor firmly against the hole wall.

E. Machine screw anchor. A hole is drilled with a masonry bit. The machine screw is removed and the anchor is inserted in the hole. A special tool is used to drive the anchor to the bottom of the hole. This forces the bottom wedge upward which tightens the anchor against the hole wall. The machine screw can then be turned into the anchor.

F. Lead screw anchor for common wood screws. This is set in the same way as the lag screw anchor.

G. Plastic anchor for fastening to dry wall, ceramic tile, etc. A hole is drilled and the anchor is inserted into it. A common screw is turned into the anchor, forcing it against the hole wall.

H. Plastic plug. This is used as a plastic anchor but has a longer screw.

I. Sureset pin. A device is used to hold the pin as it is driven directly into masonry with a hammer.

J. Ram set nail. A special gun (ram set) powered with cartridges is used to hold and shoot nails into masonry.

K. Concrete nail. This is driven directly into concrete or a mortar joint.

Staples

A staple is made by bending wire into a "U" shape. Staples are available in a wide variety of types, sizes, and finishes and come in strips or bars for easy loading. See Fig. 12-9 (K).

Staples ordinarily provide more holding power than tacks or small nails because they have two legs holding instead of one. The staple legs follow the cut of the point on each leg. Different types of points are used so that the staple legs will toe-in or flare out (diverge) to make them stronger. Some staples are clinched on the back side of materials. Fig. 12-11 illustrates how a special, long staple with divergent points clings to the wood.

Staples are used for many purposes including: fastening roofing, insulation, ceiling tile, and upholstery materials. Industry uses staples to fasten wood and numerous other materials.

Staplers

Staplers are developed for many different uses. Some staplers are spring-driven and work well for light or medium work. Other staplers, developed for heavy work, are driven with air pressure.

Stapling

A strip of staples is loaded in a stapling gun or hammer with the sharpened points

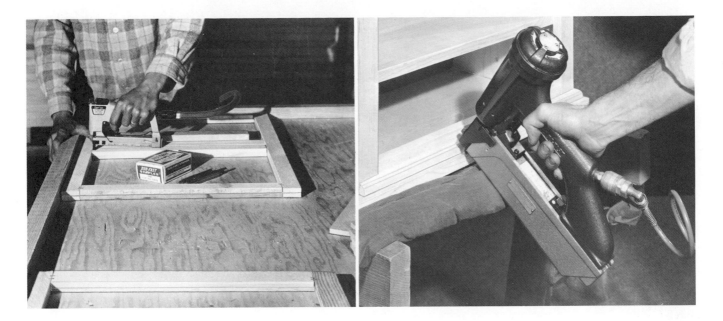

*Fig. 12-12. Stapling with a pneumatic stapler. Left. Light wood assembly.
Right. Attaching a trim strip with staples.*

facing downward. The stapler is held firmly against the work and is activated with a trigger. Fig. 12-12 shows skilled workers using pneumatic staplers.

Nailers and Nailing

Nailers operate similar to staplers. They are used to drive a variety of nails quickly and efficiently. The nails are attached together in strips. A strip of nails is mounted in a nailer with the points facing downward. The nailer is held firmly against the work and is activated with its trigger. Fig. 12-13 illustrates an air-powered nailer being used for heavy construction.

Glue Blocks

Glue blocks are small pieces of wood attached with glue or metal fasteners to strengthen joints.

Wood Dowels

Dowels are round, usually made of birch and are available in diameters of 1/8 to 1 in. and in lengths of 3 ft. Dowels are frequently used to reinforce pieces of wood fastened together with glue. Short dowel pegs with

spiral grooves are specially made for wood joints. The grooves allow air and excess glue to escape to the bottom of the holes during the clamping process.

Feathers

A feather (key) is a thin strip of wood used to strengthen and aid in the assembly of a corner joint. A saw kerf is cut across a corner joint and a thin strip of wood is fastened into the kerf with glue, locking the two pieces together.

Fig. 12-13. Using a pneumatic nailer.

Splines

A spline is a thin, rectangular strip of wood which is inserted into grooves or saw kerfs made in two adjacent parts of a joint. The spline strengthens and aids in the assembly of a joint.

Adhesives

Adhesives are used to bond materials together. A great variety of adhesives are available. Some adhesives are actually stronger than the wood itself.

BEFORE YOU USE CEMENTS OR GLUES, ALWAYS READ THE MANUFACTURER'S DIRECTIONS.

Rubber Cement

We use rubber cement to bond paper, cardboard, felt, and other light, porous materials. It is especially useful in preparing patterns. Rubber cement is available in ready-mixed, liquid form. It is applied with a brush onto the surfaces of both pieces to be attached and allowed to dry to a dull appearance. The two pieces are then carefully pressed together.

Contact Cement

A frequent use of contact cement is to fasten laminated plastic or veneer onto wood and plywood surfaces. This is available in liquid form and may be applied with a brush, roller, or spray gun. One or more thin coats (usually two coats for dry or porous surfaces) are applied to the surfaces of both pieces to be attached and then allowed to dry (usually about 30 minutes) to a dull appearance. As the name implies, this cement bonds on contact of two coated surfaces. You can keep the pieces separated by using dowel rods between them, placed close together. Another method is to use heavy wrapping paper. When the cement is dry, carefully position the two pieces. Begin at one end, pressing the two parts together. Move toward the other end, pressing from the center outward, and removing the dowels one at a time. Roll the outer surface with a large dowel or rubber roller to remove possible air pockets.

Plastics Cements

Plastics cements are useful for a variety of repair jobs using numerous materials. These cements usually come in tubes.

AIRPLANE cement is a common plastics cement. It sets quickly and hardens overnight to form a waterproof material. This can be used to bond porous or impervious materials.

EPOXY cement is one of our strongest adhesives. It is usually packed in two parts, a resin and a catalyst. These are mixed in small amounts as the cement is needed. Epoxy cement usually requires 6 to 8 hours to dry to a hard, waterproof consistency.

White Liquid Resin Glue

White liquid resin glue (polyvinyl acetate) which is available in convenient squeeze bottles spreads easily at temperatures above 60 deg. F. White glue is strong and has good gap-filling qualities. It sets and dries quickly, usually requiring only about 30 minutes of clamping time, with only enough pressure to bring the joints tightly together (about 25 psi). Polyvinyl glue dries by moisture absorption and evaporation. It dries to a flexible and colorless material which is ideal for furniture and cabinetwork. A disadvantage of this glue is its lack of resistance to heat and moisture. All excess glue should be removed before sanding to prevent clogging the sandpaper.

Animal Glue

Animal (hide) glue is made from animal hides and hooves. It is one of the oldest wood glues. Hide glue is available in liquid and dry forms. The liquid form is packaged in plastic squeeze bottles for easy application and storage. The dry form is seldom used, except by expert gluers on production jobs, because it is difficult to prepare. For use, it is dissolved in water, heated to about 140 deg. F., and applied hot.

Hide glue is excellent for furniture and cabinetwork. It is not waterproof so should be used only for interior work. Hide glue requires 3 to 4 hours clamping time at temperatures above 70 deg. F.

Plastic Resin Glue

Plastic resin glue (urea-formaldehyde) is highly moisture resistant and very strong if correctly used. It is a good glue to use for products which are exposed to a considerable amount of moisture for a short time.

This glue is available in powder form and is mixed to a creamy consistency with water for use. It is easy to use and dries to a hard, brittle substance with light brown color. Plastic resin glue dries slowly, by chemical change, which allows plenty of time to clamp the work. Only stock with well-fitted joints should be used. Work should be clamped securely for 6 to 8 hours or more at temperatures above 70 deg. F. Addition of heat aids the setting of plastic resin glue. Certain compounds of plastic resin glue are used with electronic gluing equipment. Plastic resin glue should be used only with non-oily woods.

Aliphatic Resin Glue

Aliphatic resin glue is a cream-colored, nonstaining liquid resin glue which comes in ready to use form. It is a very strong glue, resists heat and chemicals, and sands easily. This glue sets quickly, requiring only about 45 minutes at temperatures above 70 deg. F., but can be used at temperatures as low as 40 deg. F. A disadvantage is its inability to resist moisture, but it is a good glue for interior work.

Resorcinol Resin Glue

This is a powdered glue which is mixed to a creamy consistency with a liquid catalyst and water immediately before use. It is a very strong, waterproof glue so is used with materials subjected to large amounts of moisture. Resorcinol glue creates an unwanted dark glue line and requires 12 to 16 hours of clamping time at temperatures above 70 deg. F.

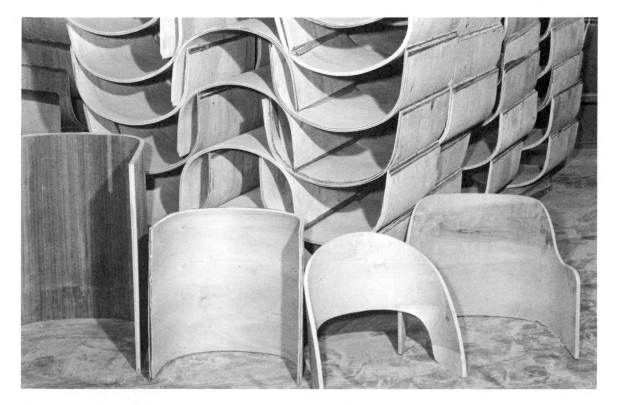

Industry photo. Laminated furniture parts are molded under pressure to desired shape.

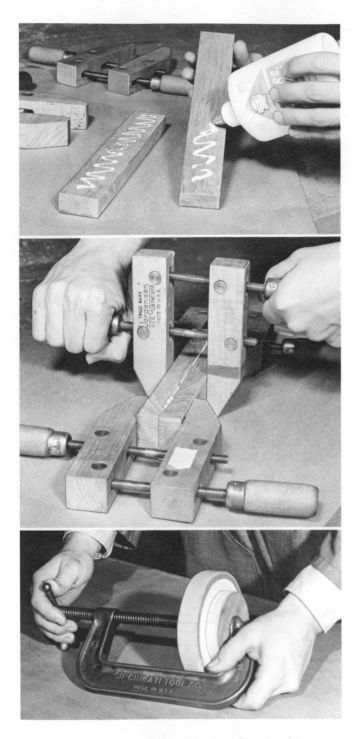

ate clamping time. Casein glue can be used at low temperatures just above freezing, but it works better at warmer temperatures. It is water resistant and especially useful with oily wood such as cypress. Casein glue has a tendency to stain woods like maple and oak.

Glue Application

Before applying glue for assembly, carefully check the fit of all parts with the necessary clamping devices in a trial-assembly.

If dry glue is being used, mix only the amount you can use in 3 to 4 hours. Using the correct amount of glue is of major importance. Too much glue results in excess squeeze-out which is messy and wasteful. Too little glue results in "starved" joints which are often weak.

Before deciding which glue to use be sure to consider the setting time. Some glues should be closed with clamps 2 to 5 minutes after glue application. Complicated assemblies should be done in several steps with the aid of a helper.

Apply glue on each piece to be attached, then spread it evenly from the center toward the edges with a brush, flat stick, or a roller. End grain should be given a second coat after about 1 minute, Fig. 12-14 (Above).

Clamping Devices

Clamping devices are available in many sizes and types. After using a clamping device, you should always remove any excess glue squeeze-out. You can do this with a damp cloth or sponge immediately after the clamping process. Another method is to wait 30 minutes or more, until the glue becomes a flexible solid, then pare it from the stock with a knife or paint scraper.

Hand Screws

Hand screws (parallel clamps) have two adjustable wood jaws which should be carefully set before use. Hand screws are used to hold fixtures and to clamp small pieces of wood, Fig. 12-14 (Center).

Fig. 12-14. Above. Applying white liquid resin glue onto a wood surface with a plastic squeeze bottle. Center. Using hand screws to clamp stock. Below. Using a C-clamp to glue stock.

Casein Glue

Casein glue is made in powder form primarily from milk curd. It is mixed with cold water, allowed to stand a few minutes, and then further mixed to a creamy consistency for use. It is a strong glue requiring moder-

C-Clamps

The C-clamp has an adjustable screw which holds stock firmly against the anvil. This is used extensively to hold fixtures and small pieces of stock, Fig. 12-14 (Below).

Spring Clamps

The spring clamp presses against stock with its fingers which are activated by a strong spring. Some spring clamps are

Fig. 12-16. Bar clamps. Above. Gluing narrow stock edge-to-edge to make a wide panel. Below. Bar clamp carrier to hold glued stock edge-to-edge for mass production of panels.

equipped with adjustable fingers for holding irregular shaped work. These clamps are especially helpful for holding small pieces in place, Fig. 12-15 (Above).

Miter Clamps

Miter clamps are useful in assembling corner joints cut for frames. Different types are available. Some are used for single corner joints, others for joining entire frames at once, Fig. 12-15 (Center and Below).

Steel Bar Clamps

Steel bar clamps (cabinet clamps) are used to join several narrow pieces of stock edge-to-edge to form a wider board or panel, Fig. 12-16. These are also used to make complete assemblies of cabinets and furni-

Fig. 12-15. Clamping devices. Above. Holding small pieces with spring clamps. Center. Forming a corner joint with a miter clamp. Below. Gluing an entire frame with a miter clamp fixture.

ture. Bar clamps are exceptionally strong. You can easily apply 500 to 600 lbs. of pressure. Pieces of scrap wood should be used between the clamp jaws and the stock to protect the stock from damage.

Space bar clamps 12 to 15 in. apart. When more than two clamps are used, alternating the clamping direction helps to prevent twisting of the panel. Small bar clamps (quick and web) are used with wood strips to hold panels straight, across the grain, Fig. 12-16 (Above).

Bar clamps are used in carriers by industry to assemble stock for mass production, Fig. 12-16 (Below).

Band Clamps

Band clamps are used to hold round or irregular shaped pieces in place, Fig. 12-17.

Fig. 12-18. A shop-made veneer press to glue veneer on wood or plywood surfaces.

Fig. 12-17. Using band clamps to assemble a chair.

Veneer Clamps

Veneer clamps can be made as needed using press screws used in a fixture. See Fig. 12-18.

Test Your Knowledge - Unit 12

1. Most of the nails we use are made from _____.
2. In indicating nail length the symbol used is the letter _____.
3. Common nails have _____ heads.
4. Finish nails have small round heads and are usually set below the surface of the wood. True or False?
5. Claw hammer size is indicated by the weight of the hammer _____.
6. Small nails 8d or less, may be removed using a _____ _____.
7. Screws are often used on jobs which need to be _____.
8. Screws will hold more than nails because they make _____ in the wood.
9. In use, the heads of round head screws fit flush with the surface. True or False?
10. The pilot hole for a wood screw should be a little _____ than the root diameter of the screw thread.
11. A staple is made by bending wire to a _____ shape.
12. Most wood dowels are made of _____.
13. A feather is a thin strip of wood used in the assembly of a _____ joint.
14. Epoxy cement usually comes in two parts, a resin and a _____.
15. Casein glue comes in _____ form

and is mixed with _____ .

16. Miter clamps are useful in assembling _____ joints.

Research and Development

1. Make a collection of as many different kinds of fasteners as you can find. Attach these to a piece of plywood to form a display.

2. What did the nails used by early settlers in the U. S. look like? See what you can find about this by searching in your library.

3. Are screws much stronger than nails? Develop a fixture, make some tests and report to your class.

4. Were you to have access to only glue in woodshop activities, which glue would you select?

Unit 13
SANDING

We sand wood to remove tool marks, to smooth and shape, to make ready for the application of finishing materials, and to smooth the materials used for finishing.

Coated Abrasives

Coated abrasive sheets, popularly called "sandpaper," are available with both natural and man-made abrasive coatings. Abrasive materials are sifted through screens to obtain particles (grit) of uniform size. These particles are then cemented to paper, cloth, or combination backing. The backing sheets are made in varying weights and degrees of flexibility.

CLOSED COAT abrasives are those which cover the entire surface.

OPEN COAT abrasives cover 50 to 70 percent of the surface. The open spaces allow chips of wood to drop out which reduces clogging.

Coated abrasives are available in the form of sheets, belts, disks and drums. Sheet size is usually 9 x 11 in.

Abrasive Materials

FLINT is a natural material (quartz) which is found in large deposits in the earth. It is low in cost, but lacks the toughness and durability of most other abrasive materials. Flint is gray-tan in color.

GARNET is a natural red silicate mineral. It is widely used in the woodworking industry, particularly for finish sanding. Garnet is tough, and durable. It comes in varying shades of red-brown.

ALUMINUM OXIDE is a synthetic (man-made) material made in an electric furnace from aluminum ore (bauxite). It is hard, tough, and durable with sharp cutting edges. Abrasive products made with aluminum oxide are often used in machine sanding.

SILICON CARBIDE, a synthetic material green-black in color, is made in an electric furnace from silica, petroleum coke, salt and wood sawdust. It is sharp, brittle and hard; in fact almost as hard as a diamond. Silicon carbide on waterproof paper is used extensively in production work.

CLASS	MESH SIZE	SYMBOL	CLASS	MESH SIZE	SYMBOL
	400	10/0		100	2/0
	360	--	Medium	80	1/0
Very	320	9/0		60	1/2
Fine	280	8/0		50	1
	240	7/0	Coarse	40	1 1/2
	220	6/0		36	2
	180	5/0	Very	30	2 1/2
Fine	150	4/0	Coarse	24	3
	120	3/0		20	3 1/2

Fig. 13-1. Abrasive mesh grit sizes.

Fig. 13-2. Fixture for tearing sandpaper.

Abrasive Grit Sizes

Standard abrasive grit sizes are indicated by a number, which is the mesh size per linear inch, or by a symbol, which represents a grit size. For example, grits that pass through a screen with 80 openings per linear inch are grit 80 - designated 80(0). The (0) is the symbol number. Some of the standard abrasive mesh grit sizes are shown in Fig. 13-1.

Steel Wool

Steel wool is made of thin shavings of steel which are packaged in pads and rolls. Grades are from very fine (4/0) to coarse (3). Steel wool is used to smooth intricate and curved surfaces, and for smoothing finished surfaces.

Polishing Compounds

Prepared polishing compounds and powdered abrasives are used to polish finishes. Powdered abrasives are applied with a cloth pad and water or mineral oil. PUMICE, derived from lava, is white in color. Grades FF and FFF are commonly used. ROTTEN-STONE is an iron oxide produced from shale. It is red-brown or gray-brown in color. Rottenstone which is finer than pumice is generally used after pumice.

Hand Sanding

Final sanding is usually done by hand, following the use of cutting tools or a machine sander. Hand sanding removes mill marks and smooths the wood ready for finishing materials.

For most sanding jobs grades 60, 100 and 150 can be used. The rough or medium grade should be used first, followed by the finer grades. Tear the sandpaper sheets into appropriate size pieces. If you tear them into thirds, the pieces can also be used in a finishing sander. Fig. 13-2 illustrates an easily made fixture which may be used to gauge and tear abrasive papers.

To smooth a flat surface, clamp the piece in a vise. Wrap a piece of sandpaper around a block of wood or fasten it in a sanding block. Using a block helps to keep the stock flat. ALWAYS SAND WITH THE GRAIN NOT

111

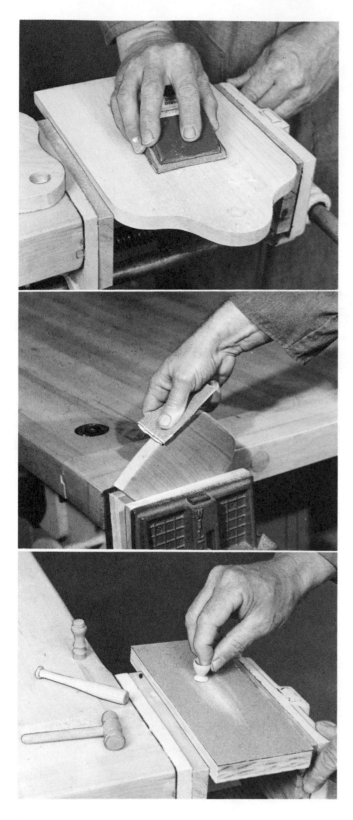

Fig. 13-3. Hand sanding. Above. Sanding a surface. Center. Sanding an edge. Below. Sanding small pieces of stock.

ACROSS IT. Sanding across the grain usually cuts deep scratches into the wood which are difficult to remove, Fig. 13-3 (Above).

To sand around a curved or irregular-shaped edge of stock, fold a piece of sandpaper into a small pad so your thumb or fingers fit the edge, Fig. 13-3 (Center).

To smooth small pieces of stock, attach a piece of sandpaper to a piece of scrap wood and clamp the wood in a vise. Move the pieces along the surface of the sandpaper. See Fig. 13-3 (Below).

Disk Sander

The disk sander is useful when shaping edges and ends of stock. Disk sander size is indicated by the diameter of the disk. A 12 in. disk sander is a common size. The disk sander is usually equipped with an adjustable table on which a miter gage is used to guide the stock when smoothing bevels and angles.

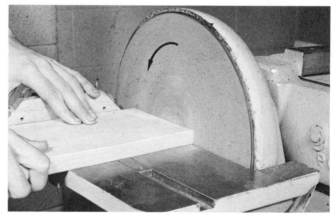

Fig. 13-4. Smoothing the end of a board with a disk sander.

To smooth the end of a board with a disk sander, place it on the sander table so the disk cuts in a downward direction. Turn on the motor and move the piece carefully into the disk with just enough pressure to keep it cutting. Move the piece sideways, slightly, to reduce heat caused by friction. When the end of the piece is smooth, remove it from the table and turn off the motor, Fig. 13-4.

Belt Sander

The belt sander is useful for smoothing surfaces and edges of stock. Its size is indicated by width of the sander belt. A 6 in.

112

belt sander is a popular size. The length of the belt varies with different types of sanders. The belt revolves on two pulleys, one of which is movable to adjust belt tracking and

Fig. 13-5. Smoothing the surface of a board with a belt sander in its horizontal position.

tension. Belt sanders are used in both vertical and horizontal positions. A table is used to hold stock in the vertical position and an end stop is used in the horizontal position.

To smooth the surface of a board with the belt sander in its horizontal position, carefully lower the board onto the sanding belt with the end of the piece held against the stop. Move the board from side to side until it is smooth, then remove it from the sander and turn off the motor, Fig. 13-5.

Portable Belt Sander

The portable belt sander is also useful when smoothing wood surfaces. Belt sander size is indicated by the width of its belt. A 3 in. belt sander is a common size. The belt turns on two pulleys, one of which can be moved to adjust belt tracking and tension.

Clamp the stock in a vise. Hold the sander over the stock and start at one side of the board surface. As you sand, move the sander carefully over the stock working with the grain. Raise the sander slightly at the end of the stroke. Begin the second stroke by lapping halfway across the width of the first stroke. Continue with succeeding strokes across the width of the board, Fig. 13-6.

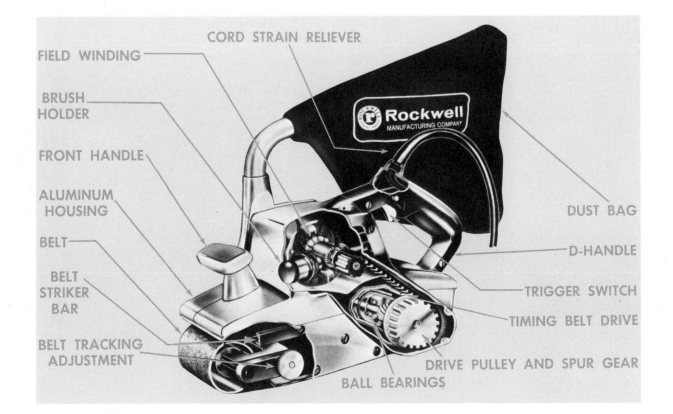

Fig. 13-6. Parts of a portable belt sander.

Finish Sanders

Both electric and pneumatic sanders are used to do smoothing before hand sanding. Some have an orbital (elliptical) stroke and others have a straight-line (straight) stroke. Finish sanders are commonly designed to use one third of a standard sheet of sandpaper.

To use a finish sander, clamp your stock in a vise. Begin at one side of the stock surface, moving the sander carefully. Use only enough pressure to keep the sander cutting. Move the sander WITH the grain of the wood, lapping each succeeding stroke, Fig. 13-7 (Above and Below).

Sanding Curved and Irregular Edges

Both curved and irregular edges can be smoothed with a drum sander fastened in a drill press or with a spindle sander, Fig. 13-8 (Left and Right).

Safety and Care of Sanders

1. Always check the motor switch to see that it is in the "off-position" before you plug in the power cord.
2. Unplug the sander when it is not in use.

Fig. 13-7. *Finishing sanders. Above. Smoothing the surface of a board with an orbital electric sander. Below. Smoothing the surface of a board with a pneumatic straight-line sander.*

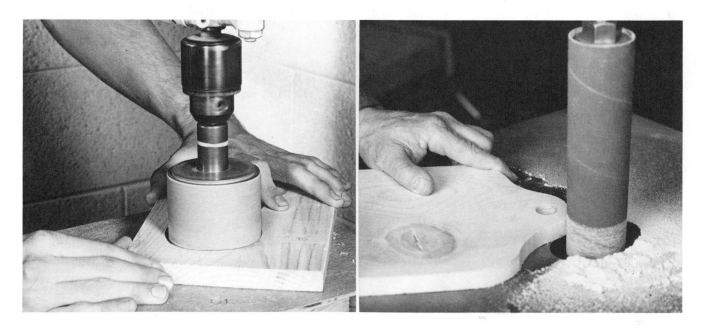

Fig. 13-8. *Smoothing curved and irregular-shaped edges. Left. Using a drum sander in a drill press. Right. Using a spindle sander.*

3. When the sander is not in use, store it on a scrap piece of hardboard, toward the center of the bench, where it will not fall or damage the bench top.

4. Use only enough pressure to keep the sander cutting.

5. Keep the sanding belt adjusted to correct alignment and tension.

6. Replace worn sanding sheets, belts and sleeves when necessary.

7. Keep the sander clean and properly lubricated.

Test Your Knowledge - Unit 13

1. Coated abrasives are available with both _____ and _____ particles.
2. Open coat abrasives allow chips of wood to fall out which reduces_____.
3. A greenish-black abrasive, almost as hard as a diamond, is _____ _____.
4. Standard abrasive grit sizes are indicated by a number which is the mesh size per linear_____.
5. Always sand with the grain, not across it. True or false?
6. Place materials to be smoothed on the disk sander table so the sander disk cuts in the _____ direction.
7. Belt sander size is indicated by the_____ of the sander belt.
8. Finish sanders are commonly designed to use one_____ of a standard size sheet of sandpaper.

Research and Development

1. Which abrasive works best on pine, on oak? To answer this try different kinds of sandpaper on the surfaces of the two woods.
2. Make a chart listing as many different kinds of abrasives as you can find. Try to obtain actual samples for a bulletin board display.
3. Which sanding methods are used most by the woodworking industry? Check library reference books and prepare a brief written report.

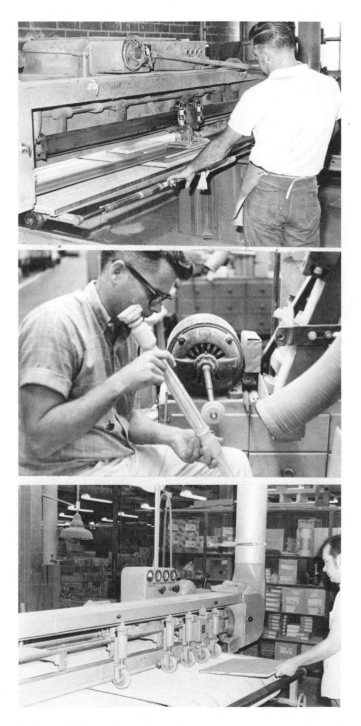

Industry photos. Above. Smoothing the surface of a wood panel with a stroke belt sander. Center. Contour sanding. Below. Power fed belt sander.

Unit 14
WOOD FINISHING

We apply finish to wood to protect the surface and enhance the natural beauty of the wood.

The wood finish to use depends on a number of considerations such as the kind of wood, appearance desired, time available for wood finishing, and wood finishing supplies and equipment available.

In this Unit we will discuss the use of a variety of wood finishing products which are being used in typical industrial arts laboratories.

In using all wood finishes, it is important to experiment on scrap stock of the same kind of wood used in constructing your project, and to make sure the product is being applied according to the manufacturer's instructions.

First Steps

Repairing Defects

Before applying finish, nail holes, small cracks and any other small defects should be repaired.

Fillers commonly used include Plastic Wood, Wood Putty, Water Putty and Stick Shellac. See Figs. 14-1 and 14-2.

Fig. 14-1. Products commonly used in repairing wood defects. Plastic Wood, Wood Putty and Water Putty.

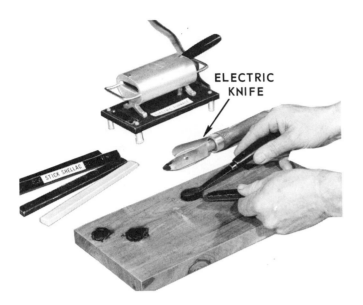

Fig. 14-2. Repairing wood defects with stick shellac.

Plastic Wood

Plastic Wood, available in several shades including natural, oak, mahogany and walnut, comes in ready-to-use form. It handles like putty and hardens like wood. Patching with Plastic Wood should be done before any finish is applied. The surface should be clean and dry. Press plastic into place using tool such as putty knife or small spatula, or a finger. To fill large holes apply Plastic Wood in thin layers. Allow each layer to dry before applying next layer. Overfill to allow for shrinkage and sanding. Keep can tightly covered when not in use.

CAUTION: Plastic Wood is extremely flammable. Avoid excessive inhalation of fumes. Use only with adequate ventilation.

Wood, Water Putties

Wood and Water Putties which come in powder form are prepared by mixing with water to form a smooth, thick paste. Mix only the amount which can be used in a short time. Adding a small amount of vinegar will retard setting. If color is required, dry colors or water stains may be added.

Prepare the cavity by removing all dirt and grease. Wet edges to give good bond. Use a putty knife to press mixture into cavity. Smooth carefully with wet putty knife or finger. The Putty is easier to sand after hardening if moistened with water.

Stick Shellac

Stick Shellac comes in various colors. To correct wood defects with stick shellac, select a stick that is slightly darker than you expect the wood will be when you apply the finish. You can dampen a small spot to help you visualize the color. Use a heated knife, or electrically heated unit to melt the shellac so it can be worked into the defect. See Fig. 14-2.

Products such as Plastic Wood, Wood Putty and Stick Shellac are used BEFORE applying the finish.

Filling Dents

Most small dents in wood can be filled prior to the application of the finish, by the application of water and heat. Lightly moisten the dented area, place a wet cloth pad over the dent and apply heat with a soldering iron, or household iron.

Water and steam cause the wood fibers to swell and spring back to approximate original shape. Allow the wood to dry, then smooth with fine sandpaper.

Putty Sticks, Pencils

Preparations such as Putty Sticks and Blend Sticks, Fig. 14-3, are generally used AFTER applying the finish, and on prefinished

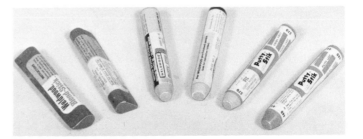

Fig. 14-3. Putty and Blend Sticks are generally used after applying finish and to fill nail holes in prefinished panels.

panels. Select a stick which best matches the finished wood. Rub the stick over the hole until it is filled, then wipe off the excess with a cloth pad.

Bleaching Wood

When it is desirable to lighten wood to remove dark streaks, and to prepare the surface for special finishes, wood bleach is used. OXALIC ACID may be used as a mild bleaching solution. It comes in powder form and a bleaching solution may be made by using 1 part oxalic acid powder to 20 parts of water.

The oxalic acid solution is usually harmless to your skin but should be kept away from your eyes. Oxalic acid bleach may be applied with a cloth pad.

COMMERCIAL WOOD BLEACH usually comes in two separate containers (sodium hydroxide and hydrogen peroxide), Fig. 14-4. The two solutions are mixed together in small amounts as needed, following the manufacturer's instructions.

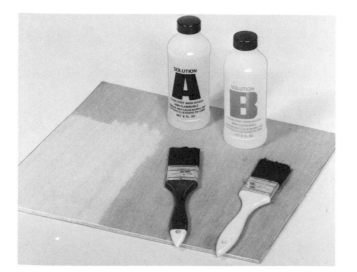

Fig. 14-4. Using commercial type wood bleach. Bleach has been used on the light-colored area at the left.

In working with commercial bleaches, always wear rubber gloves to protect your hands, and goggles for eye protection. Use bleach only in a well-ventilated area. If the

bleach accidentally comes in contact with your skin, wash immediately, using soap and water.

Sanding

To obtain a fine finish on a wood surface, the surface should be smoothed by sanding to make the surface perfectly smooth. Keep in mind the fact the finished surface will be no smoother than the surface to which it is applied.

Use a flat sanding block to hold fine abrasive paper and work WITH the grain of the wood. All traces of dust and sand may be removed by using a tack rag (tack rags available commercially are chemically treated so they will remain soft and tacky). A tack rag may be made by moistening a pad of soft cotton cloth with thinned varnish.

Brushes

Brushes come in many sizes, shapes and grades. Some have animal hair bristles, some nylon bristles. The bristles are usually set in rubber and held in place with a metal ferrule. See Fig. 14-5.

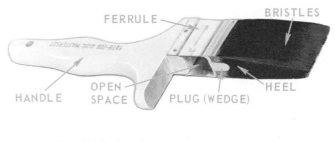

Fig. 14-5. Brush — cutaway view showing constructional details.

In wood finishing, it is important to purchase good brushes, and see to it the brushes are properly used and stored. A brush which is used regularly for the same type of finish may be stored for short periods of time by drilling a hole through the handle, inserting a wire through the hole and suspending the brush in a can or jar containing solvent. The brush should be held so the bristles will not touch the bottom of the container.

If you use a brush with a finish which dries by evaporation (shellac, lacquer, synthetic finish) you can store it in a glass jar containing the finish, by using a rubber lid, Fig. 14-6.

Fig. 14-7. Wood finishing with Deft vinyl stain.

Fig. 14-6. Storing brushes in glass jars with rubber lids.

A good way to preserve the quality of a brush, is to clean it after use and store it dry. Remove excess finish by pulling the brush lightly across the top of a container. Wash the brush in solvent (type used with finish being used) and dry it with a cloth or paper towel. Scrub the brush with soap or detergent and water, and wrap it with paper or aluminum foil to keep the bristles straight.

Finishing with Deft Vinyl Stain

If you finish your project with a commercially available finish such as Deft vinyl stain (water cleanup), a paste wood filler (as described later in this Unit) is usually not required. The first coat fills open pores and seals the surface of the wood. Deft comes in colors such as walnut, maple, cherry, fruitwood, mahogany, natural. See Fig. 14-7.

Use Deft vinyl stain as it comes in the can. Apply generously with brush, cloth or roller. While wet, wipe off excess stain with water dampened cloth. Avoid lapping by staining one area (side, top, etc.) at a time. Recoating may be done as soon as dry.. in about two hours.

Sand first coat lightly using fine (6/0 or 8/0) paper, then apply another coat of vinyl stain or finish with Deft clear semi-gloss wood finish (cannot be cleaned up with water).

Using Deft lacquer spray stain provides a quick and an easy way to stain hard to brush places, and small projects.

Fig. 14-8. Using Sealacell products in wood finishing.

Finishing with Sealacell Products

Finishing with Sealacell wood finishes, Fig. 14-8, involves three different items:

Sealacell, a moisture repellent penetrating wood seal, is used as the first application on the unfinished wood. Use a cloth and apply liberally, as the depth of penetration depends to a considerable extent on the amount applied. Ground in oil color pigments may be used in the Sealacell to add color.

Varnowax, applied next, is a penetrating blend of gums and waxes. Apply Varnowax in a circular motion with a small pad of cloth. Use only enough to lightly cover the surface.

Royal Finish which is the third and usually final coat used over the Varnowax, is a blend of gums which penetrates the wood. Royal Finish is applied in the same manner as Varnowax.

Arm-R Seal Heavy Duty, a heavy body seal, may be used as a final coat for surfaces receiving very hard usage.

Using Minwax Wood Finishes

Minwax, a quick drying wood finish which penetrates and seals is applied directly to unfinished wood. See Fig. 14-9.

Apply one coat, wait for about 12 hours until dry, then apply a second coat. Sanding between coats is unnecessary. If a soft, flat finish is desired, wait 24 hours and apply

Fig. 14-9. Using Minwax wood finish.

finishing wax. If a semi-gloss finish is desired, apply a coat of Deft clear wood finish, or varnish.

Minwax wood finish comes in several colors, also natural. Minwax colors can be mixed with natural paste wood filler to make the filler blend with the color of the project.

You can create tones of blue, green and red, by using white tint base and Americolor wood finishes by Minwax.

Wood Stains

In wood finishing, stain is used to emphasize wood grain, and to impart color to the surface of the wood.

Wood stains may be classified according to the solvent used in their manufacture. Solvents include oil, alcohol and water.

Oil Stain

Pigmented oil stains contain finely ground color particles (pigments) which do not dissolve and are mixed in a vehicle (liquid) such as linseed oil or mineral spirits. It is a common belief that stain marked walnut, mahogany, etc. will stain wood to closely resemble the wood after which it is named. Actually the name implies a color, such as a brown or reddish tint. It may be used to color any wood. The pigment colors remain on the wood surface, providing uniform color and appearance.

Stir the stain thoroughly. Apply quickly and uniformly, using a soft brush. Flow on across the grain, then make light finishing strokes WITH the grain. Check carefully for skips or spots missed. Allow the stain to set up until the surface appears to be flat or dull (5 to 10 min.). Then, wipe with a clean lint-free cloth WITH the wood grain to bring out the highlights of the wood. See Fig. 14-10. Depth of color may be controlled by the amount of stain left on the wood. Use turpentine or mineral spirits for cleanup. Allow about 24 hours for oil stain to dry before applying paste wood filler, or finish coats.

Fig. 14-10. *Applying oil stain. Wiping with lint-free cloth to bring out highlights.*

Penetrating oil stains are made by mixing oil and oil-soluble dyes. A problem experienced in using penetrating stain is that excessive quantities are absorbed by the end grain. A coat of linseed oil applied to the end grain a few minutes before using the penetrating stain will help to equalize the color.

Oil stain should be allowed to dry thoroughly and then coated with a sealer (shellac or lacquer) to prevent bleeding of the stain into finishing coats.

(NGR) Non-Grain-Raising Stains

Non-grain-raising stains, made by dissolving colored dyes in glycol and alcohol, are non-bleeding and will not raise wood grain.

Water Stains

Water stains are made by dissolving water soluble dyes in water. About 4 oz. of stain added to a gallon of water makes a gallon of ready-to-use stain.

Water stains penetrate deeply into the wood and tend to raise the wood grain. Before using water stain, the wood grain should be raised by sponging the wood lightly with water. Allow the wood to dry, then sand lightly with fine abrasive paper, working WITH the grain. Water stained surfaces may be darkened by applying extra coats. These stains do not bleach when exposed to sunlight and are inexpensive. After drying, water stained surfaces should be coated with shellac or lacquer sealer before applying other finishes.

Paste Wood Fillers

Woods consist of countless, interwoven fibers which contain holes or pores. Some woods like maple, pine and basswood (close-grained woods) have small pores. These small pores need only to be sealed (filled) with such finishing materials as shellac, lacquer, linseed oil or synthetics before applying finishing coats. Other woods like walnut, oak, ash, and mahogany have large, visible (open-grain) pores. These large pores should be filled with paste wood filler to obtain a smooth surface before applying most other finishes, Fig. 14-11.

Fig. 14-11. *Paste wood filler being used to fill pores of open-grain wood.*

Paste wood filler is made from ground silica (silex), linseed oil, turpentine or paint thinner and drier. It is packed as a heavy paste which needs to be thinned for use, to a heavy creamy consistency, using turpentine or paint thinner. Paste wood filler is available in natural (light buff color) and in colors such as oak, walnut and mahogany. The natural filler may be tinted with oil stains. Color of the paste filler should match closely with the finished wood.

To fill an open-grain wood, mix paste wood filler to the correct color and consistency. It is a good idea to try the filler on a scrap piece of wood first, before you apply it on your project. You can apply it directly onto the unfinished wood, or you might want to first apply a thin coat of sealer to the wood and let it dry before using the filler. Apply the filler along the grain, brushing it into the pores with a stiff brush, Fig. 14-11. If your project is large, coat only a small section at a time. Wait a few minutes, until the filler begins to have a dull appearance, then wipe off the excess filler. Rub ACROSS the grain using a lint-free cloth such as cheesecloth, or a piece of burlap, Fig. 14-12. Use a softer cloth to remove any remaining residue. You can clean out the corners with a piece of cloth wrapped around a pointed stick. Allow the filled wood to dry 4-6 hours, then lightly rub the surface with 6/0 sandpaper.

with alcohol and usually sold as 4 lb. cut (4 lbs. of shellac solids mixed with a gallon of alcohol). The 4 lb. cut is commonly mixed with an equal part of alcohol to form a 2 lb. cut for brush application. Lacquer sealer is usually applied by spraying, but it can be brushed on small projects. Lacquer sealer is reduced with lacquer thinner. Sealer stains are usually reduced with turpentine or paint thinner. Synthetics are reduced with various thinners according to their composition.

Wash-coating is the application of a thin (6-8 parts thinner to 1 part sealer) coat of sealer, usually shellac or lacquer sealer, which is applied over paste wood filler and some stains to prevent them from bleeding into the finish. A wash coat can also be used on wood prior to application of paste wood filler.

You can apply sealers with a brush or by spraying. Be sure to read and follow the manufacturer's instructions. See Fig. 14-13.

Fig. 14-12. Excess wood filler being removed, working ACROSS the grain.

Fig. 14-13. Applying wood stain and sealer by spraying.

Sealers

Sealers are finishes used as the base coat to fill the pores of close-grained wood such as maple, birch, pine and cherry. Shellac, lacquer sealer, sealer stains and synthetics are commonly used for this purpose. Sealers are available ready-mixed but are often reduced before application. Shellac is reduced

When LINSEED OIL AND TURPENTINE AND DANISH OIL finishes are used, these should be allowed to set about 30 minutes after application. Then, the excess material is wiped off and the remaining finish is al-

Fig. 14-14. Top coat finishes: varnish, lacquer, shellac, enamel, paint, synthetic.

lowed to dry 10-12 hours. Additional coats are applied in the same way. The linseed oil and turpentine finish penetrates the wood better if it is heated to about 140 deg. F. before it is applied. When the final coat is thoroughly dry, a coat of wax should be applied. Then the surface should be buffed to enhance its beauty and increase its durability.

Top Coat Finishes

A variety of finishes are used for top coats (over sealer). Varnish, lacquer, shellac and synthetics are often used to achieve a natural (clear) or transparent-color finish. Enamel and paint are used to obtain an opaque-color finish. See Fig. 14-14.

You can apply a top coat finish with a brush, roller or by spraying.

Most of the top coat finishes remain on the surface of the wood to form hard, durable and protective coverings, usually when more than one coat of finish is used, the finish should be smoothed between coats with 6/0-8/0 sandpaper or with 3/0-4/0 steel wool.

To smooth the final coat of varnish, lacquer, or shellac to a lustrous finish with

pumice or rottenstone, sprinkle the abrasive and rubbing oil over the finished surface, Fig. 14-15. Using a cloth or felt pad, rub the abrasive and oil over the surface. Wipe off the excess polishing material with a soft cloth, apply a coat of wax, and buff to shine.

Fig. 14-15. Using rottenstone and rubbing oil to smooth final coat.

VARNISH and ENAMEL are made from the same basic materials but pigment is added to enamel to give it color and make it opaque. Varnish and enamel are made with both natural and synthetic materials which create a hard, durable and waterproof finish. Drying time varies, but 8-10 hours is usually required. Varnish and enamel are reduced with turpentine or mineral spirits (paint thinner).

LACQUER dries fast by evaporation and is usually applied with spraying equipment, making it adaptable to mass production techniques. Lacquer can be brushed on small projects if a retarding (slow-drying) thinner is used to reduce it. Lacquer produces a clear, hard, durable film which is heat resistant. Pigments can be added to make either transparent or opaque color. Some lacquers are water resistant and some are not. Lacquer is reduced with lacquer thinner and should be applied in thin coats. Thick coats dry quickly on the outside but remain soft on the inside. About 30 minutes is usually allowed between coats.

CAUTION: Lacquer tends to soften and lift varnish, enamel and some synthetics so should not be used over them.

PLASTIC COATING, polyurethane is one of the newer finishes. This clear plastic coating dries fast, and is highly resistant to abrasion and wear. No sealer is needed, and it may be used on all kinds of wood both indoors and outdoors. Polyurethane plastic coating should be applied with a good quality, clean brush. On new wood, two or three coats are needed. Light sanding between coats to remove the gloss assures good adhesion.

SHELLAC will produce a fine finish if it is applied in thin coats (2 lb. cut), the same

as a sealer coat. It is one of our oldest finishes. It is lasting if properly cared for, but it is not water or alcohol resistant. Paste wax should be used after the final coat to enhance its beauty and protect the finish from moisture.

PAINTS are available with oil base or rubber (latex) base in a great variety of colors for both exterior and interior surfaces. Paints are often used to beautify and protect surfaces where an opaque finish is appropriate. Softwoods, wallboard, siding and masonry are often painted. Oil-base paint is reduced with turpentine or mineral spirits and usually requires 24 hours or more drying time for each coat. Rubber-base paints are thinned with water and can be recoated within a short time. Brushes used for latex paint should be cleaned in water soon after use.

Thinning Mediums

TURPENTINE is used to reduce oil stains and paints, varnish and enamels. It is obtained from yellow pine trees. Substitutes for turpentine (paint thinners) are made from petroleum.

SHELLAC SOLVENT is a combination of wood and grain alcohol, sometimes called "denatured" alcohol.

LACQUER THINNER is a combination of clear liquid used as a solvent for lacquer, lacquer sealer and contact cement.

Fig. 14-16. Thinning mediums.

Fig. 14-17. Antiquing with items which come in kit form.

RETARDING LACQUER THINNER is a special thinner used to slow the drying time of lacquer, and to help eliminate "blushing." Blushing is a white or cloudy appearance on a surface caused by trapping small particles of moisture beneath the finish.

LINSEED OIL, obtained from flax seed, is used in thinning some kinds of paint and as a drying oil in paints, fillers and stains. It is also used with turpentine as a finish. See Fig. 14-16.

Novelty Finishes

FLOCK is pulverized rayon or cellulose acetate which can be sprinkled or blown on a sticky substance such as enamel or glue resulting in a velvet-like coating. It is used on the bottom of small projects to protect furniture, as a decorative medium, and as a lining in boxes.

CRYSTALLINE FINISH can be brushed or sprayed and is similar to enamel or paint. Upon drying it forms a mass of wrinkles or crystals making an interesting and decorative finish.

Antiquing (Color Glazing)

You may apply an antique finish, which will make your project look "old" and "new" at the same time, by using a color base undercoat and color glaze. A kit containing the items needed (typical) is shown in Fig. 14-17. Various color combinations are available.

Application of a paint like latex undercoat covers the surface being finished (including old paint or varnish) and provides a base color for the second step - - the application of the color glaze. Allow the undercoat to dry thoroughly, then apply the color glaze. Wood tones and other special effects may be obtained by using a soft, lint-free cloth to wipe or texture the color glaze before it has a chance to dry. If the effect is not satisfactory, you can wipe off the glaze and start over.

Spraying Finishes

The spray gun is universally used in industry to obtain protective and beautiful coatings with maximum speed and minimum cost. It atomizes (forms into a fine mist) the finishing material so it can be applied in thin, uniform coats. To experience success by spraying finishing materials, we need to employ correct techniques with adequate equipment and properly mixed materials. Practicing on pieces of scrap lumber is highly desirable.

In spraying, hold the gun perpendicular to the surface, 6 to 8 in. away, as shown by the solid lines in Fig. 14-18. Tilting the gun up or down, as indicated by the dash lines, results in an uneven spray pattern.

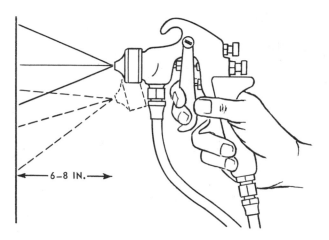

Fig. 14-18. *Using spray gun - - correct method of holding.*

Begin at one side of the practice piece and move the spray gun toward the other side. Trigger the spray gun "on" as you come to the first edge and "off" as you reach the other side. Make the necessary adjustments with the gun, mixture, or air pressure so the material is WET as it is sprayed on the surface. If the material is dry, add more solvent

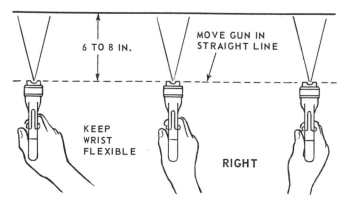

Fig. 14-19. *Using spray gun - - correct movement.*

to the mixture. Continue with succeeding strokes in the same way, lapping the previous stroke by about 50 percent, Fig. 14-19.

When spraying a large panel, it is a good idea to spray vertical bands along the ends of the piece first, then continue with right and left strokes, triggering the gun at the beginning and ending of each stroke, Fig. 14-20.

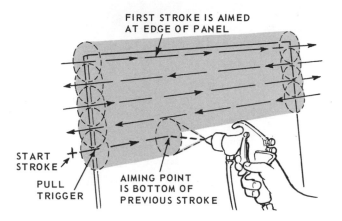

Fig. 14-20. *Panel spraying technique.*

Removing Finish

Ready-to-use materials are available that effectively remove finishes from wood or metal surfaces.

Before removing a finish, cover your workbench with sheet metal, or hardboard, and old newspapers. Obtain a pair of rubber gloves to protect your hands. Pour about a cupful of remover into a tin can.

Using a brush, apply the remover to one side of the project. Continue applying the remover until the finish begins to loosen. Then, using a piece of burlap or coarse cloth, wipe away the loosened finish. Use a putty knife or spatula if the finish is thick. An old tooth brush is helpful around intricate or irregular shapes. Continue with the remainder of your project, removing the finish from one panel at a time. Allow your project to dry 8-10 hours, then smooth it with fine sandpaper.

You can use a commercial bleach to subdue a stain left by an old finish.

Wood Finishing

Safety Notes

1. Keep sparks and flames away from the finishing area.
2. Help to see to it that all waste materials and rags are placed in a metal container.
3. Always use an exhaust fan (or work in an area that is adequately ventilated) to expel dangerous fumes while spray painting or removing a finish.
4. Wear goggles and rubber gloves when you handle strong liquids such as bleaches and finish removers.
5. Clean your brushes and store them properly after each use.
6. Tightly seal finish cans and store them in a metal cabinet.
7. Protect your clothing with a shop apron.

Test Your Knowledge - Unit 14

1. When finishing it is important to experiment on scrap stock of the _____ kind of wood as used in the construction of your projects.
2. Be sure the finishing product is being applied according to the _____.
3. Nail holes, small cracks, and any other defects should be repaired _____ applying finish.
4. Plastic Wood handles like _____ and hardens like _____.
5. Wetting the edges of the cavity gives a good _____ between Wood Putty and wood.
6. To correct wood defects with stick shellac, select a stick that is slightly _____ than you expect the wood will be when you apply the finish.
7. Putty Sticks and Pencils are generally used _____ applying the finish, and on _____ panels.
8. Oxalic acid may be used as a mild wood _____ solution.
9. When storing a brush for a short period of time in a can or jar of solvent, the brush should be held so the bristles ____ _____.
10. After using Deft Vinyl Stain, cleanup is done with _____.
11. Wood stains may be classified according to the _____ used in their manufacture.
12. To prevent excessive quantities of penetrating stain from being absorbed in end grain, apply a coat of _____ to the end grain.
13. Paste wood fillers are used on (close-grain or open-grain) woods.
14. When wiping off excess paste wood filler, wipe _____ the grain.
15. _____ are used as the base coat to fill the _____ of close-grain wood.
16. Most top coat finishes remain on the ____ of the wood and form hard, durable, and protective coverings.
17. Two bases in which paints are available are _____ base and _____ base.
18. Three wood finish thinning mediums are: _____.
19. To prevent an uneven spray pattern, hold the spray gun _____ to the surface.

Unit 15
HARDWARE

Hardware as used in constructing furniture, and in cabinetmaking, is available in many styles and qualities. In this Unit, we will discuss basic types. Some additional information on hardware may be obtained from Unit 12, on Fasteners.

Hinges

Butt hinges come in a variety of sizes. Large sizes are commonly used to swing doors in homes and in other building construction. Smaller sizes are used for doors and boxes in furniture and cabinets. Butt hinges can be used on surfaces, but they are often mounted in mortises or recesses called "gains," Fig. 15-1.

Fig. 15-1. Installing a butt hinge.

Surface type hinges may be mounted either flush or offset. This type of hinge is mounted on the face of the cabinet door and on the frame.

Semiconcealed hinges show only the joint or the small leaf and joint of the hinge when the door is closed, Fig. 15-2.

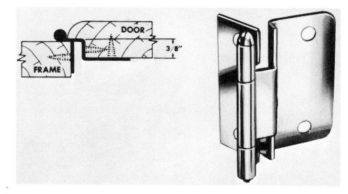

Fig. 15-2. Semiconcealed offset hinge.

Concealed pin hinges are designed for doors that completely cover the frame of the cabinet. Only a small joint shows. See Fig. 15-3 (Above and Below).

Fig. 15-3. A concealed hinge. Above. Door open.
Below. Door closed.

Fig. 15-4. Above. Contemporary cabinet and furniture trim. Fig. 15-5. Below.
Selected modern and traditional furniture trim.

Fig. 15-6. Above. Early American patterns of colonial cabinet hardware.
Fig. 15-7. Below. French Provincial cabinet and furniture trim.

Pulls

Door and drawer pulls, together with matching hinges and other hardware, are available to fit almost every need. Some contemporary patterns are shown in Fig. 15-4.

Fig. 15-5 illustrates a selection of modern, traditional and authentic period types.

Early American patterns of colonial cabinet hardware is finished to resemble hand-wrought and weathered hardware. Flat black and antique copper finish are generally used for these patterns, Fig. 15-6.

French Provincial patterns offer both grace and beauty to appropriate furniture and cabinets. A popular finish for French Provincial furniture is ivory with gold trim. Antique copper and antique English finishes are also used, Fig. 15-7.

Catches

Catches to hold furniture and cabinet doors closed are available in many styles.

Magnetic catches are popular and practical. A pull of 8 to 10 lbs. for an average size cabinet door is usually recommended. Since application of finish reduces magnetic

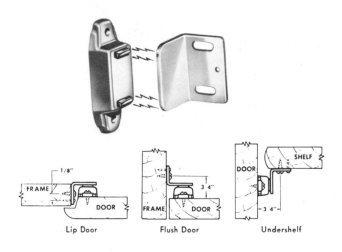

Fig. 15-8. Parts and uses of a magnetic catch.

holding power, you should keep the poles free from varnish, paint and other finishes. Fig. 15-8 shows three ways to use a magnetic catch.

Roller spring catches are available in both single and double roller types. Fig. 15-9 illustrates two methods of using a single roller spring catch.

Fig. 15-9. Parts and uses of a roller spring catch.

A simple type of friction catch is the "alligator" type. The catch is applied to the door frame or a cabinet shelf and engages the strike, usually attached to a door. See Fig. 15-10.

Fig. 15-10. Friction type "alligator" catch.

The elbow type catch is often attached to the inside of the cabinet door with the strike fastened to the frame or to a shelf of the cabinet. When the door is closed, the catch will automatically engage the strike and must be released from the inside of the cabinet door. For this reason, the elbow catch can be used on only one door of a pair of doors, Fig. 15-11.

Fig. 15-11. Elbow catch.

Sliding Tracks

Numerous kinds of sliding mechanisms are available for drawers and doors. Directions for installation supplied by the manufacturer should be followed.

Fig. 15-12 shows how one type of sliding mechanism is used with a drawer. The drawer is supported and moved on rollers attached to each side of the lower drawer rail. A third roller, attached to the drawer front, moves

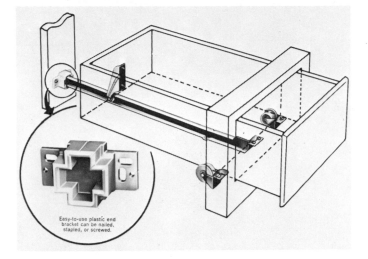

Fig. 15-12. *Drawer slide assembly.*

in a metal channel support, guiding the drawer as it is moved forward or backward. The metal channel support is fastened to the rail and to the cabinet back or vertical wood support.

Test Your Knowledge - Unit 15

1. Butt hinges are often mounted in recesses called _____.
2. Surface type hinges are mounted on the face of the cabinet door and on the frame. True or False?
3. Early American cabinet hardware finished to resemble handwrought and weathered hardware is usually finished in flat _____, or antique _____.
4. In magnetic catches a pull of _____to_____ lbs. is usually recommended.
5. Does covering the poles of a magnetic catch with varnish increase or decrease the holding power of the catch?
6. When an elbow catch is used, the catch automatically engages the strike and must be released from the _____of the cabinet door.

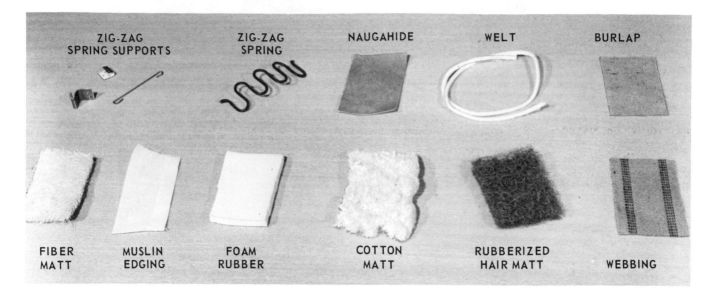

Fig. 16-1. Upholstery materials.

Unit 16
UPHOLSTERY

We upholster furniture to make it comfortable and functional.

Materials

Fig. 16-1 illustrates some of the materials commonly used in upholstery. These are identified as:

1. Zig-zag spring supports, to fasten a zig-zag spring to a wood frame.

2. Zig-zag spring, for chairs and couches.

3. Naugahide (plastic coated fabric) covering for stools, chair seats, chairs and other furniture. An assortment of colors, designs, and textures is available.

4. Welt, for use along edges of upholstered furniture. This is a cloth covered cord, usually filled with jute or cellulose. Welt is sewed inside a strip of fabric covering. This requires considerable skill and should be done with a machine.

5. Burlap, for use over springs and to hold loose materials together. This is a coarse cloth, usually woven from jute fibers.

6. Fiber matt, for use as a padding. It is often made with intermingled hemp fibers.

7. Muslin edging, to round over a cushioned edge. It is a thin, closely woven cloth usually made from cotton. A strip along the inside surface of the muslin edging is coated with a mastic so it can be attached to a foam pad.

8. Foam rubber, for use as a cushion pad. Foam plastic is also used for this purpose. Both materials are available in light to firm compression and in a variety of thicknesses.

9. Cotton matt, to result in a soft, cushioning effect over rubberized hair, wood and other materials.

10. Rubberized hair matt, for use as a cushioned pad. This is made with intermingled hair and rubber and has a cloth mesh base.

11. Webbing, to form the support for a

stool, chair or other upholstery seat. It is tightly woven and strong, similar to canvas.

Tools

Few special tools are needed for upholstery. Fig. 16-2 illustrates two tools in use. Note the upholstery hammer. This has two driving faces, one of which is a permanent magnet. The magnet face holds an upholstery tack by its head so it can be accurately started in place. The tack can then be set with the other face of the hammer. The webbing stretcher shown has a head equipped with a row of sharp nail points which grip the webbing, and a handle to use as a lever when stretching the webbing.

A stapler is shown in Fig. 16-5. The stapler is activated by a strong spring. Some staplers are powered by electricity or air.

Upholstering a Stool

Preparing the Base

Let's discuss a typical job, upholstering a stool constructed in your shop. Wood recommended for seat frame construction is a medium-hard wood, such as white pine, soft maple, or red gum. These woods are soft

enough to take the fasteners, yet hard enough to hold them.

If the base for the upholstery material is solid, like plywood, foam rubber or foam plastic may be used. If a frame base is used, webbing will be required to support the upholstery material, Fig. 16-2.

Attaching Webbing to Wood Frame

With scissors, cut enough strips of webbing to run each way, allowing about 1 in. extra length for lapping at each end.

Using size 10-12 upholstery tacks and an upholstery hammer, attach one of the pieces at one end of the frame about 1 in. from the side. Lap the end of the webbing over and drive in two more tacks.

Insert the sharp points of the webbing stretcher through the webbing, stretch the webbing taut over the other end of the frame, and fasten with three tacks. Then, lap the end over and drive in two more tacks. Use scissors to cut off the excess webbing.

Continue with the other strips of webbing in the same way. Weave each piece over and under pieces it crosses, Fig. 16-2.

Fig. 16-2. Using a stretcher to hold webbing in place over a frame as upholstery tacks are driven with an upholstery hammer.

Installing Cushion

With scissors, cut a piece of rubberized hair matt to fit the size of your stool. Then, lay the matt over the webbing.

Using your fingers, tear layers of cotton about 1/2 in. thick and attach them to the sides of the stool with size 3-4 upholstery tacks.

Tear a piece of cotton the size of your stool and about 1/2 in. thick. Lay it over the rubberized hair, Fig. 16-3.

Fig. 16-3. Applying rubberized hair matt and cotton matt over webbing.

Attaching Cover

Cut a piece of fabric large enough to lap around the frame and attach on the underneath side. Lay the stool upside down over the inside of the covering material.

Fasten the middle of each side to the frame with three upholstery tacks, size 6-8. Draw the material over snuggly with your fingers, Fig. 16-4 (Above).

Continue to fasten the cover from the center toward the corners. Fold each corner,

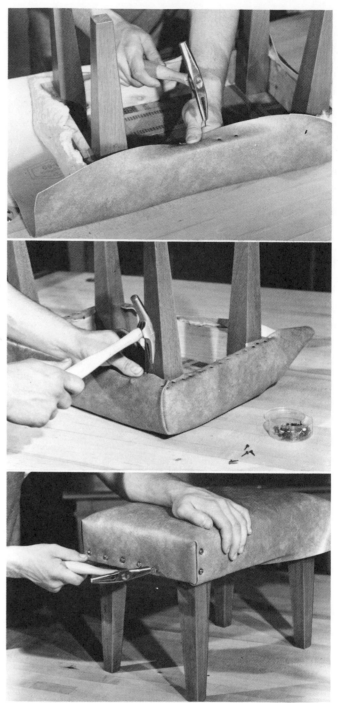

Fig. 16-4. Attaching a plastic covering. Above. Attaching centers of each side with upholstery tacks. Center. Folding and attaching a corner. Below. Driving decorative upholstery nails.

drawing the material tightly to the frame, and attach it with upholstery tacks. See Fig. 16-4 (Center).

As an option, you can drive decorative upholstery nails at each corner and along an edge of your stool, Fig. 16-4 (Below).

Installing Cushion Over Solid Base

Cover the sides of your stool with a 1/2 in. layer of cotton.

Cut a piece of foam rubber or foam plastic about 1 in. larger than the top of the stool. Attach the foam pad to the top of the stool with contact cement. Cut four pieces of muslin edging to be attached around the edges of the foam pad.

Fasten the mastic surface of the muslin edging along the edge of the foam pad. Then, pull the muslin edging down to round over the foam pad, and attach it to the sides of the stool with staples, Fig. 16-5.

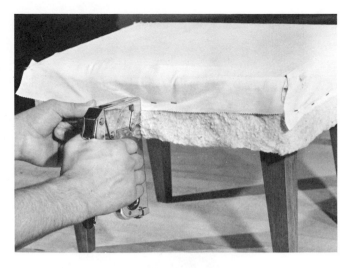

Fig. 16-5. Stapling a muslin strip to the side of a stool to round over a foam rubber edge.

Test Your Knowledge - Unit 16

1. Furniture is upholstered to make it_____ and _____.
2. Naugahyde is a type of fiber matt used for padding. True or False?
3. Burlap is a coarse material made from _____fibers.
4. _____ rubber is used extensively for making cushion pads.
5. An upholstery hammer has one face magnetized, which is used to hold _____.
6. In constructing stools to be upholstered, oak is an ideal wood to use. True or False? Why?_____.
7. In cutting webbing about_____ in. of extra material should be allowed at each end for lapping.
8. Is the foam rubber pad used for the seat cushion attached to solid base with cement or tacks?

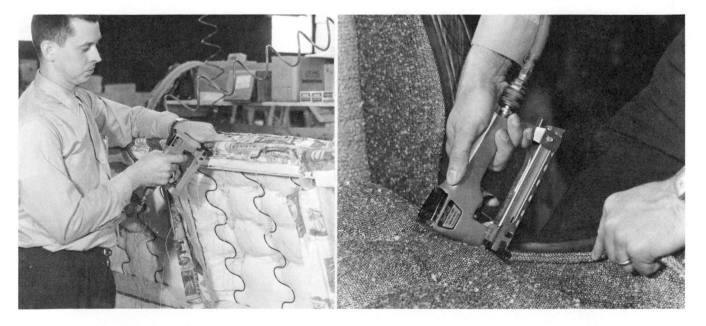

Industry photos. Left. Stapling a fabric covering onto a couch. Right. Stapling a welt around a chair arm.

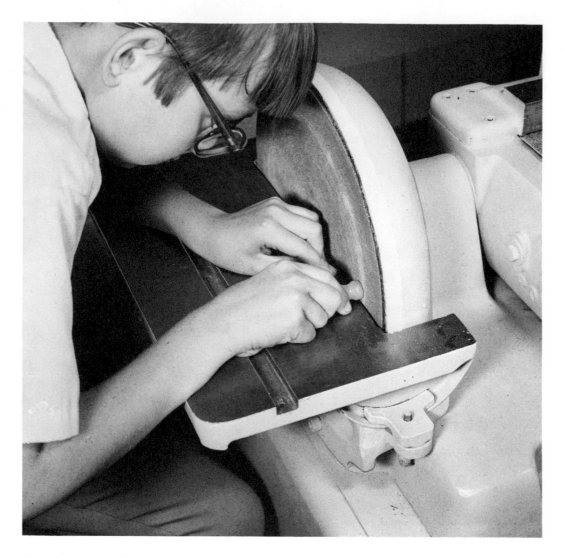

This photo shows three DON'TS...Don't use a disk sander to sand such small pieces of wood; don't get your face so close to the work; don't sand when the disk cuts in an upward direction.

Unit 17

BUSINESS EXPERIENCE ACTIVITY

In this activity you will obtain first-hand experience in the business world... experience in Organizing, Financing and Operating your own Small Manufacturing Business. You will do many of the things a large business does, on a miniature scale. You will obtain experience that will make you a better employee when you are ready for your first full-time job.

Typical Activity

The business activity discussed in this Unit may be changed to meet local conditions and restrictions.

The procedure to follow in a typical setup includes:

1. Deciding on a product.
2. Selecting a name for your new company.
3. Electing company officials.
4. Determining approximate amount of operating capital needed to finance the business.
5. Selling shares of stock to raise operating capital.
6. Determining the manufacturing steps required, and sequence of operations.
7. Providing jigs and fixtures needed for mass production.
8. Developing sales plan; promoting product sales.
9. Dissolving the business and reimbursing stockholders.

Decide on Product

At your first meeting (with your instructor serving as advisor) you should decide on the product to be manufactured. Selecting one of the tested products covered later in this Unit is suggested.

Select Company Name

The name selected should be appropriate, businesslike, and not too long.

Since this is a class activity in which all students are expected to participate, each member of the class should make an effort to come up with a good name for the new company which is being organized.

It is suggested that each class member write one or more names on a slip of paper. The slips should be collected, proposed names discussed, and a vote taken to determine which company name is to be used.

Caution: Do not include Incorporated, or Corporation after the company name. Each of these is a legal term which can be used only in cases where a state charter has been obtained.

Company Officials

If your company is to be successful, it must be operated in an efficient, business-

A-1 PRODUCTS, 123 W. Taft, South Holland, Ill. 60473

RECEIPTS

Date	Item	Quantity	Sold To	Sold By	Amount

Fig. 17-1. Business activity records -- cash receipts.

like manner. This means you will need capable company officials, also capable workers. It is suggested that you elect:

1. General Manager.
2. Office Manager.
3. Purchasing Agent.
4. Sales Manager.
5. Safety Director.

Duties of the company officials as described in the following paragraphs, should be discussed before holding an election.

Duties of General Manager

Your General Manager will be expected to:

1. Exercise general supervision over entire activity.
2. Train workers, assign workers to jobs.
3. Check on, and be responsible for product quality and manufacturing efficiency.
4. OK bills to be paid by Office Manager; OK purchase orders before making purchases.
5. Prepare and submit reports as required by your Advisor (Instructor).
6. Cooperate with your Advisor, and other Company officials.

Duties of Office Manager

The Office Manager should:

1. Maintain attendance records. Check absentees for valid excuses.
2. Keep Company's financial records (8 1/2 x 11 loose leaf notebook suggested).

3. Keep a record of all money received on RECEIPTS page of record book, Fig. 17-1.
4. All cash receipts should be deposited in a local bank and a checking account established.
5. Pay all bills, invoices previously OK'd by your General Manager, by writing checks. Make a complete record in your check book, which shows date and amount of money deposited in checking account and checks written. Show balance -- amount in bank, after each check is written. See Fig. 17-2. Be sure your figures are accu-

25	BAL. BRO'T FOR'D	48	20

Nov. 9 19____

TO *General Supply South Holland, Ill.*

FOR *Lumber*

DEPOSITS | 8 | 00

TOTAL	48	20
AMOUNT THIS CHECK	6	00
BALANCE	42	20

Fig. 17-2. Business activity records -- checkbook record of bills paid.

rate because this is the only record your Company has of the cash on hand.
6. Keep stock sales and ownership records.
7. Cooperate with your Advisor and other Company officials.

Duties of Purchasing Agent

The Purchasing Agent should:

1. Check with Advisor relative to materials and supplies needed to manufacture product selected.
2. Arrange to have printed, or run off on school duplicator, stock certificates, purchase orders, and other forms needed.
3. Have purchase orders OK'd by General Manager before issuing order.
4. Obtain materials required from school stock or purchase from outside source.
5. Cooperate with Advisor and other Company officials.

Duties of Sales Manager

The Sales Manager should:

1. After product sample is available, he should help decide on how product is to be packaged, and provide instructions on product use, to include in the package.
2. Plan sales program; help decide on price to charge for product, where and how product is to be sold. Note: All students participating in this activity will be expected to sell your Company's products (also stock).
3. Cooperate with Advisor and other Company officials.

Duties of Safety Director

The Safety Director should:

1. Enforce safety rules.
2. Stop all horseplay and call attention to undesirable conduct.

3. Be alert to hazards.
4. Take steps to eliminate possible accident causes.
5. See to it that equipment and tools are in good operating condition.
6. Check to make sure machine guards are in place and students are using eye protection and protective clothing as specified by Advisor.
7. If someone is injured, even slightly, contact Advisor immediately.
8. Cooperate with Advisor and other Company officials.

All Company officials should be provided with identification badges, Fig. 17-3.

Fig. 17-3. Identification badge for company official--typical.

Raising Capital

In operating your new business, you will need money (capital) to pay bills until you start taking in cash from the sale of your product. Most corporations raise money by selling stock to the public. It is suggested you do the same.

Getting stock certificates printed, stock sold, and keeping the necessary records, is the responsibility of your Office Manager. See Fig. 17-4.

A-1 PRODUCTS, 123 W. Taft, South Holland, Ill. 60473

STOCK RECORD

Date	Certif. No.	Sold To	Sold By	Amount

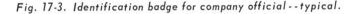

Fig. 17-4. Business activity--stock ownership record.

```
        STOCK CERTIFICATE

                A-1 PRODUCTS
One Share       South Holland, Ill.
                                        Certificate Number
Par Value 50¢
                                        _____

Redeemable Within
One Year After Issue                    Date Issued

                                        _____

This Certifies That (please print)

_____

First Name         Initial      Last Name

_____

Street Address     City         State        Zip


Is the Owner of One Share, Par Value 50¢, of the stock of A-1 Products.


_____        _____
Stockholder's Signature            for A-1 Products

Stockholder by signature, okays operation of Company by Student Officials elected
by Student Stockholders.
```

Fig. 17-5. Stock certificate, form suggestions.

Let's assume that you need $40.00. This may be raised by selling 80 shares of stock at $.50 each. See Fig. 17-5 for a suggested Stock Certificate form.

This should be run off on a duplicating machine on two different colors of stock... 100 copies of each, yellow and white suggested. Number the certificates 1 to 100.

Each student will be expected to purchase a share of stock at $.50. When starting to sell stock (on your own time) it is a good idea to make your first sale to yourself. Using a ball point pen and carbon paper, fill out the stock certificate form in duplicate, with the white copy on top. On the share you sell to yourself sign in two places, where the stockholder's signature is required, and as a representative of your company. Keep the white copy. Turn in the yellow copy (carbon) and the $.50 to your Office Manager. It is his job to keep an accurate record of stock sales, and to see to it that the cash turned in is deposited in the bank. See Fig. 17-6.

It is suggested you limit stock sales to one share per customer. The stock should

Fig. 17-6. All cash received from product sales is deposited in the bank and bills are paid by check.

```
DEPOSITED WITH

South Holland Trust & Savings Bank
        SOUTH HOLLAND, ILLINOIS

                                  |        | DOLLARS | CENTS |
NAME  A-1 PRODUCTS                | CURRENCY |    7    |  00   |
                                  | COIN     |    3    |  40   |
ADDRESS SOUTH HOLLAND, ILL.       | CHECKS   |         |       |
                                  |          |         |       |
                                  |          |         |       |
                                  | TOTAL    |   10    |  40   |
                                  | LESS CASH DEDUCTION |  |   |
DATE    11-1    19                | TOTAL DEPOSIT |  10  |  40  |

    ACCOUNT NUMBER           LIST ADDITIONAL CHECKS ON REVERSE SIDE
      _487_                  CHECKS DEPOSITED CANNOT BE DRAWN AGAINST
                            UNTIL THEY HAVE BEEN COLLECTED BY THE BANK.
```

Fig. 17-7. Project suggestion — Tic-Tac-Toe game.

be divided so each student has approximately the same number of shares to sell. In contacting prospective purchasers . . . local business men, parents, neighbors, friends, be businesslike. Describe your Company and its operations briefly. Be enthusiastic. Try to give your prospect the impression he is buying a share in a GOING BUSINESS, and is NOT "donating to charity." Tell him you cannot guarantee results in advance, but that your Company expects to operate profitably and when the business is closed out to redeem the stock at full par value ($.50 per share) and pay a small dividend.

After a share of stock has been sold, fill out the stock certificate as previously described. Be sure to print. Ask your purchaser to read the certificate to make sure everything is understood and is agreeable, then ask him to sign. Hand the top (white) copy to your purchaser. As you leave don't forget to say "thank you" (like you really meant it).

Establishing Price, Selling Product

In establishing a selling price for your product, it is suggested you determine the total cost per item, then add to this about 25%. The extra 25% is to cover the cost of material wasted, and to pay a dividend to stockholders when the business is closed out.

Each student participating in the project (all are stockholders) is expected to help sell the company's product.

If the product selected is small such as the two items described in this Unit, you will probably find it advisable to make up the products in advance so you can provide "on the spot" delivery.

Keep an accurate record of all sales -- quantity sold, name of customer, and amount collected. Turn these records and the cash collected over to your Office Manager for handling.

Mass Production in the School Shop

Two projects for mass production with proven student interest are the Tic-Tac-Toe Game, Fig. 17-7, and the Golf Tee Tie Rack, Fig. 17-22.

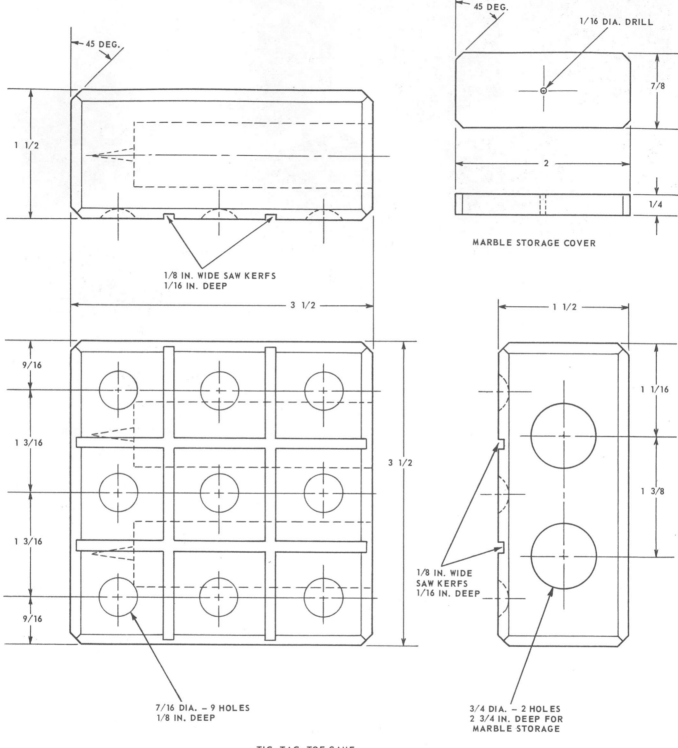

45 DEG.

1 1/2

1/8 IN. WIDE SAW KERFS
1/16 IN. DEEP

3 1/2

9/16

1 3/16

1 3/16

9/16

3 1/2

7/16 DIA. – 9 HOLES
1/8 IN. DEEP

45 DEG.

1/16 DIA. DRILL

7/8

2

1/4

MARBLE STORAGE COVER

1 1/2

1 1/16

1 3/8

1/8 IN. WIDE
SAW KERFS
1/16 IN. DEEP

3/4 DIA. – 2 HOLES
2 3/4 IN. DEEP FOR
MARBLE STORAGE

TIC–TAC–TOE GAME

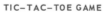

Fig. 17-8. Working drawing for Tic-Tac-Toe game.

Mass Producing Tic-Tac-Toe Game

See Fig. 17-8 for working drawings of the tic-tac-toe game. Note that one piece of stock, 3 1/2 x 3 1/2 x 1 1/2 in. (piece of 2 x 4) is required for each game. White pine is suggested, but almost any 2 x 4 stock without knots may be used. As you will note marbles used in playing the game are stored in the body or main member.

In our mass production we can use hand tools, but the work can be done faster and better by using power tools. In working with power tools, considerable time may be saved by using jigs and fixtures (devices that hold the work and guide the tools during the cutting operations). In this Unit the holding devices will all be referred to as fixtures. In our mass produced project we should do as industry does - - look for ways to step up production, and quality of our product.

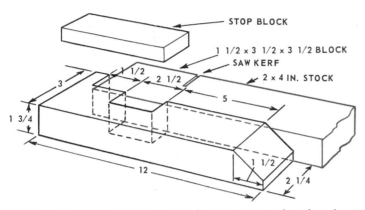

Fig. 17-9. Fixture to be used in cutting stock to length.

Fig. 17-9 shows a simple fixture designed to aid in cutting the 2 x 4 stock to length. Fig. 17-10 shows the fixture in use. Screws are used to fasten the fixture to the miter gauge of the band saw, which is set to an angle of 90 deg. A stop block is clamped to the table in an appropriate location.

In sawing, hold a piece of 2 x 4 stock firmly against the fixture and push the stock into the moving saw blade. When the blade cuts through the stock and reaches the stop block,

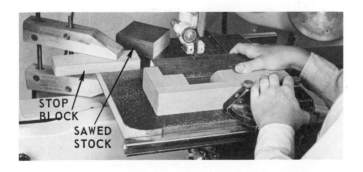

Fig. 17-10. Fixture in use on band saw. If students are not permitted to use a band saw the fixture should be redesigned for use on a jig saw.

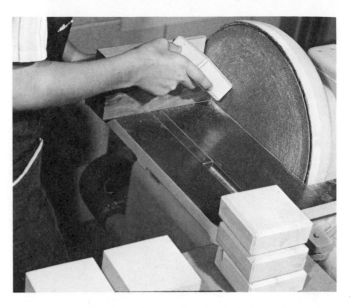

Fig. 17-11. Chamfering edges with disk sander.

return the miter gauge to the beginning position. Readjust the 2 x 4 stock and repeat the procedure to make additional cuts.

Smoothing Ends by Sanding

Use a disk or belt sander to smooth the ends of the stock. Set the sander miter gauge at a 90 deg. angle. In sanding, hold each piece firmly against the miter gauge.

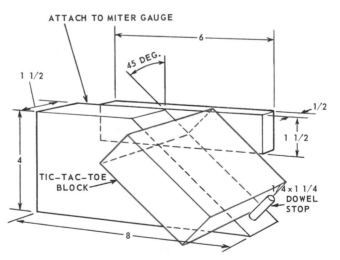

Fig. 17-12. Fixture for sanding chamfers (beveling edges).

Chamfering Edges

In chamfering (beveling) the edges, a fixture as shown in Figs. 17-11 and 17-12, will come in real handy. The fixture is screwed to the miter gauge. Rotation of the disk sander, Fig. 17-11, is counterclockwise.

143

Applying Wood Finish

Examine all surfaces and edges and sand as required to provide smooth, ready-for-finishing surfaces. Apply the finish of your choice. The games shown in Fig. 17-7, were finished by simply applying sealer stain to all surfaces.

Fig. 17-15. Drilling holes in block to take marbles (self-storing feature).

Fig. 17-13. Using circular saw to "dress up" the blocks by making saw kerfs in top surface. The saw guard has been removed to show the action.

Adjust the circular saw blade to make a cut about 1/16 in. deep. Insert a piece of stock in the fixture. Hold the fixture firmly against the circular saw fence and push the fixture forward to move the stock across the revolving blade. Turn off the saw, revolve the piece 90 deg. and make another cut. Continue in the same way until four cuts as shown, have been made.

Drilling Holes for Marbles

Holes for storing the marbles used in playing the tic-tac-toe game are made by using a drill press, and another fixture. See Figs. 17-15 and 17-16.

Cutting Saw Kerfs

Making saw kerfs in the top surface of the wood blocks with a circular saw, to divide the surface into thirds, is shown in Fig. 17-13. Dimensions of the fixture used are given in Fig. 17-14.

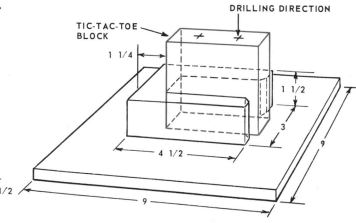

Fig. 17-16. Fixture used in drilling holes in block.

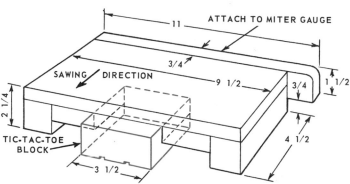

Fig. 17-14. Fixture for making saw kerf in surface of block.

Clamp the fixture to the drill press table. Install a 3/4 in. diameter speed bit in the drill press. Insert one of the pieces of stock in the fixture and make the necessary adjustment for drilling.

Holding the stock firmly against the fixture, pull the revolving bit into its edge until the hole is drilled to the correct depth. Turn the stock 180 deg. and drill another hole in the same way.

Drilling Playing Recesses

Drilling recesses to take marbles used in playing the game is shown in Figs. 17-17 and 17-18. Clamp the fixture to the drill press table. Install a 7/16 in. diameter twist drill in the drill press. Insert one of the pieces of stock in the fixture and make the necessary adjustment for drilling a 1/8 in. deep recess into one corner.

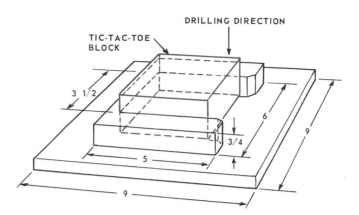

Fig. 17-18. Fixture for drilling playing recesses.

turning the piece for drilling the four locations.

Readjust the fixture and drill the center recess in each piece.

Attaching Marble Compartment Cover

Figs. 17-19 and 17-20 show drilling of holes in cover for marble storage compartment. Install a 1/16 in. twist drill in the drill press. Insert one of the covers in the fixture and make the necessary adjustment for drilling.

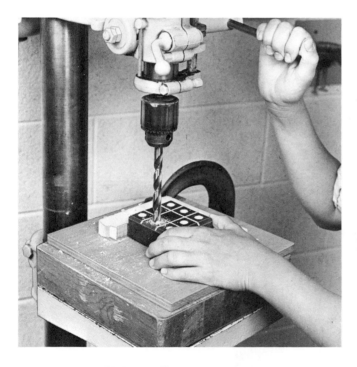

Fig. 17-17. Drilling playing recesses.

Holding the stock firmly against the fixture, pull the revolving bit into the stock. Turn the stock 90 deg. and drill the second hole. Repeat the process for the remaining two corners.

Readjust the fixture to drill the center recess along one of the face edges of the stock. Drill into the face of the stock as before,

Fig. 17-19. Drilling hole in marble compartment cover.

Using a push stick, hold the cover firmly in the fixture and pull the revolving bit into the cover.

145

Smooth the compartment covers using fine sandpaper.

Attach compartment cover to each piece of stock with a No. 17 - 3/4 in. wire nail or a small wood screw.

Complete your tic-tac-toe game by applying a coat of clear wood finish.

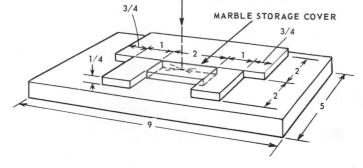

Fig. 17-20. *Fixture to use in drilling hole in cover for marble storage compartment.*

Mass Producing Golf Tee Tie Racks

Making Rack Sides

Each of the golf tee tie racks, built from the suggested layout in Fig. 17-21 and shown in Fig. 17-22, was made from a piece of hardwood 1/2 x 2 x 12 3/4 in., and 18 multicolor

golf tees. Plastic tees made by injection molding are also well suited for the purpose.

Using the suggested layout, Fig. 17-21, as a guide, make a full-size cardboard template

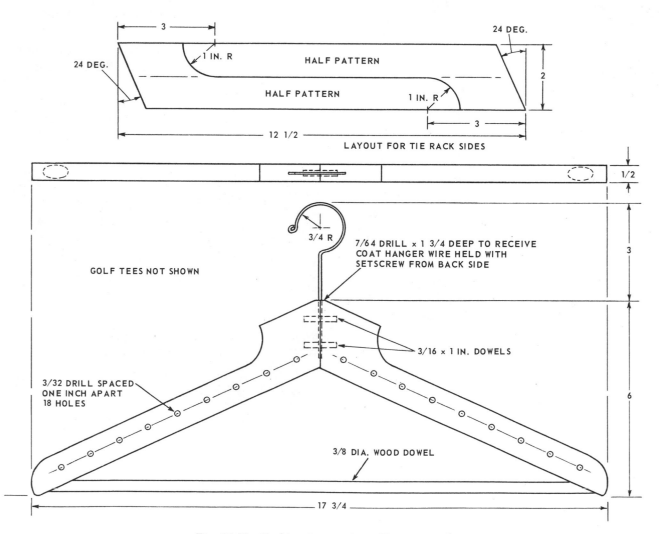

Fig. 17-21. *Working drawing for golf tee tie rack.*

Fig. 17-22. Golf tee tie rack.

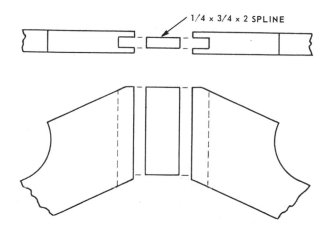

1/4 x 3/4 x 2 SPLINE

Fig. 17-23. Alternate method of joining tie rack sides.

for the rack sides. An alternate method of joining the rack sides is shown in Fig. 17-23.

Using appropriate tools and machines, cut pieces of hardwood to make the desired quantity of tie racks.

Cutting Stock to Rough Length on Band Saw

Attach fixture, Fig. 17-24, to a band saw miter gauge with screws. Set the miter gauge to an angle of 66 deg. (24 deg. from right angle). Insert a piece of stock into the space provided in the fixture.

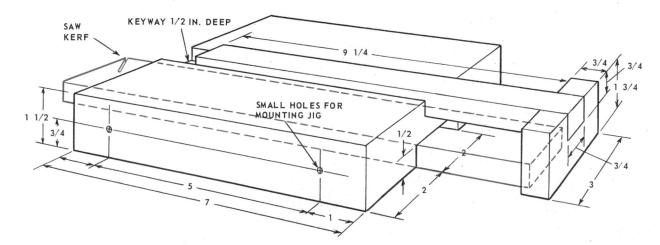

Fig. 17-24. Fixture for cutting tie rack stock to length.

Holding the stock firmly, push the stock carefully into the moving saw blade. When the end of the stock is completely cut, return the miter gauge to its beginning position, reverse ends of the stock in the fixture, and cut off the other end of the stock in the same way, Fig. 17-25.

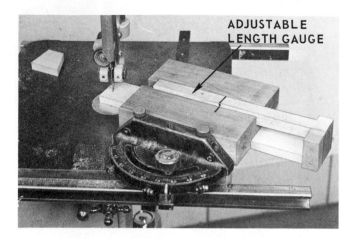

Fig. 17-25. Cutting stock to length, using fixture shown in Fig. 17-24.

Smoothing Ends with Sander

Set sander miter gauge to angle of 66 deg. Holding the stock firmly against the miter gauge, smooth the ends of each piece with a disk or belt sander, Fig. 17-26.

Fig. 17-26. Using disk sander to smooth ends of stock.

Transferring Template Onto Hardwood Stock

Lay template over the face surface of the stock and trace around its shape with a pencil, Fig. 17-27.

Sawing Sides from Hardwood Stock

Using a jig saw or band saw, cut along the lines previously traced, Fig. 17-28.

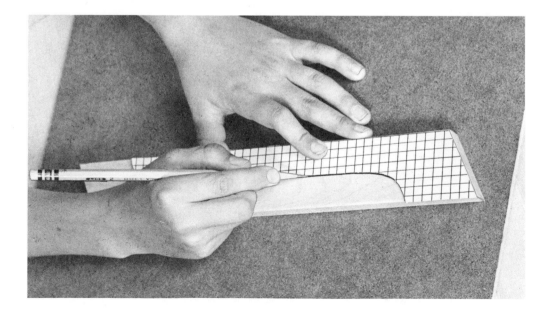

Fig. 17-27. Tracing around template onto hardwood used to make rack parts.

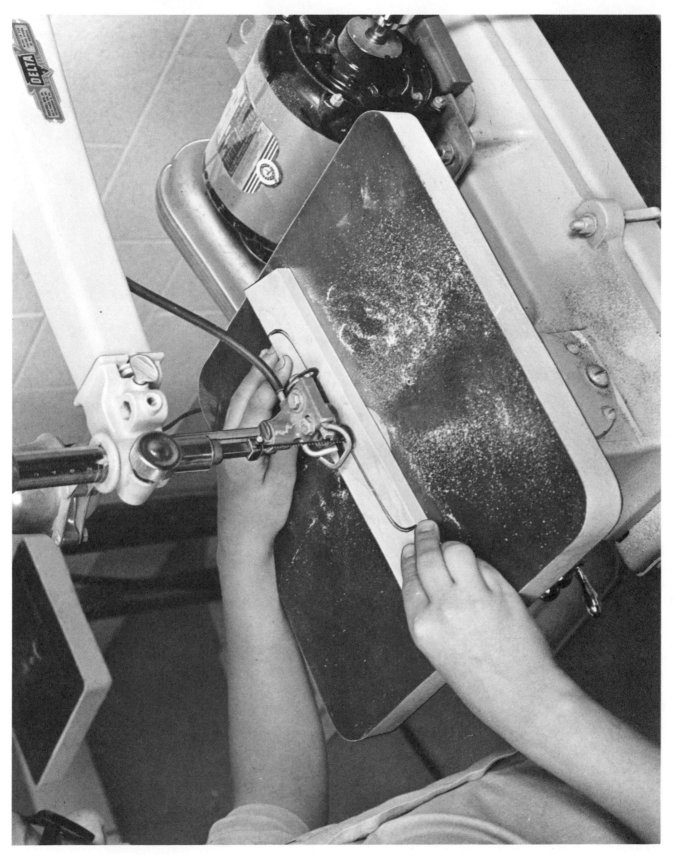

Fig. 17-28. One cut on jig saw forms both halves of rack.

Smoothing Curved Edges of Sides

Using a spindle sander or sleeve sander, smooth the curved edges of the sides. See Fig. 17-29.

Fig. 17-29. Smoothing curved edges with a spindle sander.

Drilling Holes to Receive Golf Tee Tie Supports

Fasten fixture as shown in Fig. 17-30, to the drill press table. Install a 3/32 in. diameter drill in the drill press. Place one of the

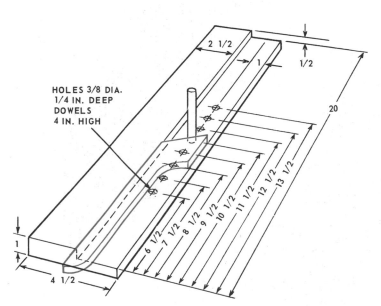

HOLES 3/8 DIA.
1/4 IN. DEEP
DOWELS
4 IN. HIGH

2 1/2 1 1/2 20

6 1/2 7 1/2 8 1/2 9 1/2 10 1/2 11 1/2 12 1/2 13 1/2

1 4 1/2

Fig. 17-30. Fixture for drilling holes in rack sides to take golf tees.

side pieces on the fixture, locate the position for drilling the first hole, and set the drill press depth gauge.

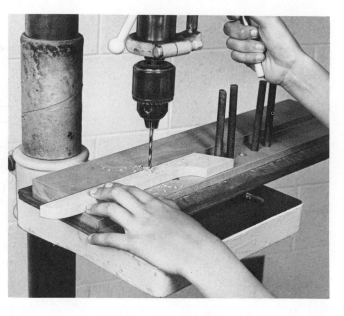

Fig. 17-31. Using fixture dimensioned in Fig. 17-30.

Holding the stock firmly against the fixture, pull the revolving bit into the stock. Remove the first dowel rod stop, reposition the stock against the next dowel rod stop, and drill a second hole. Continue in the same way to drill the remaining holes, Fig. 17-31.

Drilling Holes to Join Sides with Dowels

Clamp fixture, Fig. 17-32, to drill press table. Fit 3/16 in. diameter twist drill in the drill press. Insert one of the sides into the cavity provided in the fixture. Carefully make

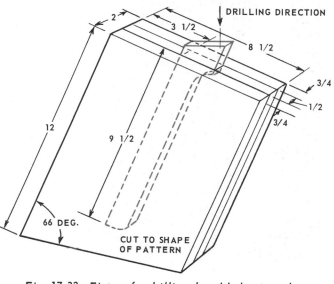

2 3 1/2 8 1/2 DRILLING DIRECTION

3/4 1/2 3/4

12 9 1/2

66 DEG. CUT TO SHAPE OF PATTERN

Fig. 17-32. Fixture for drilling dowel holes in ends of side pieces.

the necessary adjustments for drilling the first hole.

Pull the revolving bit into the stock, drill the hole to the correct depth, then remove the bit. Drill the first hole in the other sides in the same way. Then adjust the bit in the correct position for drilling the second hole, and drill the second hole into all side pieces, Fig. 17-33.

Fig. 17-33. Drilling hole in end of side to receive dowel.

Assembling Sides with Dowels

Cut a sufficient number of 3/16 in. diameter dowels to a length of 1 in. Assemble the sides with glue and appropriate clamps. Strong rubber bands may be used as clamps.

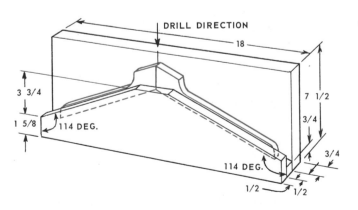

Fig. 17-34. Fixture to use in drilling hole for wire hanger.

Drilling Hole to Receive Hanger Wire

Attach fixture, Fig. 17-34, to the drill press table and install 7/64 in. diameter twist drill. Position the assembled sides into the fixture and make the necessary adjustments for drilling.

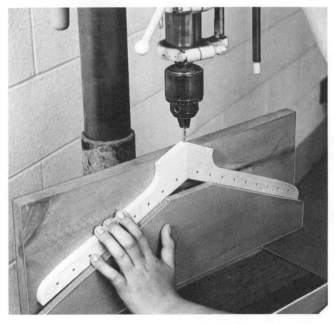

Fig. 17-35. Fixture, dimensioned in Fig. 17-34, being used to drill hole for wire hanger.

Carefully pull the revolving bit into the stock, drill the hole to the correct depth, then remove the bit from the stock. See Fig. 17-35.

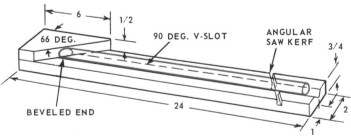

Fig. 17-36. Fixture to be used in sawing tie-supporting dowels to length.

Cutting Tie Supporting Dowel Rod to Length

Fasten fixture, Fig. 17-36, to a bench top. Place 3/8 in. diameter dowel rod in the V-groove provided in the fixture.

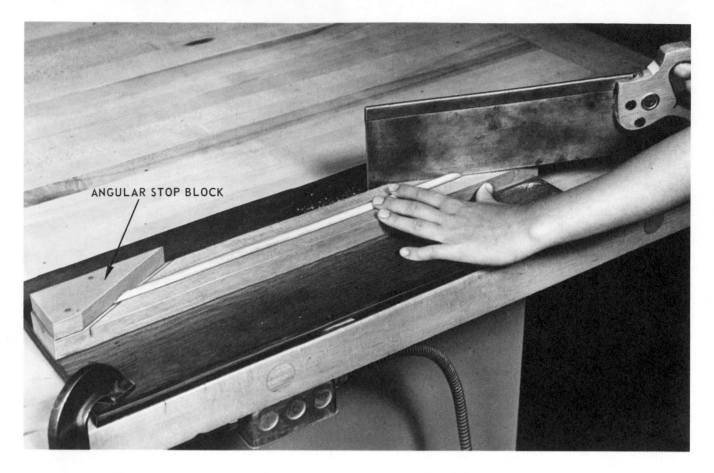

ANGULAR STOP BLOCK

Fig. 17-37. Using fixture shown in Fig. 17-36.

Using the saw kerf made in the fixture as a guide, saw one end of the dowel rod at the desired angle. Then turn the cut end around and place its bevel against the angled board on the fixture. Saw the second end of the dowel rod support to its correct angle and length, Fig. 17-37.

Drilling Hole at End of Dowel Rod

Clamp fixture, Fig. 17-38, to the drill press table. Install a 1/8 in. diameter twist

drill in the drill press. Place a dowel rod support in the V-groove provided in the fixture. Slide one end of the dowel rod support through the hole and against the beveled end of the fixture. Position the fixture and bit for drilling.

Fig. 17-39. Using fixture shown in Fig. 17-38.

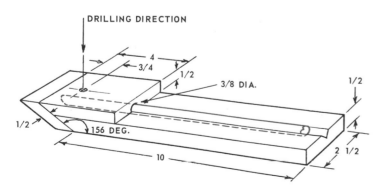

DRILLING DIRECTION

4
3/4
1/2
3/8 DIA.
1/2
1/2
156 DEG.
10
2 1/2

Fig. 17-38. Fixture for drilling holes in tie-supporting dowel for screws.

Holding the dowel rod firmly in the fixture, pull the revolving bit into the stock. Drill through the stock and remove the bit.

Insert the other end of the dowel rod in the fixture and drill a hole through the other end in the same way, Fig. 17-39.

Assembling Dowel Rod Tie Support

Fasten the dowel supporting rod to the sides with two No. 4 x 3/8 in. round head brass screws.

Bending and Installing Hanger Wire

Cut the desired number of pieces of heavy wire to lengths of 6 - 7 in. You can obtain wire from used wire coat hangers.

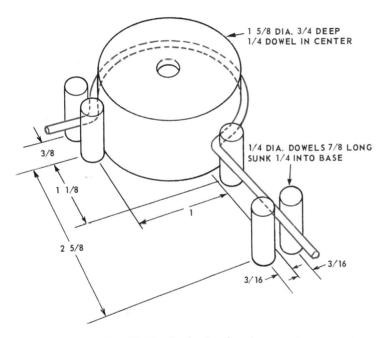

1 5/8 DIA. 3/4 DEEP
1/4 DOWEL IN CENTER

1/4 DIA. DOWELS 7/8 LONG
SUNK 1/4 INTO BASE

3/8

1 1/8

1

2 5/8

3/16

3/16

Fig. 17-40. Jig for bending hanger wire.

Place jig, Fig. 17-40, on a bench top. Bend one end of a piece of wire at an angle. Insert this end between the dowels on the jig. Bend the wire around the large dowel and between the small dowels until you obtain the correct shape, Fig. 17-41.

Fig. 17-41. Using jig dimensioned in Fig. 17-40.

Push the hanger wire into the hole drilled to receive it. Install a No. 3 x 1/4 in. brass screw against the hanger wire from the back side as a setscrew to hold the wire, or let the wire extend through the rack and bend it toward the back so it will be out of sight.

Completing Assembly

Apply finish of your choice and glue golf tees in holes to complete the project.

Unit 18
CAREERS IN
WOODWORKING INDUSTRIES

The field of woodworking offers many opportunities for employment. New and improved uses of forest products are developed each year. Production, service, and maintenance of forest products requires a variety of professional, skilled, and semiskilled workmen.

Our forest products industry ranks sixth among all American industries in the number of full-time employees and total salaries and wages paid.

Fig. 18-2. Loading logs for removal from the forest.

Fig. 18-1. Forester measures a mature tree he has marked to cut.

Professional positions usually require a college education or its equivalent. Skilled and semiskilled jobs require specialized training and experience.

154

Fig. 18-3. Building construction. Carpenters building new homes.

Forestry

Several hundred new foresters are needed every year. Foresters do many kinds of work, both indoors and out. They are concerned with growing and protecting trees, planting seedlings, building roads, fighting fires, and controlling insects. They help decide when trees are ready to harvest and make provision for the next crop of timber. Foresters also help decide on the best use for each log, whether it be lumber, paper, or other. See Fig. 18-1.

Forest Service Management

The Forest Service is a Federal agency dedicated to the best use, development and conservation of our nation's forest lands. Rangers, fallers, loggers and many other intriguing jobs are available for those who enjoy being outdoors, Fig. 18-2.

Building Construction

Demands for homes and other structures provide a considerable need for carpenters and other woodworking craftworkers. Almost four out of five single family homes are built with wood construction. Each home averages about 13,000 board feet of lumber. Other areas requiring skills and wood products include farm structures, fences, decking, schools, churches, and commercial buildings, Figs. 18-3, 18-4, and 18-5.

Fig. 18-4. Carpenter installing cabinets made with solid wood.

Fig. 18-5. Skilled worker installing ceiling tile.

Exploring Woodworking

Industrial Education Teacher

Teaching industrial education provides an opportunity to help guide students toward becoming a part of our industrial democracy. The industrial education teacher acquaints his students with materials, tools, machines and processes used by industry.

Engineer

Engineers are needed to analyze and test forest products and to explore and develop new products through research.

Fig. 18-6. Construction specialists. Unloading a laminated truss for a large building. (Truss on derrick is 62 ft. long and weighs 3 1/2 tons.)

Construction Specialist

Skilled workers are needed to construct, handle and install building components and laminated beams used in large buildings. See Fig. 18-6.

Industrial Woodworker

The cabinet and furniture manufacturing plants offer rewarding futures to professional, skilled, and semiskilled workers who help fabricate the thousands of products turned out by these plants.

Patternmaker

Our industries need skilled patternmakers --workers who can shape wood to dimensions of close tolerances. Patterns are used in making metal castings for many of the products we use.

Research Technician

Technicians who perform a variety of tasks are needed in the analysis and testing of forest products.

Research and Development

1. Without becoming a professional, how can we contribute toward the conservation of our natural resources?
2. Make a list of as many occupations as you can which are a result of forest products or related materials.
3. Select an occupation for which you have interest. Then investigate its offerings in an "Occupational Outlook Handbook" or other up-to-date source.
4. Check to see which schools offer educational programs in the area of woodworking and write for descriptive literature.
5. If there is a home being constructed in your neighborhood discuss with the carpentry supervisor on the construction job, carpentry apprenticeship requirements, and report to your class.

Unit 19

PROJECTS

Designing and constructing projects will teach you to THINK and to PLAN. You will experiment, do research with materials, and learn to solve numerous problems. Your completed projects will reflect your personality and application of thought. It is important that you do your best work on every project. Successful accomplishment will result in joy and satisfaction.

Choosing a Project

Your projects should be something you are interested in making. They should be useful upon completion. In quality they should compare favorably with similar items available commercially. In selecting projects you should consider such matters as: Are necessary materials and tools available to make it? Can I plan and construct the project during the time allotted? Is it worth the time, effort, and cost of material? Is it within my ability?

This unit is presented as an aid to you in choosing suitable projects and developing the necessary plans. You will be expected to do some creative work...add improvements and innovations to project designs you select.

Be sure to use your imagination freely. Carefully plan the details of your project. Make up drawings needed, an outline of proposed procedure, and get your instructor's approval before you begin construction.

After you gain some experience with materials and tools by planning and constructing projects, you may want to join with other members of your class in building a project on a production basis and setting up a small business, as discussed in Unit 17.

Napkin or Letter Holder

A napkin or letter holder, Figs. 19-1 and 19-2, is a useful project. If you decide to use the squirrel design you can provide a full size pattern by sketching the design freehand into 1/2 in. squares.

If you choose to start with one of the alternate designs, Fig. 19-3, you can provide a pattern by placing a piece of tracing paper with 1/4 in. squares over the design and sketching the design into 1/2 in. squares.

You may want to change shape of the back piece or use another squirrel-shaped piece in its place.

If you want to allow more room for napkins or letters, you can move the squirrel-shaped piece toward the front of the base piece.

STOCK LIST:

Quantity	Part	Size (inches) S2S
1	Back	1/2 x 5 3/4 x 6 1/2
1	Base	1/2 x 3 1/4 x 6
1	Squirrel	1/2 x 5 3/4 x 6 1/2

WOOD: willow, white pine, poplar, redwood

OTHER MATERIALS:

Quantity	Description	Size
4	Flathead screws	No. 6 x 1"
	Abrasive paper	60, 100, 150 grits
	Finish	

Fig. 19-1. *Napkin or letter holder.*

TOOLS NEEDED: Coping saw, try square, compass, crosscut saw, rip saw, files, hand drill and bit, countersink, screwdriver.

PLAN OF PROCEDURE:

1. Make stock cutting list.
2. Prepare a full size template. Cement paper design onto cardboard and cut out with scissors.
3. Select stock, being careful to use grain direction affording the greatest strength.
4. Lay out stock to rough dimensions.
5. Saw stock to rough dimensions with crosscut and rip saws.
6. Transfer the squirrel-shape to stock. Place template on stock and trace around it with a pencil.
7. Cut out the curved edges with a coping saw or jig saw.
8. Using a wood straightedge as a guide, cut the straight edges to finish sizes.
9. Use file on all edges to smooth saw marks.
10. Sand edges and surfaces with 60, 100, and 150 grit paper.
11. Draw, then woodburn design detail lines on the squirrel-shaped front piece.
12. Lay out, drill and countersink for No. 6 x 1 flathead wood screws.
13. Assemble the parts with wood screws and a screwdriver.
14. Apply finish desired.
15. Attach felt or other protective material to the bottom surface of the base.

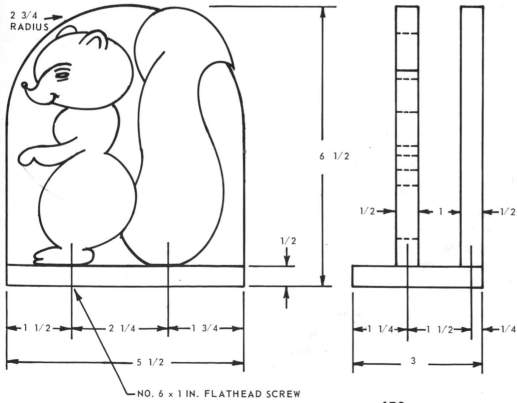

1/2 SQUARES

Fig. 19-2. *Working drawing for napkin or letter holder, shown in Fig. 19-1.*

158

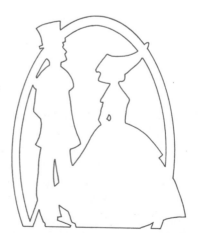

Fig. 19-3. Napkin, letter holder, alternate design suggestions.

Fig. 19-4. Bookends.

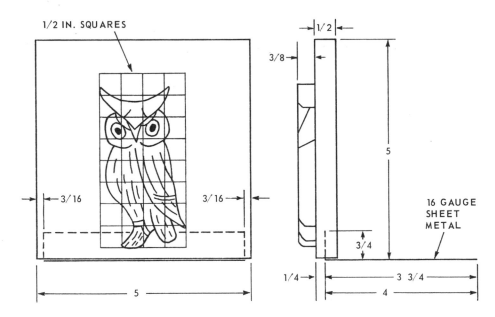

1/2 IN. SQUARES

3/16

3/16

5

1/2

3/8

5

3/4

1/4

3 3/4

4

16 GAUGE SHEET METAL

Fig. 19-5. Working drawing for bookends, shown in Fig. 19-4.

Bookends

You probably have certain books that you would like to keep in a convenient or prominent place. You can design and make bookends or a bookrack that will be well suited to your specific needs.

Bookends should be designed to blend with other furnishings. You may want to use one of the design suggestions shown in Fig. 19-4 or 19-6, and improve upon it.

A variety of bases can be used with bookends and bookracks. Fig. 19-5 illustrates the use of a piece of metal beneath each bookend. The stored books provide sufficient weight to stabilize the bookends. You can fasten the metal base with glue or with small countersunk flathead screws. A piece of felt, leather, or sponge rubber should be attached under each base to prevent scratching of other furniture.

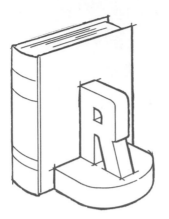

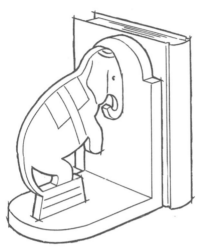

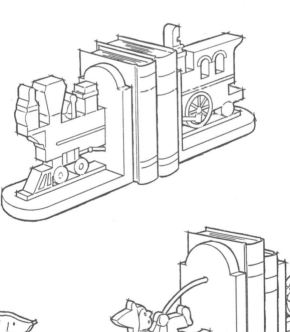
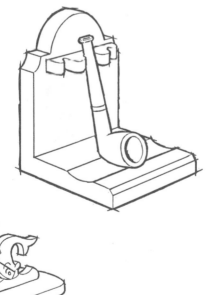

Fig. 19-6. Bookends, alternate design suggestions.

Fig. 19-7. Key holder.

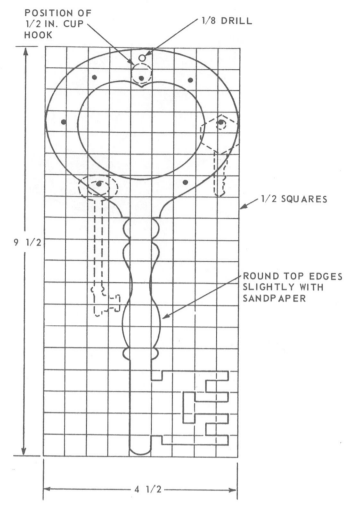

Fig. 19-8. Working drawing for key holder, shown in Fig. 19-7.

Key Holder

This little project is handy to hold keys that you only need on occasion. You can make it with a single piece of wood or plywood. If you use solid wood, choose a kind that resists splitting. Be careful as you saw out its shape so that only a minimum of filing and sanding is necessary. You might want to redesign its shape. See Figs. 19-7 and 19-8.

Salad Tools (Lamination and Wood Bending)

You can make the salad tools shown in Figs. 19-9 and 19-10 by using either wood lamination or wood bending.

To make a salad tool by lamination, cut three or more strips of wood veneer of suitable size. Apply glue (aliphatic is preferable) to the veneer surfaces to be bonded. Using a protective paper over the outside pieces, clamp the veneer in a forming jig. You can form the resulting laminated sandwich with tools to the desired shape.

To make a salad tool by wood bending, cut a piece of suitable wood 1/4 x 2 1/2 x 10 1/2. Soak the piece in hot water 2 - 4 hours, then steam it about 30 minutes. Clamp the steamed piece in a forming jig and allow it to dry overnight. Form the resulting bent piece with tools to the desired shape.

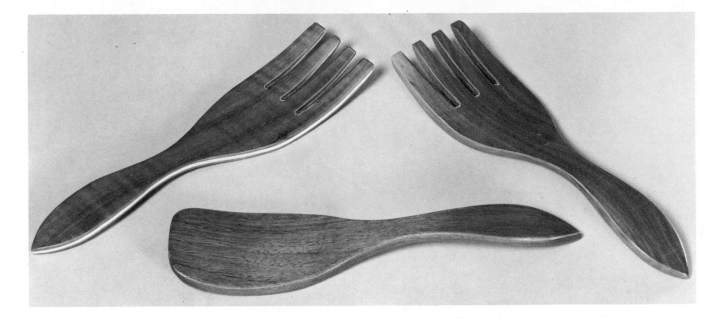

Fig. 19-9. Salad tools (laminating and wood bending).

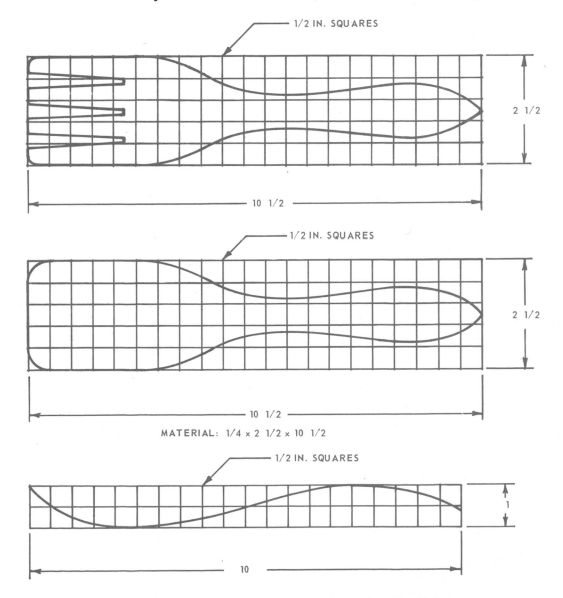

1/2 IN. SQUARES

2 1/2

10 1/2

1/2 IN. SQUARES

2 1/2

10 1/2

MATERIAL: 1/4 x 2 1/2 x 10 1/2

1/2 IN. SQUARES

1

10

Fig. 19-10. Working drawing for salad tools, shown in Fig. 19-9.

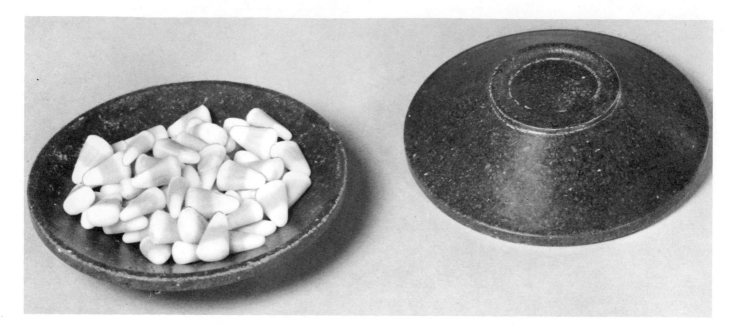

Fig. 19-11. Wood flour bowls (castings).

Bowls (Wood Flour Molding)

The bowls shown in Fig. 19-11 are castings formed in a mold illustrated in Fig. 19-12 by using a process called wood flour molding. Refined wood obtained from sawdust and other wood waste is combined with powdered plastic binders, placed in suitable molds under pressure and heat, and transformed into valuable products. Serving trays, dishes, desk tops, chair seats and backs, croquet balls and many other products we use are made by wood flour molding.

BILL OF MATERIALS FOR WOOD FLOUR BOWL:

No.	Size	Kind	Part
1	30 grams	Wood flour	Bowl
1	60 grams	Melamine resin	

PROCEDURE FOR MAKING A WOOD FLOUR BOWL:

1. Preheat the platens of the press to 325 deg. F.
2. Weigh the materials for a casting. Check the empty weight of the can first, then add 30 grams of wood particles and 60 grams of melamine resin.
3. Mix the contents of the can thoroughly by hand and fill the lower portion of the mold with the mixture.
4. Press the upper half of the mold over the mixture and place the mold between the platens of the press.
5. Using the press, slowly close the mold (during a one-minute period) to allow gases in the mixture to escape. Apply 2,000 psi pressure to the mold (maximum) for one minute, then turn off the heating elements.
6. Cool the mold with the platen cooling system to about 125 deg. F. (about 3 minutes). Then using asbestos gloves, release the pressure and remove the mold from the press.
7. Carefully separate the two parts of the mold using a screwdriver in the slots provided in the mold.
8. Turn the mold over and tap the casting release disk to remove the bowl.
9. Smooth any rough spots with 280 grit abrasive paper.
10. Apply paste wax and buff to polish.
11. Turn off the press.

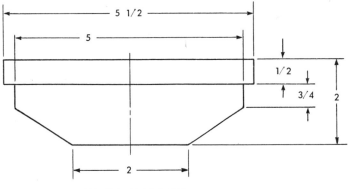

UPPER (MALE) PART

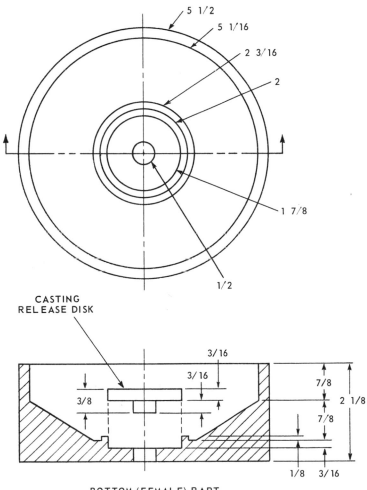

CASTING
RELEASE DISK

BOTTOM (FEMALE) PART

Fig. 19-12. Working drawing for two-part aluminum mold to make the wood flour bowls, shown in Fig. 19-11.

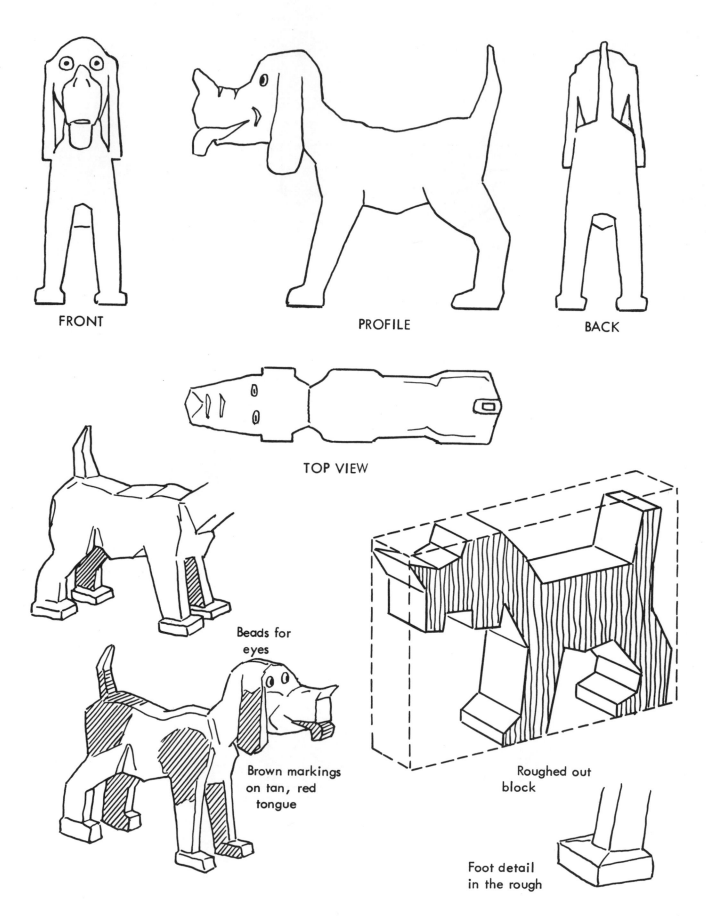

FRONT

PROFILE

BACK

TOP VIEW

Beads for
eyes

Brown markings
on tan, red
tongue

Roughed out
block

Foot detail
in the rough

Fig. 19-13. Sketches and full-size patterns for
carving animal caricature.

Carving Animal Caricatures

Carving animal caricatures (carvings in which distinguishing characteristics are emphasized) is a fascinating hobby. You can enjoy this hobby tremendously without being an expert or spending a lot of money for tools and equipment.

WOOD TO USE. Woods best suited for carving are straight-grain sugar pine, white pine, basswood, poplar and cottonwood. After you get some experience you can use harder woods, such as walnut, mahogany, and sweet gum.

TOOLS. The principal tool needed is a sharp knife. A sharp knife cuts better and is safer to use than a dull knife. You can use also a sloyd knife, an X-acto knife with interchangeable blades, or an ordinary pocket knife. See Figs. 7-5 and 7-6.

PROCEDURE:

1. Trace the outline of the design onto tracing paper, Fig. 19-13. If you choose an alternate design from Fig. 19-14, place an overlay with 1/4 in. squares over the design, and enlarge it onto paper with 1/2 in. squares.
2. Cut around the outer edge of the design with scissors, then use rubber cement to fasten the pattern onto wood. Be sure the wood grain runs parallel with the thinnest portions of the design.
3. Cut out the profile with a coping saw or jig saw.
4. Using a pencil, draw the front, top and end views on the wood.
5. Use a coping saw to cut away excess wood wherever possible.
6. Whittle with a series of short cuts. The rough appearance adds charm to your carving. See also Unit 7, Figs. 7-5 and 7-6.
7. Observe the drawing of the completed caricature. Try to shape your carving as shown. Take it easy. It is better to make two light cuts than one heavy cut. Rotate the wood as you carve, and work on the carving as a whole.
8. Protect tender spots on your hands with adhesive tape, until they become calloused.
9. Lightly sand your carving after you complete the whittling.
10. You can apply a natural finish using a thin coat of shellac and wax. If color is desired, a flat finish is preferable - - flat enamel or water color.
11. Whittle a different caricature at your first opportunity. Try out some of your own design ideas.

Fig. 19-14. Carving animal caricatures, alternate design suggestions.

Fig. 19-15. Hand carved tray.

Hand Carved Trays

You can easily design your own wood tray to be hand carved by drawing a freehand shape variation of round, oval, square, rectangular or triangular. You may want to reproduce the design shown in Figs. 19-15 and 19-16. You can develop your own design by sketching variations of conventional shapes.

Basswood, sweetgum, walnut and mahogany are good woods to use for hand carved trays. Recommended wood thickness is from 3/4 to 1 1/4 in. Here are two ways to shape

hand carved trays:

1. Drill uniformly spaced 1/4 in. diameter holes to the required depth. Remove the remaining wood with a gouge and smooth the gouged surfaces with sandpaper. Cut and shape the outside edges.
2. Cut out the tray divisions with a jig saw and smooth the edges with cutting tools and abrasive paper. Then use a piece of 1/4 in. plywood for the bottom and shape the outside edges.

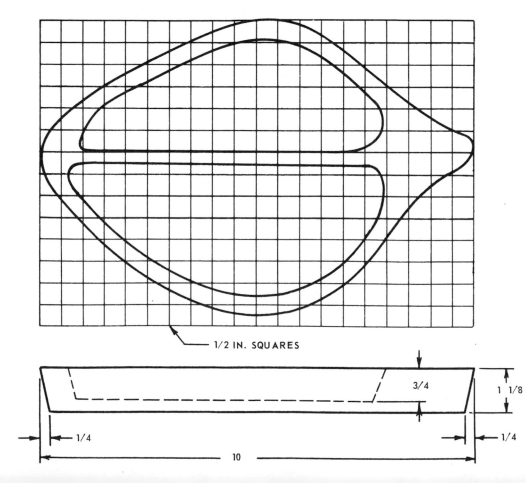

1/2 IN. SQUARES

Fig. 19-16. Working drawing for hand carved tray, shown in Fig. 19-15.

3/4

1 1/8

1/4

1/4

10

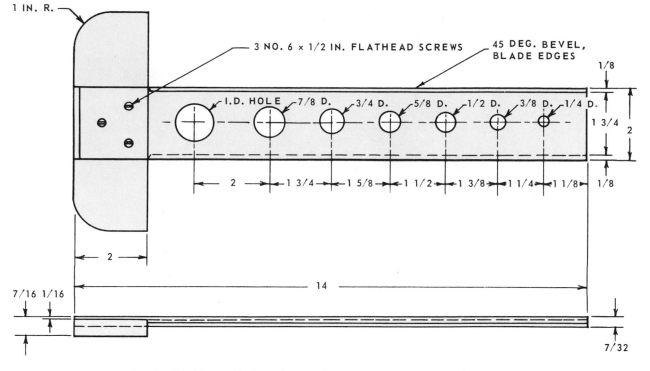

Fig. 19-17. Above. Working drawing for miniature T-square. Below. Miniature T-square and drawing board.

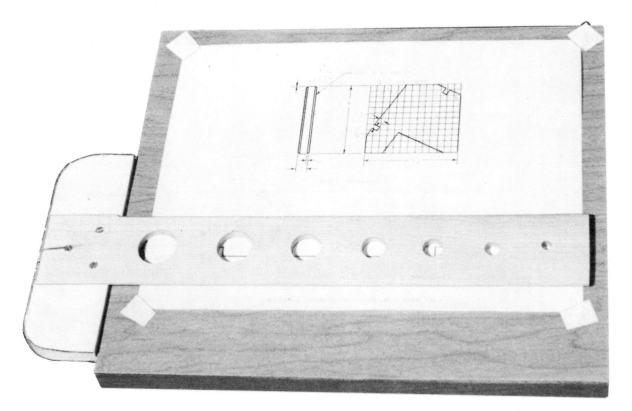

Minature T-square and Drawing Board

Developing your ideas into sketches and working drawings are conveniently accomplished with this little project. You can use it to straighten sketch lines or to prepare working drawings. Both pieces are easily carried under arm or in a brief case.

Hard maple is an excellent wood for construction of the T-square. Plywood covered with plastic or wood veneer results in a handsome, serviceable drawing board. Be sure sides of board are squared. See the working drawing and illustration in Fig. 19-17.

Fig. 19-18. Serving tray.

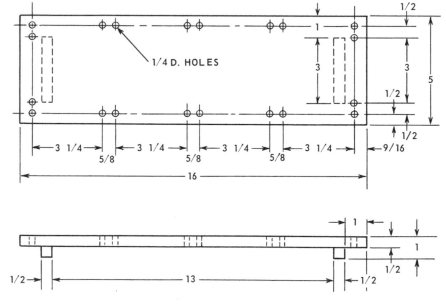

1/4 D. HOLES

Fig. 19-19. Working drawing for serving tray, shown in Fig. 19-18.

Serving Trays

Design possibilities for serving trays are almost unlimited. Fig. 19-18 illustrates a serving tray of unique and simple design. Construction details for making this tray are given in Fig. 19-19.

Perhaps you would like to make a serving tray similar to one of the trays shown in Fig. 19-20. Prepare several sketches. Try to improve on the designs given, then complete plans necessary to make the tray.

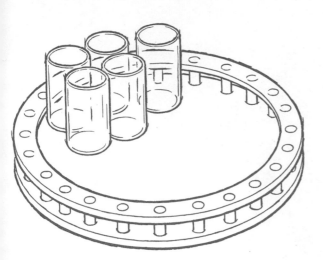

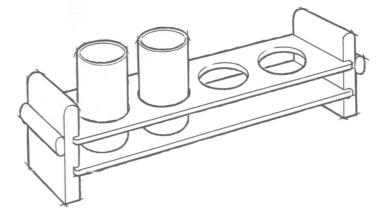
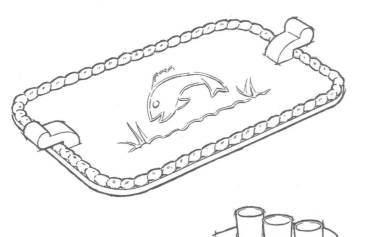
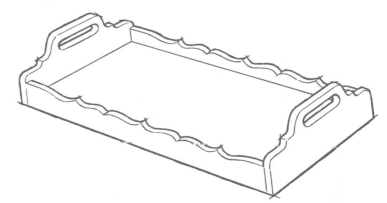
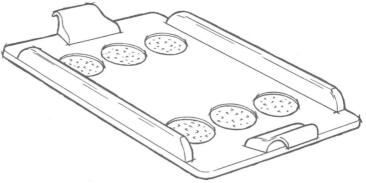

Fig. 19-20. Serving tray, alternate design suggestions.

Fig. 19-21. Novelty box.

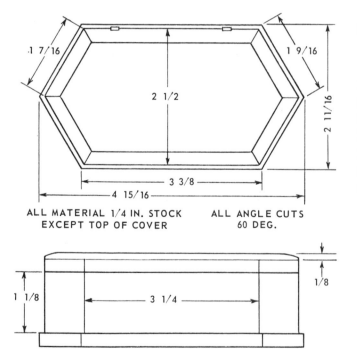

.1 7/16   1 9/16

2 1/2   2 11/16

3 3/8
4 15/16

ALL MATERIAL 1/4 IN. STOCK   ALL ANGLE CUTS
EXCEPT TOP OF COVER   60 DEG.

1 1/8   3 1/4   1/8

Fig. 19-22. Working drawing for a
novelty box, shown in Fig. 19-21.

Fig. 19-23. Box hinge made from wire brads.

Novelty Boxes

The little novelty boxes, shown in Figs. 19-21 and 19-25, are ideal for safely storing stamps, coins, jewelry, and other small items. Constructional details for making the hexagon-shape novelty box shown in Fig. 19-21, are given in Fig. 19-22. Other design shapes and completed novelty boxes are illustrated in Figs. 19-24 and 19-25.

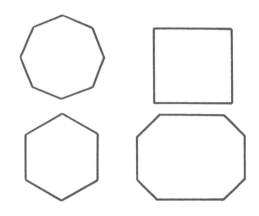

Fig. 19-24. Novelty box, alternate design shapes.

Fig. 19-25. Novelty box, alternate design suggestions. (Designed by Charles H. Wise, Industrial Arts Instructor, Kansas City, Missouri Schools)

Fig. 19-26. Bird feeder.

Bird Feeders

By helping to feed our feathered friends, we not only aid in preserving them, but also receive a great deal of personal enjoyment.

The bird feeder shown in Figs. 19-26 and 19-27, is designed with a hopper so the bin below is kept full by gravity. The top is easily removed for filling. A piece of clear plastic is used so you can observe the food supply. If desired, you could design and make a wire hanger to hold suet and attach it to the outside of the feeder.

Fig. 19-28 illustrates design suggestions. Make several sketches, then make detailed plans for the one you decide to construct.

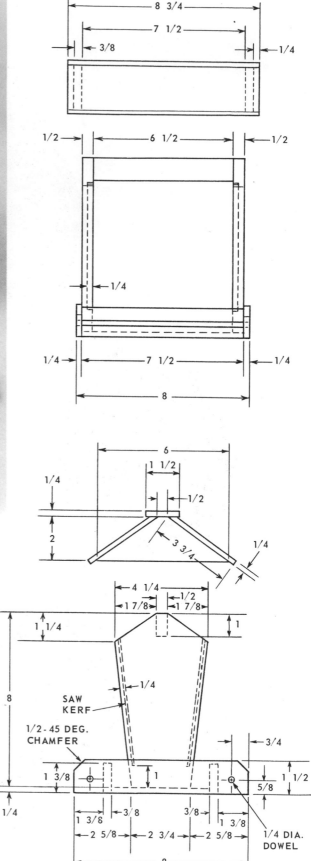

Fig. 19-27. Working drawing for bird feeder, shown in Fig. 19-26.

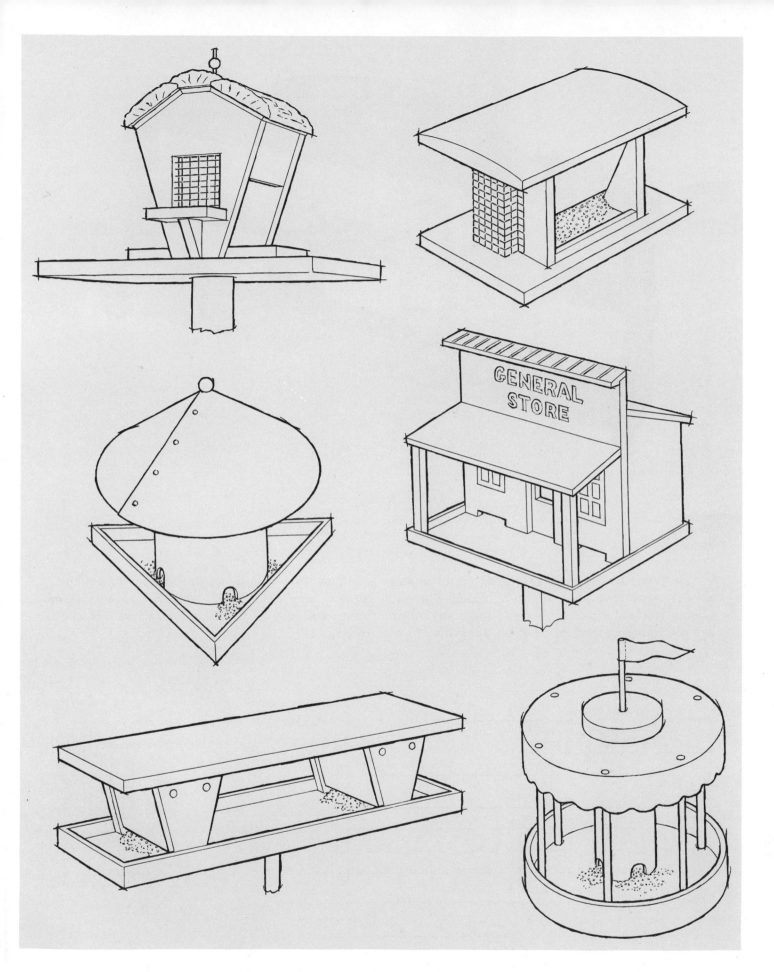

Fig. 19-28. Bird feeder, alternate design suggestions.

Fig. 19-29. Spice shelf.

Shelves

Shelves are among the most popular and useful products that we can make. Spices, books, dishes, clocks, radios, and many other articles are stored or held on shelves.

You may want to build the spice shelf shown in Figs. 19-29 and 19-30, or design your own shelf, following suggestions given in Fig. 19-31.

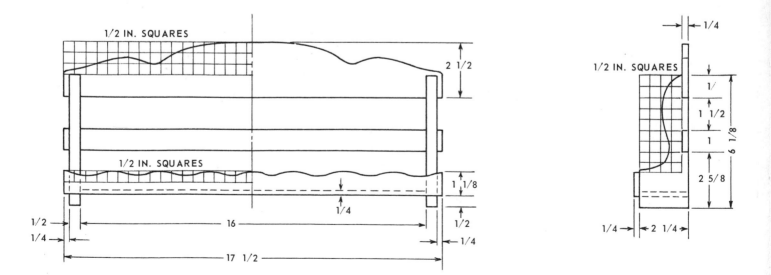

Fig. 19-30. Working drawing for spice shelf, shown in Fig. 19-29.

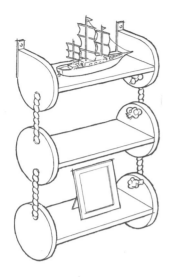

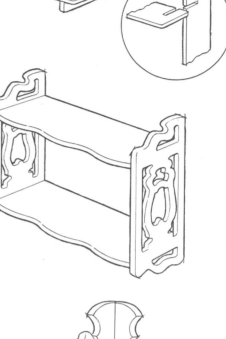

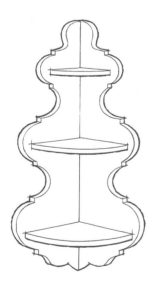

Fig. 19-31. Shelf, alternate design suggestions.

Fig. 19-32. Pelican thread and scissors holder.

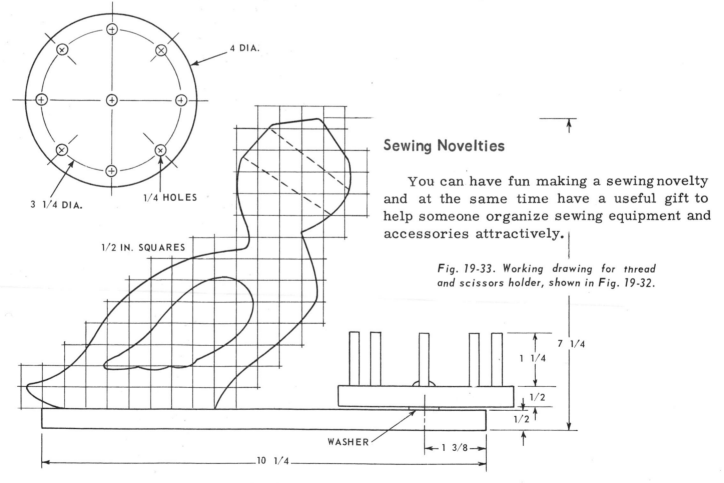

4 DIA.

3 1/4 DIA.   1/4 HOLES

1/2 IN. SQUARES

Sewing Novelties

You can have fun making a sewing novelty and at the same time have a useful gift to help someone organize sewing equipment and accessories attractively.

Fig. 19-33. Working drawing for thread and scissors holder, shown in Fig. 19-32.

7 1/4

1 1/4

1/2

1/2

WASHER

1 3/8

10 1/4

Fig. 19-34. Sewing novelty, alternate design suggestions.

Fig. 19-35. Floral planter.

Planters for Artificial Flowers or Potted Plants

A small floral planter makes a nice gift.

You can easily make the floral planter shown in Figs. 19-35 and 19-36, or you may want to design your own making use of some of the design suggestions, Fig. 19-37. Show your sketches to your instructor and get approval before you proceed with the actual construction.

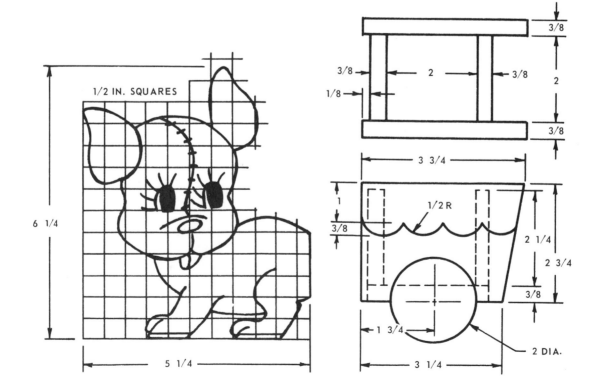

Fig. 19-36. Working drawing for floral planter, shown in Fig. 19-35.

Fig. 19-37. Floral planter, alternate design suggestions.

Flower Stand or Table

Constructing the attractive table shown in Figs. 19-38 and 19-39, involves the use of a variety of hand and power tools.

You can make the legs by wood lamination, wood bending, or by cutting them from solid stock. The legs may be fastened to the top with metal braces or with wood dowels.

Fig. 19-38. Flower stand.

Fig. 19-39. Working drawing for flower stand, shown in Fig. 19-38.

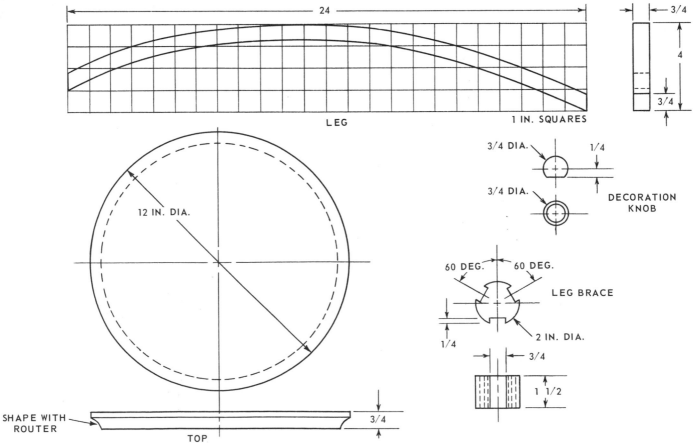

LEG

1 IN. SQUARES

24

3/4

4

3/4

12 IN. DIA.

SHAPE WITH ROUTER

TOP

3/4

3/4 DIA.

1/4

3/4 DIA.

DECORATION KNOB

60 DEG.   60 DEG.

LEG BRACE

1/4

2 IN. DIA.

3/4

1 1/2

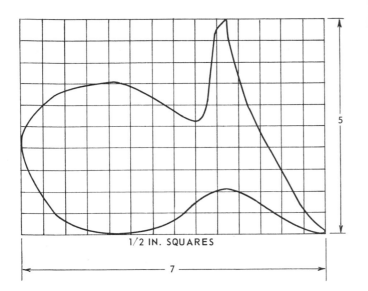

1/2 IN. SQUARES

7

5

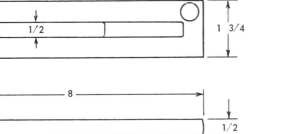

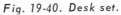

1/2

1 3/4

8

1/2

BASE

Fig. 19-41. Working drawing for desk set.

Fig. 19-40. Desk set.

Desk Set

Figs. 19-40 and 19-41 show an interesting and useful project which involves the use of a number of hand tools.

The base may be used with other animal forms and figures. It may also be redesigned to hold additional pens or other desk accessories.

Fig. 19-42. Cabinet for cassette tapes.

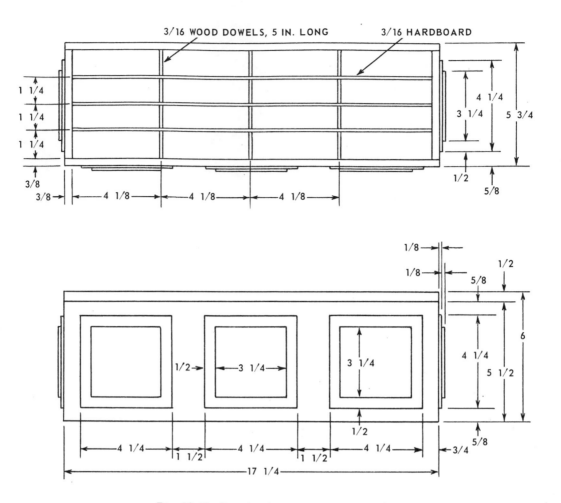

Fig. 19-43. Drawing for a cassette tape cabinet, shown in Fig. 19-42.

Cassette Tape Cabinet

The little cabinet, Figs. 19-42 and 19-43, will provide a good place to store your cassette tapes. You may want to redesign the cabinet to accommodate additional or larger tapes.

Note the thin pieces of wood attached to the front and ends of the cabinet. You may want to use wood veneers of contrasting colors as a design variation.

Curio Shelf With Drawers

Most every kitchen wall is enhanced by the addition of a Curio Shelf. Enumerable decorative pieces are easily and casually displayed.

You can use the drawers as accessible storage for keys, grocery list, etc.

Stained ponderosa pine or yellow poplar are very appropriate for this project, Figs. 19-44 and 19-45.

Fig. 19-44. Curio shelf with drawers.

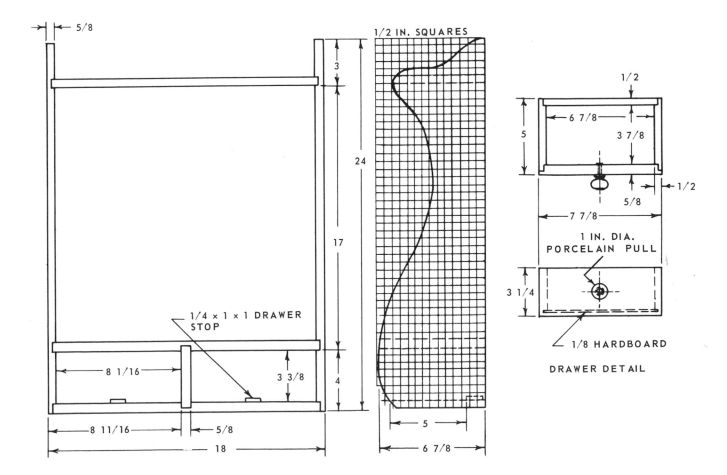

5/8

1/2 IN. SQUARES

3

24

17

1/4 x 1 x 1 DRAWER STOP

8 1/16

3 3/8

4

8 11/16

5/8

18

5

6 7/8

1/2

6 7/8

3 7/8

5

7 7/8

1/2

5/8

1 IN. DIA.
PORCELAIN PULL

3 1/4

1/8 HARDBOARD

DRAWER DETAIL

Fig. 19-45. Working drawing for curio shelf shown in Fig. 19-44.

Salad Cutting Board

You can make a hit with your favorite cook by making her a salad cutting board of the type shown in Figs. 19-46 and 19-47.

Note that the cutting board base tilts toward the hole cut in the corner so sliced vegetables can be easily collected on wax paper underneath. The feet are short for easy storage.

Fig. 19-46. Salad cutting board.

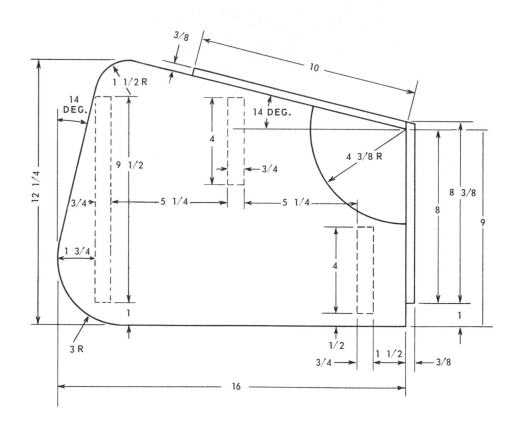

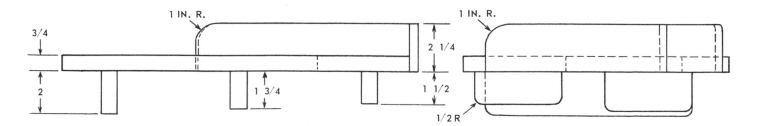

Fig. 19-47. Working drawing for salad cutting board, shown in Fig. 19-46.

186

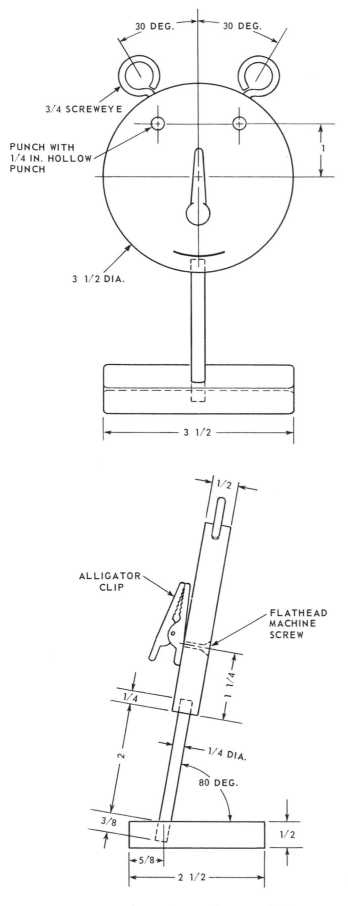

Fig. 19-48. Recipe holder.

Recipe Holder

The little holder, Figs. 19-48 and 19-49, provides a clever way to keep the cook's recipes in position for easy reading and use.

Other faces or animal figures can be used as alternate designs. Make several sketches, then decide on the design to use.

Fig. 19-49. Working drawing for recipe holder, shown in Fig. 19-48.

Fig. 19-50. Laminated wood candle holder.

Candle Stands

Candle stands beautify mantles and make attractive dining settings. Note the smooth, trim lines of both the turned and the laminated candle stands which harmonize with most modern or contemporary furnishings, Figs. 19-50 to 19-53. Each turned holder is made from one solid piece of wood. The laminated holder is made by forming and bonding alternate thin strips of two kinds of wood.

Fig. 19-51. Turned candle holders.

188

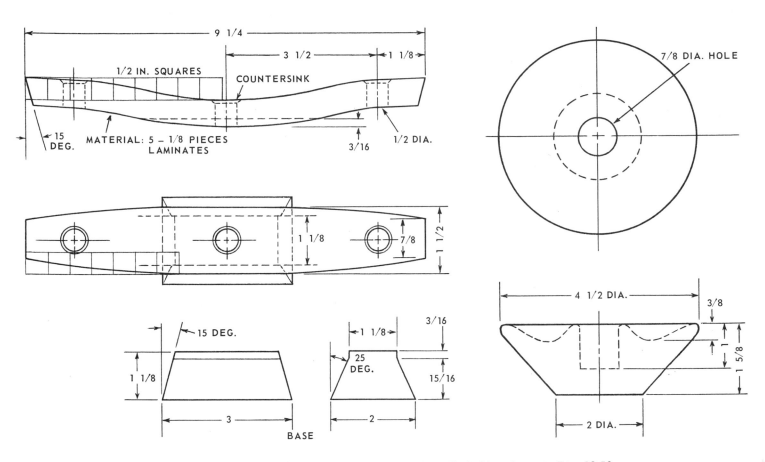

Fig. 19-52. Left. Working drawing for laminated wood candle holder shown in Fig. 19-50.
Fig. 19-53. Right. Working drawing for turned candle holders shown in Fig. 19-51.

Napkin Holder

The small rack shown in Figs. 19-54 to 19-56 holds paper napkins. You may increase the size to fit magazines.

Note the use of wood dowels in the rack to form partitions. The feet can be turned in a wood lathe by using a chuck block as shown in Fig. 11-8, page 94.

Fig. 19-54. Napkin holder.

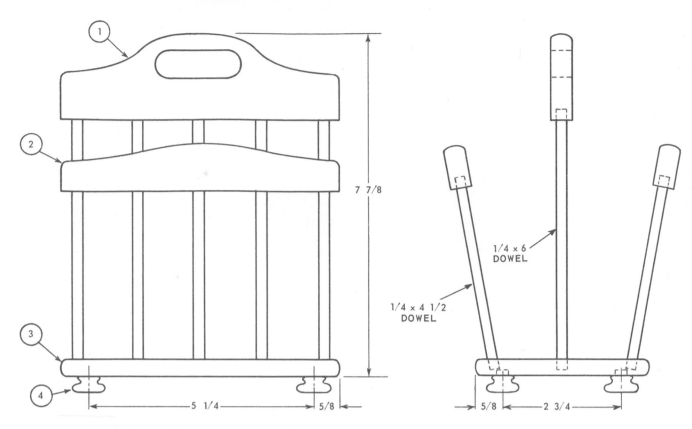

Fig. 19-55. Assembly working drawing for the napkin holder, shown in Fig. 19-54.

Fig. 19-56. Working drawing for napking holder shown in Fig. 19-54.

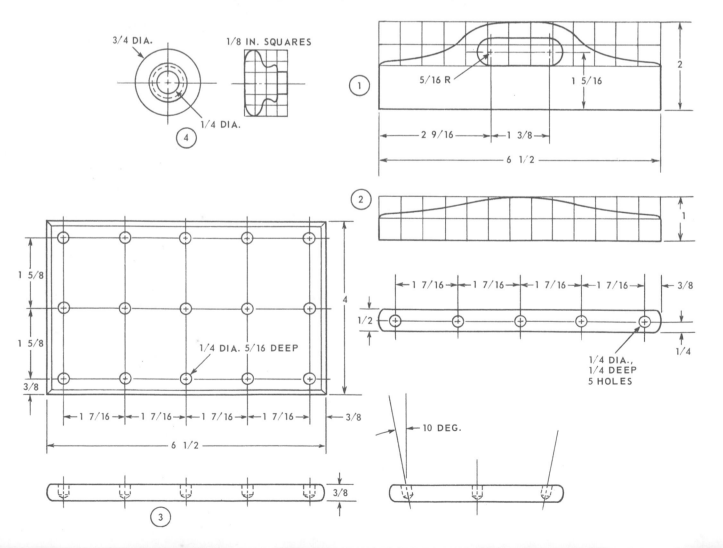

Sconce

With this project, you can decorate a wall and experience a delightful touch of the past. During special events you might want to light its candle to enhance the surroundings. Stained yellow poplar or ponderosa pine are very suitable for this project, Figs. 19-57 and 19-58.

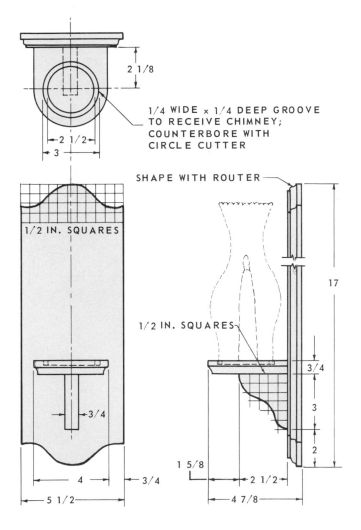

2 1/8

1/4 WIDE x 1/4 DEEP GROOVE TO RECEIVE CHIMNEY; COUNTERBORE WITH CIRCLE CUTTER

2 1/2

3

SHAPE WITH ROUTER

1/2 IN. SQUARES

17

1/2 IN. SQUARES

3/4

3

2

3/4

1 5/8

2 1/2

4 7/8

3/4

4

5 1/2

Fig. 19-57. Working drawing for sconce shown in Fig. 19-58.

Fig. 19-58. Wall sconce

PLANTER, which combines a variety of wood and metalworking processes into a functional product. Fig. 19-59, above, shows the completed project; Fig. 19-60, below, provides constructional details.

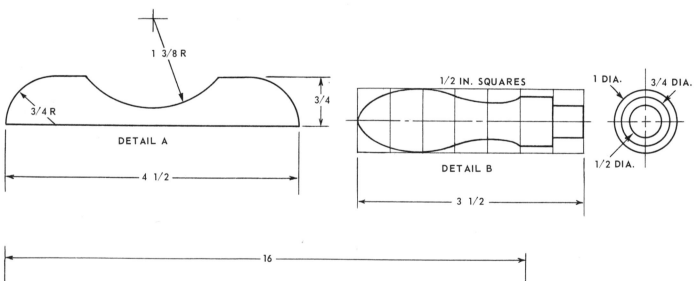

1 3/8 R

3/4 R

3/4

DETAIL A

4 1/2

1/2 IN. SQUARES

DETAIL B

3 1/2

1 DIA.

3/4 DIA.

1/2 DIA.

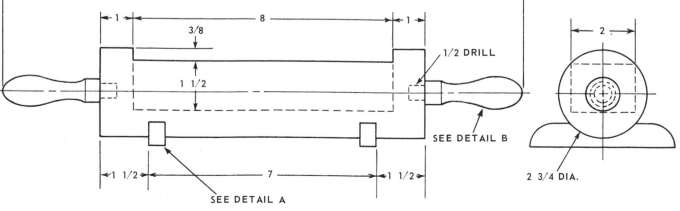

16

1

8

1

3/8

1 1/2

1/2 DRILL

SEE DETAIL B

1 1/2

7

1 1/2

SEE DETAIL A

2

2 3/4 DIA.

DRESSER CADDY. *The dresser caddy, Fig. 19-61, above, provides convenient temporary storage for personal belongings. Drawings below, Fig. 19-62, provide constructional details. You can make the recesses with hand tools, or with a power router. You may want to join with others in your class to build the caddies on a mass-production basis. Identical pieces can be carved with a router guided by using a cutting template and guide held in a prepared fixture, as shown in Figs. 19-63 and 19-64 on the next page.*

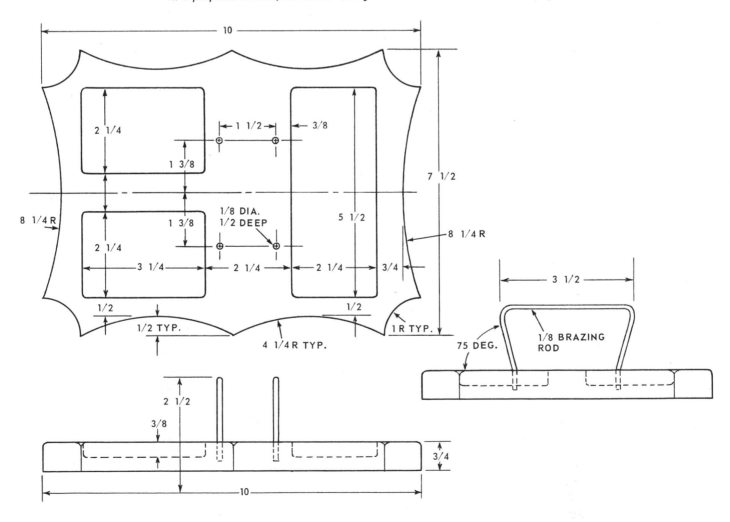

MASS PRODUCING DRESSER CADDY. *Left. Fig. 19-63. Inserting stock in fixture in preparation for template routing. Right. Fig. 19-64. Using router with fixture, template and template guide to cut uniform recesses in dresser caddy stock.*

Veneered Canisters and Pencil Holders

Attractive and pleasing projects can be made by attaching wood veneer to metal cans which are ordinarily thrown away, Figs. 19-65 and 19-66. Canister sets, pencil holders, and flower planters are but a few of the projects you can make in a short time. Lids can be turned on the wood lathe.

PROCEDURE FOR VENEERING METAL CAN:

1. Select size and shape of can which best fits your need.
2. Wash and dry the can, then apply a finish to the inside surfaces.
3. Select wood veneer and cut it to correct size. The grain should run vertically. De-

Fig. 19-65. Veneered and turned canisters and veneered pencil holder.

Fig. 19-66. Attaching wood veneer onto metal can.

Fig. 19-67. Ecology box.

termine size of veneer needed by measuring the circumference of the can with a string. Allow extra 1/8 in. length for lap. Scissors or tin snips cut well across the grain. A sharp knife used with a straight-edge may be used to cut with the grain. Protect your bench top with a scrap piece of hardboard or plywood.

4. Apply masking tape to the outside surface of the veneer to help prevent breaking.
5. With a sanding block, bevel the ends of the veneer to be lapped, then wrap the veneer around the can to test the fit.
6. Roughen the outside of the can for better adhesion, then apply two coats of contact cement to the outside of the can and the underside of the veneer, allowing them to dry to a dull appearance.
7. Attach the wood veneer to the can, Fig. 19-66.
   a. Stick one end to the surface of the can holding the beveled edge toward you.
   b. Carefully press the veneer around the can rubbing from the center outward.
8. Finish as desired.

Ecology Box

This ecology box can be constructed to suggest and emphasize conservation, and at the same time become a distinguished ornament for display, Figs. 19-67 and 19-68.

You can use a less expensive wood such as willow, basswood, or ponderosa pine to make your ecology box then stain it to match

any desired decor. Partitions are easily changed to vary compartment sizes or shapes. Mellow, mature grains make interesting displays along with dried, textured vegetables which grow unattended.

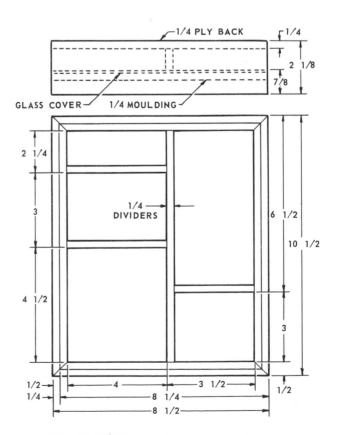

Fig. 19-68. Working drawing for ecology box.

195

Fig. 19-69. Completed Lazy Susan.

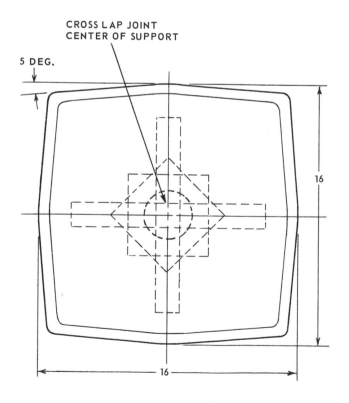

CROSS LAP JOINT
CENTER OF SUPPORT

5 DEG.

16

16

Fig. 19-70. Working drawing for Lazy Susan,
shown in Fig. 19-69.

Lazy Susan

You can make the graceful Lazy Susan tray, Figs. 19-69 and 19-70, with hand carving tools (Unit 7) or with a router. If you choose to use a router, begin cutting the recess in the center of the tray, gradually enlarging it toward the outside edges. This affords a firm rest for the base of the router.

A Lazy Susan bearing attached under the tray and to the base, allows the tray to turn freely.

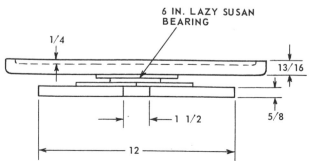

6 IN. LAZY SUSAN
BEARING

1/4

13/16

1 1/2

5/8

12

FOLD AND CARRY STOOL, Fig. 19-71, above, is functional in use, folds flat for easy carrying or storage. A stool handy for picnics, camping, and numerous other occasions. Construct it by yourself or as a member of a team in a mass production unit. Oak, maple, and birch are good woods to use for its construction. These woods are strong, durable and have beautifully figured grain patterns. Fig. 19-22, below, provides constructional details.

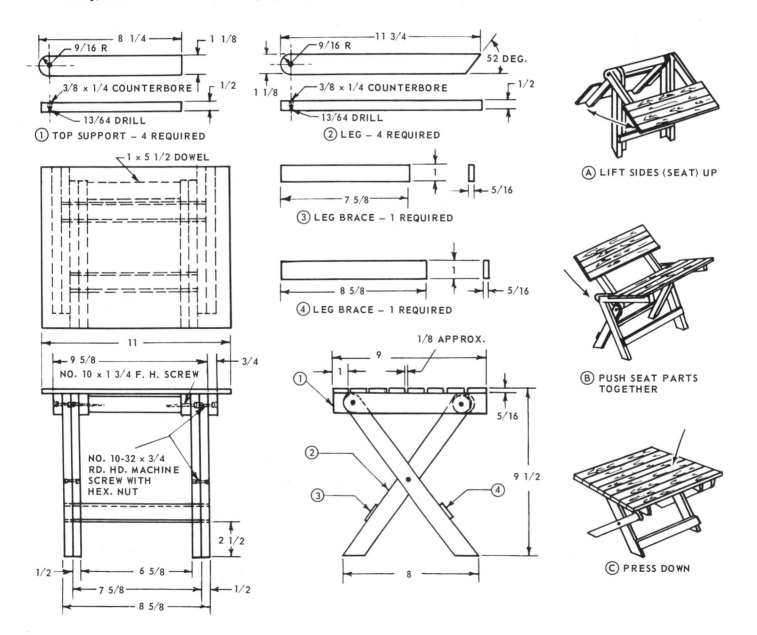

① TOP SUPPORT – 4 REQUIRED

② LEG – 4 REQUIRED

③ LEG BRACE – 1 REQUIRED

④ LEG BRACE – 1 REQUIRED

Ⓐ LIFT SIDES (SEAT) UP

Ⓑ PUSH SEAT PARTS TOGETHER

Ⓒ PRESS DOWN

CONVERSION TABLE ENGLISH TO METRIC

WHEN YOU KNOW	MULTIPLY BY: * = Exact		TO FIND
	VERY ACCURATE	APPROXIMATE	
LENGTH			
inches	*25.4		millimetres
inches	* 2.54		centimetres
feet	* 0.3048		metres
feet	*30.48		centimetres
yards	* 0.9144	0.9	metres
miles	* 1.609344	1.6	kilometres
WEIGHT			
grains	15.43236	15.4	grams
ounces	*28.349523125	28.0	grams
ounces	* 0.028349523125	.028	kilograms
pounds	* 0.45359237	0.45	kilograms
short ton	* 0.90718474	0.9	tonnes
VOLUME			
teaspoons		5.0	millilitres
tablespoons		15.0	millilitres
fluid ounces	29.57353	30.0	millilitres
cups		0.24	litres
pints	* 0.473176473	0.47	litres
quarts	* 0.946352946	0.95	litres
gallons	* 3.785411784	3.8	litres
cubic inches	* 0.016387064	0.02	litres
cubic feet	* 0.028316846592	0.03	cubic metres
cubic yards	* 0.764554857984	0.76	cubic metres
AREA			
square inches	* 6.4516	6.5	square centimetres
square feet	* 0.09290304	0.09	square metres
square yards	* 0.83612736	0.8	square metres
square miles		2.6	square kilometres
acres	* 0.40468564224	0.4	hectares
TEMPERATURE			
Fahrenheit	*5/9 (after subtracting 32)		Celsius

CONVERSION TABLE METRIC TO ENGLISH

WHEN YOU KNOW	MULTIPLY BY: * = Exact		TO FIND
	VERY ACCURATE	APPROXIMATE	
LENGTH			
millimetres	0.0393701	0.04	inches
centimetres	0.3937008	0.4	inches
metres	3.280840	3.3	feet
metres	1.093613	1.1	yards
kilometres	0.621371	0.6	miles
WEIGHT			
grains	0.00228571	0.0023	ounces
grams	0.03527396	0.035	ounces
kilograms	2.204623	2.2	pounds
tonnes	1.1023113	1.1	short tons
VOLUME			
millilitres	0.06667	0.2	teaspoons
millilitres	0.03381402	0.067	tablespoons
millilitres		0.03	fluid ounces
litres	61.02374	61.024	cubic inches
litres	2.113376	2.1	pints
litres	1.056688	1.06	quarts
litres	0.26417205	0.26	gallons
litres	0.03531467	0.035	cubic feet
cubic metres	61023.74	61023.7	cubic inches
cubic metres	35.31467	35.0	cubic feet
cubic metres	1.3079506	1.3	cubic yards
cubic metres	264.17205	264.0	gallons
AREA			
square centimetres	0.1550003	0.16	square inches
square centimetres	0.00107639	0.001	square feet
square metres	10.76391	10.8	square feet
square metres	1.195990	1.2	square yards
square kilometres		0.4	square miles
hectares	2.471054	2.5	acres
TEMPERATURE			
Celsius	*9/5 (then add 32)		Fahrenheit

DICTIONARY OF TERMS

ABRASIVE: A material used to smooth stock surfaces and to polish wood finishes.

ACROSS THE GRAIN: Perpendicular to the length of a board and its fibers. Across the diameter of a log.

ADHESIVE: A sticky substance used to bond materials together. A paste, cement or glue.

AGAINST THE GRAIN: Opposite the grain direction or growth pattern of wood fibers.

AIR-DRYING: Seasoning of lumber by natural means. Lumber is stacked in layers separated with cross strips to allow free passage of air.

AIR-TRANSFORMER: A device used with spray finishing equipment to regulate air pressure, remove dirt and moisture from compressed air, and compressor pulsations.

ALKYD RESIN: A synthetic material widely used as a vehicle in paints and enamels to increase durability.

ALLIGATORING: Cracks formed in a finished surface resulting in a mottled pattern somewhat similar to the skin on the back of an alligator. Caused by unequal expansion and contraction of separate coats of finish.

ALUMINUM OXIDE (Al_2O_3): An efficient abrasive made by fusing Bauxite ore in an electric furnace. It is used to make abrasive paper, abrasive cloth, and grinding wheels.

AMERICAN TREE FARM SYSTEM: An organization sponsored by woodworking industries. A national system of forest management affording better protection and use of our forest resources and assuring a future supply of timber.

ANILINE DYES: Oily, synthetic coloring agents produced chemically, used in making permanent type wood stain.

ANNUAL GROWTH RING: A growth ring of a tree formed in a single year, formed by springwood and summerwood.

ARBOR: A spindle, shaft or axle on which another revolving part or a cutting tool may be mounted.

ARRIS: The sharp edge formed by the meeting of two surfaces. Example - - edge of a board.

ATTACHING PLATE: A metal plate designed for fastening a leg to a table with a hanger bolt.

ATOMIZATION: The process of reducing paint or other liquids to minute particles forming a fine mist for spraying.

BAGASSE: A fibrous by-product of sugar cane useful in producing insulation. Plant residue left after juice has been extracted.

BARE-FACED TENON: A tenon having only one shoulder, exposing one side.

BATTEN: A thin strip of wood used to seal or strengthen the edge joint assembly of two adjacent boards or panels.

BEAD: A projecting band or rim formed on an edge, cylinder, or molding.

BEVEL: Angle one surface or line makes with another when the angles are not right angles.

BILL OF MATERIAL: A detailed list of the items needed to construct a project.

BLADE CLEARANCE: Width of cut made by saw beyond thickness of saw blade.

BLEACHING: Chemical solution applied to wood to make it lighter in color.

BLEEDING: The transfer of color from one finish coat to another. For example, varnish applied over an unsealed penetrating oil stain dissolves part of its color resulting in discoloration of the varnish coat.

BLEMISH: Any imperfection or small defect which mars the appearance of a surface.

BLIND DADO: A dado which is cut part way across a surface rendering it invisible from one or both sides.

BLUE STAIN: Discoloration caused by a fungus growth in unseasoned lumber.

BLUSHING: A whitish cast formed in a finish, often clear spraying lacquer, which dries too fast as it is applied. Particularly on humid days, humidity in the air is condensed and trapped with the finish. A retarding thinner can be added to lacquer as a preventative. A clouded appearance on a varnished surface.

BOARD FOOT MEASURE: A standard unit of measurement for most lumber. A board foot is one square foot of area one inch or less in thickness.

BOILED LINSEED OIL: Certain metallic driers are added to raw linseed oil. The oil is then heat treated and aged for use in the manufacture of varnish and enamel.

BUILDING-TRADES CRAFTSMEN: These constitute our nation's largest group of skilled craftsmen composed of carpenters (largest), painters, plumbers, bricklayers, electricians, operating engineers, structural workers, roofers, cement masons and others.

BULL-CHAIN (ALSO JACK LADDER): A conveyor for pulling logs lengthwise into the sawmill.

BURL: A protruding lump on a tree which when sliced produces veneer with highly figured grain.

BURLAP: A coarse cloth, usually woven from jute or hemp fibers.

CALIPER: A tool for measuring round stock.

CAMBIUM LAYER: A growth area near the bark of a tree where new cells are formed. The inside of this layer forms new wood cells and the outside forms new bark cells.

CANT: A log which has been slabbed (cut flat) on two or four sides, ready for further processing into lumber or veneer.

CAPILLARY ACTION: Movement of a liquid in contact with a solid which causes the liquid to wet the solid surface.

CATALYST: A substance which starts and aids in the control of chemical action between two other substances.

CATCHES: Devices used to hold furniture and cabinet doors closed.

CAUL BOARDS: Waxed pieces of wood or metal inserted between press platens or plywood collections to protect or shape laminated assemblies.

CENTRIFUGAL FORCE: The force that tends to drive rotating objects outward from the center of rotation.

CERTIFIED TREE FARMS: See American Tree Farm System.

CHALKING: Decomposition of paint film which leaves loose powder on the surface.

CHAMFER: The edge-surface formed by planing or sawing at an angle across one arris of a square edge.

CHECKS: Cracks along the grain at the end of a board and at about right angles to the annular growth rings.

CHUCK: A work holding device attached to rotating headstock of lathe or other machine.

CLEARANCE BLOCK: A piece of stock used as a gauge in cutting duplicate parts, to prevent binding.

CLEAT: A piece of wood attached to another piece, often as a brace or holding device.

CLINCH: Bending over the protruding ends of driven nails.

CLOSE-GRAIN: Wood having fibers which are fine and are held closely together.

COLLAPSE: A breakdown of wood cell structure caused by improper seasoning which results in a wood defect.

COLLAR: A ring or flange fastened under the nut on an arbor or spindle as an aid in securing a cutting tool.

COLLAR BEAM (ALSO RAFTER TIE): A horizontal plank used to strengthen and connect pairs of rafters.

COLONIAL FURNITURE: The kind of furniture made and used during the period of American Colonization.

COMMON GRADE (ALSO UTILITY GRADE): Lumber ranging in grade numbers from one to five depending on size, shape, and condition of knots. Common grade lumber is often used for structural purposes.

COMPATIBILITY: A term used to denote the ability of finishes to mix together without harmful chemical reactions.

CONIFER: A tree which bears cones. Lumber from conifers is designated as softwood.

CONSTRUCTION SPECIALISTS: The skilled workmen who handle and install building components and laminated beams.

CONTEMPORARY FURNITURE (ALSO MODERN): Modern day furniture made with characteristic smooth, trim lines and simple construction.

COPE: A term in foundry indicating the top half of a flask, pattern, or mold.

CORE: The center layer of plywood consisting of solid wood, hardboard, particleboard, or veneer.

COTTON MATT: A soft layer of combed cotton used over rubberized hair or other upholstery materials to produce a cushioning effect.

COUNTERBORING: To enlarge part of the length of a hole by boring, using same center as original hole.

COUNTERSINKING: To form a cone-shaped recess for receiving the head of a flat head screw or bolt.

COVE: An inside curve (concave) shape formed on an edge, surface, cylinder or molding.

CRACK (ALSO SPLIT): A narrow break or opening along the grain in the surface or at the end of a board.

CROOK: The warped edge of a board that is curved lengthwise.

CROTCH: The angle formed by two parting branches in a tree. Crotch lumber is prized for its highly figured grain.

CRYSTALLINE FINISH: A novelty finish which when drying forms a mass of wrinkles or crystals.

CUP: The warped surface of a board that is curved across the grain.

CUP CENTER: Tailstock center for a wood lathe.

DADO: A groove with square corners cut across the grain of a board.

DAYLIGHT: A title referring to the opening between the platens of a press.

DECAY: Decline (breakdown) of a substance caused by the action of fungi.

DECIDUOUS: Hardwood trees (broad leaved) which lose their leaves after each season of growth.

DEFECTS: Imperfections in lumber such as knots, splits, decay, and warp which lessen its usefulness or value.

DENATURED ALCOHOL: A combination of wood and grain alcohol.

DENSITY: The quantity of matter in a given volume.

DESIGN: A scheme or plan in which ideas and thinking are incorporated as direction for creating with materials and tools.

DIMENSION LUMBER: That which is graded primarily for framing of buildings in sizes from 2 to 5 in. thick and up to 12 in. wide.

DOVETAIL JOINT: A strong and attractive joint consisting of wedge-shaped projections, shaped like a dove's tail, which fit into matching recesses.

DOWEL: A cylinder of wood, usually birch, manufactured in a variety of diameters by a standard length of 36 in. Dowels are often used to strengthen wood joints.

DOWEL PEG: A short dowel made especially for wood joints.

DOWEL POINT: A metal cylinder with a flange and a sharp center point. It is used to mark the location of a mating hole for a dowel joint.

DRAG: The bottom half of a foundry mold or flask.

DRIER: A catalyst added to a finishing material to speed its curing and drying time.

DRIP CAP: A molding used over a door or window to shed water away from its exterior side.

DUTCHMAN: A piece used in a wood surface to correct an error or repair a defect.

EARLY AMERICAN FURNITURE: The type of furniture made and used as industry developed during the period of American Revolution.

EARTH PIGMENTS: Coloring matter used in wood finishes mined from the earth, such as ochre, sienna and umber.

ECCENTRIC: A circular piece having an off center rotation of axis. It is used to transform a circular motion to a straight motion.

EMULSION: Suspension of minute particles of one liquid, such as oil, in another, such as water.

EMULSION PAINT: An oil, resin, varnish or lacquer which is emulsified so that it can be mixed with water.

ENAMEL: A finishing material creating a hard, durable, waterproof finish. It is made by adding pigments to varnish to give it color and opacity.

EQUILIBRIUM MOISTURE CONTENT: The point at which wood reaches a balance in moisture content with the surrounding air.

ESCUTCHEON: A decorative plate fastened around hinges and locks.

EVAPORATION: The conversion of a liquid to a gas. A paint thinner evaporates from the paint solids leaving a paint film.

EXTENDER: A material used as a filler in paint or glue to provide body and increase its coverage.

FACE SURFACE (ALSO TRUE OR WORKING SURFACE): The first surface of a board which is planed to remove warp resulting in a flat, true surface. It becomes the reference surface for truing the remaining edges and surfaces.

FACTORY LUMBER (ALSO SHOP LUMBER): Lumber which is prepared especially for windows, doors, interior trim, or other components.

FEATHER (ALSO KEY): A reinforcing strip installed in a groove across the corner into both edges of a miter joint.

FEATHER BOARD: A safety device used in ripping, planing, and shaping operations. This can be made by cutting one end of a board at an angle of 20-30 deg., then ripping a series of kerfs about 6 in. long into that end to make it flexible.

FELTING PROCESS: Small particles of a substance, mixed with water and chemicals, are flowed on a screen and formed into sheets of material as excess water is removed.

FENCE: An adjustable bar or strip attached to the table of a machine to guide stock as it is processed.

FIBER: A single cell in wood.

FIGURE: The design shape yielded in a wood surface by the nature and arrangement of its fibers, its growth rings, wood rays and knots.

FINISH GRADE (ALSO SELECT GRADE): Ranges from A through D, the best grade being B or better in softwood. In white pine C or D select applies to lumber 4 in. wide or more with a medium stain covering one third of the face being permissible.

FIRST AND SECONDS (FAS): Best grade in hardwood. Minimum widths of 6 in. and lengths of 8 ft. At least 83 1/3 percent of face is clear stock. No more than 10 percent of an order can be of minimum dimension.

FIXTURE: A device used to hold material as it is processed with a tool or machine.

FLASHING: Sheet metal or other material used around openings in roof or wall construction to prevent the penetration of water.

FLATTING AGENT: A substance used in paints, lacquers and varnish to reduce its gloss and give it a rubbed appearance.

FLEXIBILITY: A characteristic or quality of a material that permits it to be bent.

FLITCH: A semicircular slab cut from a huge log which is further processed into lumber or veneer.

FLOATING CONSTRUCTION: A technique of construction which allows materials to expand or contract without damage. For example, screws set in slotted holes during assembly.

FLOCK: Pulverized or fibrous strands of rayon, plastic or wool which are blown onto a surface freshly coated with adhesive or paint to produce a velvet-like finish.

FLOW (FINISHING): The quality of a material to spread or move evenly into a uniform and level coating.

FLUTING: Rounded parallel grooves formed in a wood surface.

FOAM RUBBER: A soft, cellular and highly resilient (capable of returning to original shape after being deformed) material providing a cushioning effect. Used extensively in upholstery.

FORESTRY: A profession concerned with the conservation, care, development, management, and production of forest lands.

FOREST SERVICE MANAGEMENT: A Federal agency dedicated to the best use, development and conservation of our nation's forest lands. This includes wild life protection, water and soil conservation, recreation, research.

FRENCH POLISH: A type of wood finish produced with white shellac, boiled linseed oil, and denatured alcohol.

FRENCH PROVINCIAL FURNITURE: Furniture built and used during the reigns of Louis XIV - XVI. It has simple, curved lines and has no ornate carvings.

FURRING: Narrow strips attached to a ceiling, wall or floor as a nailing base for other material such as paneling. Also used to level a surface, or form an air space between two surfaces.

GAIN: The notch or mortise made to receive a hinge, other hardware, or another structural member.

GLAZING: (1) The process of installing glass in a window; (2) The application of transparent or translucent coatings over another finishing medium to obtain a blended effect.

GLOSS: A finished surface with a high luster and good light reflecting quality.

GLUE BLOCKS: Small triangular or rectangular-shaped pieces glued into place, often at right angles, to reinforce joints.

GRAIN: Arrangement, direction, quality, appearance, and size of the fibers in wood.

GROOVE: A square cornered channel cut in a piece of wood.

GUARD: That part of a tool or machine designed to protect its operator from a cutting edge or moving part.

GUSSETT: A reinforcing member of wood or

metal, often made as a panel or bracket, and attached to the corners and intersections of a frame.

HANGER BOLT: A threaded fastener used to attach a leg to a table.

HARDBOARD: Composition board made by compressing shredded wood chips to form flat sheets. Lignin, a natural resin, is used to hold the rearranged fibers together.

HARDWOOD: The classification of lumber which comes from broadleaf trees.

HARDWOOD PLYWOOD: Plywood with the outside veneer being a hardwood.

HARMONY: A design term implying that characteristics of parts in an object are in conformity or form a pleasing arrangement.

HEADRIG: The mechanism which holds and manipulates logs as they are being cut at the sawmill.

HEADSAW: The beginning saw in a sawmill which cuts logs into slabs, cants, or flitches.

HEARTWOOD: Wood between the pith and the sapwood in a tree or log.

HINGE: A piece of hardware used to fit parts together so that one can swing free of another as a door or window.

HOLIDAYS: Spots or places missed during application of a finish.

HOLLOW-CORE CONSTRUCTION: A method of making lightweight doors. Plywood, hardboard or other sheet material is fastened to a frame of solid wood.

HOLLOW-GROUND: The concave, sharpened edge on a cutting tool left by the circular shape of a grinding wheel.

HOLLOW-WALL SCREW ANCHOR: A fastener used to attach an object to a hollow wall. As it is assembled, the part inside the wall spreads and the fastener tightens.

HONE: The final or finish sharpening of a cutting tool on a whetting stone.

HOOK (SKIP) TOOTH: A saw blade, usually band saw, made with extra space between its teeth.

INDUSTRIAL EDUCATION TEACHER: One who teaches industrial arts or industrial occupational education.

INDUSTRIAL WOODWORKER: A person who earns his living by working in a plant which manufactures wood products such as cabinets or furniture.

INLAY: An ornamental decoration fitted into a recess and finished flush with a surface.

INSERT PLATE: An access plate used in the top of a machine around the cutting tool.

INSPECTION: A critical examination of workpieces and assemblies to detect errors in fabrication.

INSULATION: A material used in building construction to prevent the escape of heat, cold, or sound.

INTERCHANGEABILITY: Parts or devices made to dimensions of close tolerances, often by mass production, that will fit into more than one assembly.

JACK LADDER: See Bull Chain.

JIG: A device used to help perform a process such as guiding a tool to form or assemble parts.

KEELSON: A longitudinal brace used to strengthen the frame structure of a boat keel (center member at bottom).

KERF: The cut made in material by the teeth of a saw blade.

KEY: See Feather.

KILN: An enclosure with controlled heat and humidity for drying lumber, veneer, and other wood products.

KILN-DRYING: Seasoning of lumber, veneer and other wood products in a kiln.

KNOT: A hard, circular area, revealing the cross-section of a limb or branch imbedded in wood during the growth of the tree.

LAC: Resinous substance formed by an insect, used to make shellac.

LACQUER: A hard, durable finishing material made of nitro-cellulose. Drying occurs by evaporation of its solvents.

LAG SCREW: A heavy, round shank wood screw with a square head.

LAMINATE: A product made by bonding thin layers (plies or laminations) of material together with an adhesive.

LAZY SUSAN: A tray which revolves on a central bearing attached to a base.

LEAD SCREW ANCHOR: An anchor made from lead which is tapped into a hole in a wall and used to hold an object with a screw.

LEDGER: A horizontal member attached to vertical framing (studs) and used to support horizontal framing (joists).

LEVELING (FINISHING): The formation of a smooth film, free of brush marks, on a finished surface.

LIGNIN: An essential compound in wood which acts as a bonding agent and holds the fibers together.

LINEAR: Pertaining to the nature of a line. Measurement in one direction, along a length.

LINSEED OIL: A valuable oil obtained by pressing flax seeds. This oil, in its boiled form, is used alone as a wood finish. It is also extensively used in oil-base paints and finishes.

LINTEL: The horizontal beam used as support over doors, windows, and fireplaces. It rests at both ends on vertical supports.

LUMBER: Boards and planks cut from logs.

LUMBER CORE PLYWOOD: Plywood made with an inner core of solid lumber.

MACHINE: An assemblage of parts designed to apply power with tools in modifying materials by sawing, planing, shaping, turning, drilling, or sanding.

MANDREL: An arbor or spindle on which work can be mounted for rotation.

MARQUETRY: An ornamental decoration consisting of a variety of veneers forming a design or picture.

MASONRY NAIL: A spiral, fluted, steel nail with high tensile strength which can be driven into masonry.

MASS PRODUCTION: Production of parts or products in quantity.

MATERIAL: Supplies needed such as lumber, plywood, nails, etc. to construct a part or product.

MEDULLARY RAY (ALSO WOOD RAY): Rows of cells that run perpendicular to the annual rings toward the pith.

MESH: Openings formed by the crossing or weaving of a series of parallel threads or wires as in a sieve.

MILLWORK: Parts or products made in a manufacturing plant (mill) using wood materials. Examples are moldings, door frames, doors, and sashes, and window units.

MINERAL SPIRITS: A petroleum product used as a solvent in oil-base paint and varnish as a substitute for turpentine.

MITER OR MITRE: A joint formed by two members at an evenly divided angle. A cut generally made at an angle of 45 deg.

MODERN FURNITURE: See Contemporary Furniture.

MOLDING OR MOULDING: Piece of wood cut to a special shape or pattern.

MORTISE: Recess cut into a surface, usually rectangular, to receive another part, such as a tenon.

MOSAIC: A surface decoration arranged in a pattern or design, composed of pieces of materials such as glass and stone. Usually set in a mastic.

MULLION: A vertical dividing strip used to separate window units.

MUNTIN: A dividing strip used to separate panes of glass in a window, or panels in panel construction.

NAPTHA: A volatile petroleum solvent (between gasoline and benzine) used as a thinner to reduce enamel, oil-base paint, and varnish.

NATURAL RESINS: Gums and resins, used in finishes, which are emitted from trees.

NOMINAL SIZE (ALSO ROUGH SIZE): The commercial size by which lumber is known and sold.

OIL STAIN: A stain having an oil base. Two kinds are available, penetrating and pigmented.

ON CENTER (OC): A layout method used in carpentry to indicate spacing of structural members (studs, joists and rafters) from the center of one to the center of the next.

OPEN GRAIN: Wood having fibers with holes or pores which are visible without magnification.

ORANGE PEEL (FINISHING): A spraying defect resembling the texture of an orange peel caused by improper mixture or application of finish.

OXIDIZE (FINISHING): A chemical reaction caused by materials uniting with oxygen. This is part of the curing and drying process of such finishes as varnish, enamel, and oil-base paint.

PAINT: A common term referring to all protective coatings. More specifically, it is a mixture containing pigment and a vehicle which can be spread in a thin film on surfaces.

PALLET: A low cost decking built on skids. It is used to stack and ship various materials.

PARTICLEBOARD: A manufactured board composed of wood particles and shavings bonded together with a synthetic resin.

PARTITION: A wall used to divide space within a structure.

PASTE WOOD FILLER: A material used to fill open grained wood in preparation for other finish. It consists of ground silicon (silex) linseed oil, thinner, drier, and coloring.

PATTERNMAKER: A specialized craftsman who builds patterns, usually for use in the foundry.

PENNY (d): A term referring to nail size, abbreviated by letter d.

PERIPHERAL SPEED: The speed, usually given in feet per minute, of a point on the circumference of a rotating shaft or wheel.

PICTORIAL SKETCH: A method of sketching resulting in a view of an object which appears approximately as it would by eye.

PIGMENT: Fine solid particles in paint which are insoluble in the liquid portion.

PILASTER: A built-in column or pillar used to reinforce a masonry wall.

PITCH POCKET: An opening in lumber, along its annual rings, which holds or has held a resinous material.

PITH: The center point in the cross-section of a log or tree.

PLAIN-SAWED (FLAT SAWED): Lumber made by sawing entire log end to end, into lumber.

PLAN OF PROCEDURE: Operations for making a product, listed in a logical sequence.

PLANING MILL: A machine used to smooth the surfaces of rough lumber.

PLANK: A heavy, thick board that is 2 to 4 in. in thickness and 8 in. or more in width.

PLASTIC WOOD: A manufactured material used to repair cracks, holes and defects in wood.

PLUMB: Perpendicular to a level plane, or exactly vertical.

PLYWOOD: A manufactured product made with crossbanded layers (plies) of veneer or solid center stock bonded together with glue. An odd number (3, 5, 7, etc.) of plies is used.

PNEUMATIC: Related to, or operated with air pressure.

POINTS PER INCH: The number of teeth points per inch for a saw or saw blade.

POLYMERIZATION: A chemical action in which molecules combine to form larger molecules. Part of the curing and drying process of certain finishing materials.

PROCESS: A planned operation performed in the development or fabrication of a problem or product.

PROPORTION: The ratio of the dimensions of a piece.

PULL: A device used as a handle to open a drawer or door.

PUMICE: An organic substance made by pulverizing lava rock. It is used as a fine abrasive to smooth final coats of certain finishes.

QUARTER ROUND: A trim molding with one square corner and a cross-section which forms one fourth cylinder.

QUARTER SAWED: A log is first cut into quarters and then each quarter is sawed into boards.

QUILL: The hollow sleeve on a drill press which rotates, carrying the spindle or mandrel.

RABBET: An L-shape recess cut at the end or along the edge of a board.

RADIAL: A machine or body part extending outward from a center, or following the course of a radius.

RAFTER TIE: See Collar Beam.

RAISED GRAIN: Swelled and loosened fibers on a wood surface caused by moisture.

RAM-SET NAIL: A fastener driven into masonry with a special gun (ram-set) powered by a powder cartridge.

RAPPING PLATE (PATTERNMAKING): A metal plate attached to a pattern and used to help loosen and draw the pattern from a mold.

RATCHET: A mechanical device which allows a hand tool (as a brace or screwdriver) to impart motion in a close-quarter space. The teeth of a gear engage in a pawl to effect motion in one direction only.

REDUCE (FINISHING): To lower the viscosity (thickness) of a finishing material with a thinner or solvent.

RELATIVE HUMIDITY: The ratio of water vapor present in the air related to the maximum quantity of water vapor the air can hold at a given temperature.

RELIEF CUT: A cut made to ease the cutting action of a saw blade around a sharp curve.

RESAWING: Ripping a board to reduce its thickness or to make two thinner pieces.

RESEARCH TECHNICIAN: One who performs analyses and tests with forest products.

RESILIENCE: The capability of wood placed under stress to return to its original shape.

RESPIRATOR: A breathing shield to filter harmful particles from the air.

RETARDER (FINISHING): A substance added

to a finishing material to prolong its curing and drying time.

ROTARY CUT: A method of cutting veneer by turning a log in a huge lathe against a broad knife with a continuous cut.

ROTTENSTONE: A rubbing and polishing compound made from finely pulverized limestone. It is used to smooth the final coat of certain finishes. Also known as tripoli.

ROUGH SIZE: See Nominal Size.

ROUT: To cut recesses into the surfaces or edges of wood including dados, rabbets, veins, coves and mortises.

RUBBERIZED HAIR MATT: A cushioning material used in upholstering and carpeting.

RUNS (FINISHING): Abnormal flow of finishing material usually caused by excess application.

SABER SAWING: Cutting with a portable jigsaw with a heavy blade mounted in the lower chuck of the saw.

SAFETY FIRST: A slogan often used around an industrial plant, construction site, or school laboratory. It implies that safety is of utmost importance in considering any task.

SANDWICH CONSTRUCTION: A method of building panels by laminating facing materials with core stock.

SAPWOOD: The outer portion of a log or tree which contains active cells. This is located between the heartwood and cambium layer.

SAW-SET: A term referring to the process of bending (toward alternate sides) the teeth of a saw blade to provide for clearance of the blade when sawing.

SCAFFOLD: A framework or support for a workman and his materials during the construction or repair of a building.

SCRAPING CUT: A cut made with the tool cutting edge held at a near right angle to the material.

SEALER (FINISHING): A finishing material used to seal the pores of close grain wood. This is also used over stain or filler to prevent bleeding.

SEALER STAIN: A wood finish which combines a sealer and a stain.

SELECT GRADE: See Finish Grade.

SHAKE: A defect in wood which runs parallel to the annual growth rings of a board or log.

SHELLAC: A natural finishing material made by dissolving refined lac in denatured alcohol.

SHOP LUMBER: See Factory Lumber.

SHORING: An assembly of posts and boards used as a prop to afford temporary support during construction. Concrete forms are often supported by a group of shores.

SHEARING CUT: Cut in which fibers are severed directly with a sharp cutting edge.

SILEX: A hard stone (flint or quartz) which when finely ground is used in paints and paste wood filler.

SILICON CARBIDE (SiC): A synthetic compound (bluish in color) made by fusing coke and silica at high temperatures. It is an extremely hard material used on tools where sharp, durable, cutting edges are needed. It is also crushed and used for abrasive paper and grinding wheels.

SLEEPER: One of several strips of wood set in or on a concrete base to which a subfloor or finished floor is attached.

SLICED (VENEER): A thin flat piece of wood cut from a log. Veneer can be cut from a log with a slicing action.

SLIDING TRACK: A track on which a drawer, door or window slides or rolls.

SLIPSTONE: A small whetstone having a

cross-section like that of a wedge. It is used to sharpen gouges and other cutting tools.

SLOYD KNIFE: A single blade woodworker's knife used for carving, trimming, and slicing. Originated in Scandinavian countries.

SOCKET CHISEL: Chisel having a tapered hollow tang (socket) to receive a handle.

SOFFIT: The lowered section of a ceiling or the underside of a cornice, beam, or arch.

SOFTWOOD: Wood which comes from one of the evergreen, needle or cone bearing trees, called conifers.

SOFTWOOD PLYWOOD: A plywood made entirely of softwood. There are some thirty species of softwoods used in the manufacture of plywood.

SOLIDS (FINISHING): The material remaining in a paint after its liquids have evaporated. In a paint formula solids are usually indicated by percentage of weight.

SPIKE: A large size common nail, 16 d to 60 d.

SPINDLE: A shaft, arbor, or axle on which another revolving part or a cutting tool can be mounted.

SPIRIT STAIN: An aniline dye mixed with denatured alcohol to color wood.

SPLAT: A wide, flat, vertical section, often ornamental, used in the center of a chair back.

SPLAYED: Pertains to the leg of a chair or table which angles outward in two directions from its seat or top.

SPLINE: A thin reinforcing strip of wood set in grooves cut in adjacent edges of a joint.

SPLIT: See Crack.

SPRAY GUN (FINISHING): A device which atomizes (forms a fine mist) finishing material so it can be applied by spraying in thin, uniform coats.

SPRINGWOOD: That part of the growth of wood in a tree which occurs early during the growing season.

SPUR CENTER: The headstock (drive) center which fits into the headstock spindle of a wood lathe.

STAGGER: To place alternately (offset) from one side to the other of a line.

STAPLE: A U-shaped fastener used in a stapler to attach such materials as roofing, tile, and insulation.

STARVED JOINT: A joint which lacks a sufficient amount of glue to make a strong bond.

STEAMED: A process used particularly with green walnut lumber. It is steamed in vats to distribute part of the natural coloring pigments of the heartwood into the sapwood.

STICKERS: Strips of wood used between layers in a pile of lumber to allow air to circulate around each board.

STICK SHELLAC: Shellac in stick form to fill imperfections around knots and other defects. It is available in a variety of colors.

STOCK CUTTING LIST: Pieces of lumber given in the bill of materials, which have similar dimensions, are grouped together into larger pieces. This saves time and material when the pieces are cut to finish dimensions.

STORY POLE: A strip of wood used to lay out and transfer measurements for door and window openings, stairways, and courses of shingles and siding.

STRAIGHTEDGE: A strip of wood or metal with at least one true edge. It is used to lay out and check parts being processed.

STRESSED WOOD: Wood which is artificially stained and marked to make it appear to be old.

STRETCHER: A horizontal piece used as a

Dictionary of Terms

tie in a framed structure to reinforce the legs of a table, chair, or desk.

STRUCTURAL LUMBER: Similar to yard lumber but is over 5 in. in thickness and in width.

SUMMER WOOD: That part of the growth of wood in a tree which occurs late during the growing season.

SURFACED ON FOUR SIDES (S4S): A term applied to lumber which is smoothed (surfaced or planed) on four surfaces.

SWING: The diameter of the largest piece that can be turned, or the largest circle that can be made by a tool or machine part.

SYNTHETIC: Man-made.

TANG CHISEL: Chisel having a solid, tapered tang which is fitted into handle.

TAPER: A gradual and uniform narrowing in size from one end toward the other of a hole, cylinder, or rectangular piece.

TEMPERA COLORS: A finishing medium which is mixed with water for application. Pigments or colors are usually mixed with an albuminous (water soluble protein) vehicle.

TEMPLATE: A piece of cardboard, metal, hardboard, or other material used as a guide to cut work, transfer a pattern, or check the accuracy of work.

TENON: The protruding part of a mortise and tenon joint.

TENSILE STRENGTH: Resistance of a board or other material to longitudinal stress (pulling).

THERMOPLASTIC: A resin which softens and becomes flexible each time it is heated.

THERMOSETTING: A resin which cures, sets, and becomes hard when subjected to heat. Once hardened, it will not resoften when exposed to heat.

THINNER: A liquid for reducing the consistency of a finishing material such as paint.

TIMBERS: Construction lumber with a large cross section, 5 in. or more in thickness and in width.

TOENAILING: Attaching the end of a vertical piece to the surface of a horizontal piece with nails driven at an angle.

TONGUE: The protruding part of a tongue and groove joint.

TOOL: A device or instrument used to perform, or aid in the performing of a manual or machine process.

TOOL REST: A mechanism for holding or positioning tools to perform cutting operations, such as a lathe tool rest.

TRACKING: The alignment of a blade on the wheels of a band saw or the belt on the drums of a belt sander.

TRADITIONAL FURNITURE: Furniture created in Europe, particularly during the 18th and 19th centuries. It is named for the rulers who ordered it built or for the craftsmen who originated it. Typical decorations include gilt, fretwork, carvings, claw and ball feet and extravagant fabrics.

TREE FARMER: One who grows, protects and manages trees for continuous crops.

TRIAL ASSEMBLY: Dry (without glue) assembly of parts to check accuracy and function before final (bonding) assembly.

TRIM: A general term referring to a variety of decorative moldings and strips used to finish door and window openings, corners, and edges along walls, ceilings, or floors.

TRUE EDGE (ALSO WORKING EDGE): One that is straight, accurate and forms an angle of 90 deg. to the working (face) surface.

TUNG OIL: A drying oil (also called Chinawood oil) used in water resistant paints and varnishes. It is obtained from the nut of the Tung tree.

TURNING: A term referring to the use of cutting and shaping tools on the wood lathe.

TURPENTINE: A volatile solvent used to reduce varnish, enamel and oil-base paints. It is made by distilling gum obtained from certain pine trees.

TWIST (ALSO WIND): The warp in a piece of lumber when both surfaces and edges are curved lengthwise.

UTILITY GRADE: See Common Grade.

VARNISH: A durable, water resistant finishing material composed of copal gums or synthetic resins; a vehicle, usually linseed oil or tung oil; and a thinner such as turpentine.

VARNISH STAIN: Varnish with pigments added so that both stain and varnish are applied at one time.

VEHICLE: Portion of wood finish such as paint which is liquid.

VENEER: A thin sheet of wood often laminated to core stock to make plywood or paneling. It is cut, sliced, or sawed from a log, cant, or flitch. When united in plywood it is sometimes referred to as a ply.

VENEER CORE PLYWOOD: A plywood made by bonding crossbands of veneers, each band being at right angles to the adjacent bands.

VESSELS: Continuous tubes formed in wood by large wood cells being attached together. Openings in these vessels on the surface of wood are called pores.

VOLATILE LIQUID: Liquid that evaporates.

WAINSCOT: Paneling or other material attached to the lower three to four feet of an interior wall.

WANE: A defect in wood characterized by bark or lack of wood along an edge or at a corner of a board.

WARP: Any variation of shape in lumber from a true surface or edge. This includes cup, bow, wind (twist), and crook.

WASH COAT: A thin coat of sealer, usually shellac or lacquer sealer, applied over stain or paste wood filler.

WATER PUTTY: A dry powder which is mixed with water to form a paste. Used to fill defects in wood surfaces.

WATER STAIN: Wood stain made by dissolving water-soluble colored pigments in water.

WATER WHITE: Clear, transparent as water. A term used to describe an exceptionally clear finishing material.

WEB (PATTERNMAKING): A thin section in a pattern linking two heavier sections to provide greater strength in a metal casting.

WEBBING: A thin, woven strap used to form the support for a stool, chair, or other upholstery seat.

WELT: A cloth covered cord used to form edges in upholstery.

WIND: See Twist.

WING TOGGLE BOLT: A device for anchoring something to a hollow wall.

WITH THE GRAIN: Toward the direction or growth pattern of wood fibers.

WOOD BENDING: Forming wood by twisting or curving.

WOOD FLOUR MOLDING: Molding sawdust particles with certain thermosetting resin binders.

WOOD LAMINATING: Bonding together thin strips or layers of wood.

WOOD RAY: See Medullary Ray.

WORKING DRAWING: An orthographic drawing, drawn to scale, usually with two or more views.

WORKING SURFACE: See Face Surface.

YARD LUMBER: Lumber usually available at retail lumber yards consisting of select (finish) grades and common (utility) grades.

Acknowledgments

Generous assistance has been given by numerous individuals and companies during the preparation of this book.

Grateful acknowledgment is given to my wife, Lois, our son, Tom, and our daughter, Judy for their patience, understanding and help.

Distinctive acknowledgment is given to Terry Redell for his work in the preparation of project drawings and to Jack Hedblade for his photography.

Special thanks is given to Dr. Dempsey Reid, Chairman, Department of Industrial Education and Technology, and other colleagues of Western Illinois University for their interest and cooperation.

Appreciation is acknowledged to the many students and individuals who in one way or another contributed to the preparation of this book. Special credit is due: Douglas Moews, Jim Davis, Dale Doty, Harold Dorsey, Edward Doonan, John Modlin, Richard Snyder, Jerry Boice, Keith McMillen, Marion Cornelius, Richard Kerr, Robert Anderson, Kurt Meintzer, Wesley Knight, Don Reynolds, Jim Brady, John Psaute, Phil Essington, Steve Jacobsen and Rob Meline.

Sincere gratitude is expressed to Miss June McSwain, Director, Educational Services, Forest Products Institute and Mr. John G. Shope, National Forest Products Association for their time and effort in editing the woods unit.

Contributions from the following companies and organizations are appreciated:

Adjustable Clamp Company, Chicago, Illinois
American Forest Institute, Washington, D. C.
American Plywood Association, Tacoma, Washington
American Wood Working Company, Montello, Wisconsin
Amerock Corporation, Rockford, Illinois
Auto-Nailer Company, Atlanta, Georgia
Binks Manufacturing Company, Chicago, Illinois
The Black Brothers Company, Inc., Mendota, Illinois
Brett Guard Corporation, Bergenfield, New Jersey
Brodhead-Garrett Company, Cleveland, Ohio
Buss Machine Works, Inc., Wabash, Indiana
Coe Manufacturing Company, Painesville, Ohio

Peter Cooper Corporations, Gowanda, New Jersey
DeVilbiss Company, Toledo, Ohio
Diehl Machines, Inc., Wabash, Indiana
Drexel Enterprises, Inc., Drexel, North Carolina
Educational Lumber Company, Inc., Asheville, N. C.
E. I. du Pont de Nemours & Company, Inc., Wilmington, Del.
Fastener Corporation, Franklin Park, Illinois
Fine Hardwoods Association, Chicago, Illinois
Foley Manufacturing Company, Minneapolis, Minnesota
Forest Products Laboratory, Madison, Wisconsin
The Franklin Glue Company, Columbus, Ohio
Greenlee Tool Company, Rockford, Illinois
Hardwood Plywood Manufacturers Association, Arlington, Va.
Huther Brothers Saw Manufacturing Company, Rochester, N.J.
Insulation Board Institute, Chicago, Illinois
Lufkin Rule Company, Apex, North Carolina
Masonite Corporation, Chicago, Illinois
Mattison Machine Works, Rockford, Illinois
Medalist Industries, Nash, Bell, Challoner Division, Oshkosh, Wisconsin
Ben Miller Lumber Company, Kansas City, Missouri
Millers Falls Company, Greenfield, Massachusetts
Myrtle Desk Company, High Point, North Carolina
National Forest Products Association, Washington, D. C.
National Particleboard Association, Washington, D. C.
National Woodwork Manufacturers' Association, Chicago, Ill.
Newman Machine Company, Inc., Greensboro, North Carolina
Nicholson File Company, Providence, Rhode Island
Norton Coated Abrasive Division, Troy, New Jersey
Oliver Machinery Company, Grand Rapids, Michigan
Frank Paxton Lumber Company, Chicago, Illinois
H. K. Porter Company, Inc., Pittsburgh, Pennsylvania
Powermatic, Inc., McMinnville, Tennessee
Rockwell Manufacturing Company, Pittsburgh, Pennsylvania
Skil Corporation, Chicago, Illinois
Southern Forest Products Association, New Orleans, La.
Stanley Tools, New Britain, Connecticut
Sumner Rider and Associates, Inc., Chicago, Illinois
James L. Taylor Manufacturing Company, Poughkeepsi, N. J.
U. S. Department of Labor, Bureau of Labor Standards, Washington, D. C.
U. S. Plywood Corporation, New York, New York
Western Wood Products Association, Portland, Oregon
Weyerhaeuser Company, Tacoma, Washington
Yates-American Machine Company, Roscoe, Illinois

INDEX

A

Abrasive grit sizes, 111
Abrasive materials, 110
Adhesives, 104
Airplane cement, 104
Aliphatic resin glue, 105
Aluminum oxide, 110
American Tree Farm System, 8
Animal caricatures, 166, 167
Animal glue, 104
Antiquing (color glazing), 125
Auger bit, sharpening, 50
Auger bits, 47
Automatic (push) drill, 49
Awls, 30

B

Backsaw, 36
Band clamps, 108
Bandsaw, 38
  safety and care, 40
Belt sander, 112
Bevel gauge, 31
Beveling with circular saw, 43
Bevels, planing, 64
Bill of Materials, 23
Bird feeders, 174, 175
Bleaching wood, 118
Blend sticks, 117
Block plane, 61
Bookends, 160, 161
Boring, 47
  holes at an angle, 48, 52
  straight holes, 47, 52
Bowls, 164, 165
Box joints, 81
Box nail, 97
Brace, 47
Brads, 97
Brushes, 118
Building construction, 155
Business experience activity, 137
Butt hinge, 128
Butt joints, 74

C

Cabinet scraper, 65
Calipers, 32
Candle stands, 188, 189

Canisters, veneered, 194, 195
Careers in woodworking, 154
Carving, 56, 58
Carving animal caricatures, 167
Casein glue, 106
Cash receipt records, 138
Casing nail, 97
Cassette tape cabinet, 184
Catches, 130
C-clamps, 107
Certified Tree Farms, 8
Chalk line, 32
Chamfers, planing, 64
Changing circular saw blade, 42
Changing design size, 32
Checkbook records, 138
Chisel safety and care, 60
Chiseling, 56, 59
Choosing a project, 157
Chuck for turning small pieces, 94
Circle cutter, 52, 53
Circular saw, 40
  changing blade, 43
  grooves and dados, 44
Clamping, 97, 106
Clamping devices, 106
Classification of wood, 7
Coated abrasives, 110
Color and grain characteristics of
    different wood species, 16
Combination square, 29
Common nail, 97
Company name, business activity, 137
Company officials for business
    activity, 137
Computing lumber measurement, 22
Concepts of business, 137
Concrete fasteners, 100
Concealed hinge, 128
Construction specialist, 156
Contact cement, 104
Coping saw, 34
Countersinking, 50
Crosscut saw, 35
Crosscutting with circular saw, 41
Crystalline finish, 125
Curio shelf with drawers, 185

Cutting list, 24
Cutting veneer, 13
Cutting with wood chisels, 59

D

Dado joints, 77, 78
Dados, cutting on circular saw, 44
Deciding on product for business
    activity, 137
Defects, wood, 11
Deft vinyl stain, 119
Design considerations, 18
Designing appropriate projects, 19
Designing products, 18
Disk sander, 112
Dividers, 31
Dovetail joints, 80
Doweled miter joint, 76
Dowels, 103
Draw knife, 57
Dresser caddy, 193, 194
Drill bits, 49
Drill press, 51
  safety and care, 53
Drilling, 47
  round stock, 52
Driving nails, 98
Drying lumber, 11
Durability, design, 19

E

Ecology box, 195
Edge-doweled joint, 74
Edge joint, 74
Elbow catch, 130
Enamel, 123
Engineer, 156
Equipment safety, 27
Escutcheon nail, 97
Expansive bit, 49

F

Feathers, 103
File, using, 56
Filling dents before finishing, 117
Finish nail, 97
Finish sander, 114
Flat sawed, 10
Flint, 110
Flock, 125
Flower stand or table, 182, 183
Fold and carry stool, 197
Folding rule, 29
Fore planes, 62
Forest service management, 155
Forestry, 155
Forstner bit, 48
Friction "alligator" catch, 130
Function, design, 18
Furniture styles, 19

G

Garnet, 110
General Manager duties, 138
General safety, 27, 28
Glue application, 106
Glue blocks, 103
Gluing, 97, 104
Golf tee tie rack, 146
Gouge, 57, 91

Grinding lumber, 12
Groove joints, 79
Grooves, cutting on circular saw, 44
Growth of wood, 7

H

Hand crosscut saw, 35
Hand drill, 49
Hand ripsaw, 35
Hand sanding, 111
Hand scraper, sharpening, 66
Hand screws, 106
Hardboard, 15
Hardware, 128
Hardwoods, 8
Head sawyer, 9
Headstock turning, 93
Hinges, 128

I

Identification of wood, 7, 16
Industrial education teacher, 156
Industrial worker, 156
Installing screws, 100
Insulation board, 16
Internal cut, sawing, 37

J

Jack planes, 61
Jig saw, 36
  safety and care, 38
Jointer, 67
  depth of cut limitations, 68
  planes, 62
  safety, 70
  stock size limitations, 68
Jointing edges, 68
Joints, 74

K

Key holder, 162
Kind of wood, design, 18

L

Laboratory safety, 27
Lacquer, 124
  thinner, 124
Lamination and wood bending, 162
Lap joints, 76
Lathe, 90
  safety and care, 95
  speeds, 91
Laying out tools and processes, 29
Lazy susan, 196
Letter holder, 157, 158, 159
Linseed oil, 125
Lumber manufacturing process, 8
Lumber measurement, 22

M

Machine drill bits, 51
Machine safety, 28
Magnetic catch, 130
Manufacturing business, 137
Marking gauge, 30
Mass producing golf tee tie rack, 146
Mass producing tic-tac-toe game, 142
Mass production, 137, 141
Metal fasteners, 97
Metric conversion tables, 198
Minwax wood finishes, 120
Miscellaneous fasteners, 100

Index

Miter box saw, 36
Miter clamps, 107
Miter joints, 76
Mitering with circular saw, 42
Modeler's plane, 61
Moisture content, 11
Mortise and tenon joints, 80

N

Nail hammers, 97
Nail sets, 97
Nailers, 103
Nailing, 103
Nails, 97
Napkin holders, 157, 158, 159, 189, 190
Non-grain-rasing stains, 121
Novelty boxes, 172, 173
Novelty finishes, 125

O

Office Manager duties, 138
Oil stains, 120
Opportunities in woodworking industries, 154

P

Particle board, 15
Parting tool, 91
Paste wood fillers, 121
Patternmaker, 156
Pencil holders, veneered, 194, 195
Pictorial sketch, 20
Plain sawed, 10
Plan of Procedure, 24
Plane iron, sharpening, 66
Planer, 70
  safety and care, 71
Planes, care and adjustment, 62
Planing
  chamfers and bevels, 64
  edge, 64
  ends, 64
  lumber, 11
  second surface, 64
  surface, 62, 63, 69
  tapers, 69
  tools and machines, 61
Planning, 18
Planters, 180, 181, 192
Plastic
  cements, 104
  resin glue, 105
  wood, 117
Plywood, 12, 14
Polishing compounds, 111
Portable
  belt sander, 113
  circular saw, 44
  electric drill, 53, 54
  jig saw, 38
  jointers, 70
Portable router, 83
  installing bits and adjusting base, 84
Price for business activity product, 141
Projects, 157
  bird feeders, 174, 175
  bookends, 160, 161
  bowls, 164, 165
  candle stands, 188, 189
  carving animal caricatures, 166, 167

  cassett tape cabinet, 184
  curio shelf with drawers, 185
  desk set, 183
  dresser caddy, 193, 194
  ecology box, 195
  flower stand or table, 183
  fold and carry stool, 197
  hand carved trays, 168, 169
  key holder, 162
  lazy susan, 196
  letter holder, 157, 158, 159
  napkin holder, 157, 158, 159, 189, 190
  novelty boxes, 172, 173
  planters, 180, 181, 192
  recipe holder, 187
  salad cutting board, 186
  salad tools, 162, 163
  sconce, 191
  serving trays, 170, 171
  sewing novelties, 178, 179
  shelves, 176, 177
  T-square and drawing board, 169
  veneered canisters and pencil holders, 195
Projects, selecting, 19
Proportion, design, 18
Pulling nails, 99
Pulls, 129
Pumice, 111
Purchasing Agent duties, 139
Push drill, 49
Putty sticks, 117

Q

Quarter sawed, 10

R

Rabbet joints, 76, 77
Rabbet planes, 62, 65
Rabbeting, 69
Radial circular saw, 45
Recipe holder, 187
Removing finish, 126
Repairing defects before finishing, 116
Resawing on circular saw, 43
Research technician, 156
Resorcinol resin glue, 105
Retarding lacquer thinner, 125
Ring nail, 97
Ripping with circular saw, 42
Ripsaw, 35
Roller spring catch, 130
Rottenstone, 111
Router bits, 83, 84
Router planes, 62, 65
Router safety and care, 86
Router, trimming laminated plastic, 85
Router, trimming wood veneer, 85
Routing, 83
Routing a groove, 84
Routing, using templates, 85
Rubber cement, 104
Rules, 29

S

Saber saw, 38
Safety Director duties, 139
Safety in the laboratory, 27
Safety with machines, 28
Safety with tools and equipment, 27

Salad cutting board, 186
Salad tools, 162, 163
Sales Manager duties, 139
Sander safety and care, 114
Sanding, 110, 118
  curved and irregular edges, 114
Sawing, 34
  an internal cut, 37
  lumber, 10
Sconce, 191
Screwdrivers, 99
Screw nail, 97
Screws, 99
Sealacell finishing, 120
Sealers, 122
Selecting appropriate projects, 19
Selling business activity product, 141
Semiconcealed offset hinge, 128
Serving trays, 170, 171
Sewing novelties, 178, 179
Shaper, 86
  forming irregular edges, 88
  forming straight edges, 88
  installing bits, 87
  position ring guard, 88
  safety and care, 89
Shaping, 83, 86
Shaping an edge, 84
Shaping bits, 83, 87
Sharpening auger bit, 50
Sharpening hand scraper, 66
Sharpening plane iron, 66
Shellac, 124
Shelves, 176, 177
Shrinking, 11
Silicon carbide, 110
Size, design, 18
Sketching projects, 20
Skew, 91
Sliding T-bevel, 31
Sliding tracks, 130
Sloyd knife, 58
Smoothing planes, 61
Softwoods, 8
Spindle turning, 92
Splines, 104
Spokeshave, 57
Spraying finishes, 125, 126
Spring clamps, 107
Squares, 29
Standard thickness and width of
  softwood lumber, 12
Standard thickness of surfaced
  hardwood lumber, 12
Staplers, 102
Staples, 102
Stapling, 102
Steel bar clamps, 107
Steel rule, 29
Steel wool, 111
Stick shellac, 117

Stock certificate form suggestion, 140
Stock cutting list, 24
Stock ownership records, 139
Stool, fold and carry, 197
Structure of wood, 7
Surface carving, 58
Surfacer, 70
Surfacer safety and care, 71
Swelling, 11

T

Tape rule, 29
Templates, 32
Templates, router, 85
Thinning mediums, 124
Tic-Tac-Toe game, 141
Tool safety, 27
Tool selection, 24
Top coat finishes, 123
Trammel points, 31
Trays, hand carved, 168, 169
Trimmer saws, 10
Try square, 29
T-square and drawing board, 169
Turning tools, 91
Turning wood, 90
Turpentine, 124

U

Upholstering a stool, 133, 134, 135
Upholstery, 132
  materials, 132
  tools, 133
Usefulness, design, 18
Utility knife, 58

V

Varnish, 123
V-block, 34
Veneer, 12, 13
Veneer clamps, 108

W

Warping, 11
Water putty, 117
Water stains, 121
White liquid resin glue, 104
Whittling, 58
Wire nails, 97
Wood
  defects, 11
  dowels, 103
  files, 56
  finishing, 116
  finishing safety, 127
  flour molding, 164
  for turning, 90
  identification, 16
  joints, 74
  lathe, 90
  putty, 117
  stains, 120
  turning, 90
Woods, 7
Working drawing, 20, 21